Bloom's Modern Critical Views

African American
Poets: Wheatley-
Tolson
Edward Albee
American and
Canadian Women
Poets, 1930–present
American Women
Poets, 1650–1950
Maya Angelou
Asian-American
Writers
Margaret Atwood
Jane Austen
James Baldwin
Honoré de Balzac
Samuel Beckett
Saul Bellow
The Bible
William Blake
Jorge Luis Borges
Ray Bradbury
The Brontës
Gwendolyn Brooks
Elizabeth Barrett
Browning
Robert Browning
Italo Calvino
Albert Camus
Lewis Carroll
Willa Cather
Cervantes
Geoffrey Chaucer
Anton Chekhov
Kate Chopin
Agatha Christie
Samuel Taylor
Coleridge
Joseph Conrad
Contemporary Poets
Stephen Crane
Dante
Daniel Defoe

Don DeLillo
Charles Dickens
Emily Dickinson
John Donne and the
17th-Century Poets
Fyodor Dostoevsky
W.E.B. DuBois
George Eliot
T. S. Eliot
Ralph Ellison
Ralph Waldo Emerson
William Faulkner
F. Scott Fitzgerald
Sigmund Freud
Robert Frost
Johann Wolfgang
von Goethe
George Gordon, Lord
Byron
Graham Greene
Thomas Hardy
Nathaniel Hawthorne
Ernest Hemingway
Hispanic-American
Writers
Homer
Langston Hughes
Zora Neale Hurston
Aldous Huxley
Henrik Ibsen
John Irving
Henry James
James Joyce
Franz Kafka
John Keats
Jamaica Kincaid
Stephen King
Rudyard Kipling
Milan Kundera
D. H. Lawrence
Ursula K. Le Guin
Sinclair Lewis
Bernard Malamud

Christopher Marlowe
Gabriel García
Márquez
Cormac McCarthy
Carson McCullers
Herman Melville
Arthur Miller
John Milton
Molière
Toni Morrison
Native-American
Writers
Joyce Carol Oates
Flannery O'Connor
Eugene O'Neill
George Orwell
Octavio Paz
Sylvia Plath
Edgar Allan Poe
Katherine Anne
Porter
J. D. Salinger
Jean-Paul Sartre
William Shakespeare:
Histories and
Poems
William Shakespeare:
Romances
William Shakespeare:
The Comedies
William Shakespeare:
The Tragedies
George Bernard Shaw
Mary Wollstonecraft
Shelley
Percy Bysshe Shelley
Alexander
Solzhenitsyn
Sophocles
John Steinbeck
Tom Stoppard
Jonathan Swift
Amy Tan

Bloom's Modern Critical Views

Alfred, Lord Tennyson

Henry David Thoreau

J. R. R. Tolkien

Leo Tolstoy

Mark Twain

John Updike

Kurt Vonnegut

Alice Walker

Robert Penn Warren

Eudora Welty

Edith Wharton

Walt Whitman

Oscar Wilde

Tennessee Williams

Thomas Wolfe

Tom Wolfe

Virginia Woolf

William Wordsworth

Richard Wright

William Butler Yeats

Bloom's Modern Critical Views

DON DeLILLO

Edited and with an introduction by
Harold Bloom
Sterling Professor of the Humanities
Yale University

CHELSEA HOUSE
PUBLISHERS
A Haights Cross Communications Company
Philadelphia

A Haights Cross Communications ✕ Company

Printed and bound in the United States of America
10 9 8 7 6 5 4 3 2 1

Library of Congress Cataloging-in-Publication Data

Don DeLillo / edited with an introduction by Harold Bloom.
      p. cm. -- (Bloom's modern critical views)
Includes bibliographical references and index.
   ISBN: 0-7910-7038-7
   1. DeLillo, Don--Criticism and interpretation. I. Bloom, Harold.
II. Series.
   PS3554.E4425 Z64 2002
   813'.54--dc21

                                                2002013046

Chelsea House Publishers
1974 Sproul Road, Suite 400
Broomall, PA 19008-0914

http://www.chelseahouse.com

Contributing Editor: Aaron Tillman

Cover designed by Terry Mallon

Cover: Deborah Feingold/Getty Images

Layout by EJB Publishing Services

Contents

Editor's Note   vii

Introduction   1
    Harold Bloom

Don DeLillo's Search for Walden Pond   5
    Michael Oriard

Preface and Don DeLillo   13
    Robert Nadeau

Don DeLillo's America   21
    Bruce Bawer

White Magic: Don DeLillo's Intelligence Networks   29
    Greg Tate

Myth, Magic and Dread: Reading Culture Religiously   33
    Gregory Salyer

The Romantic Metaphysics of Don DeLillo   51
    Paul Maltby

For Whom the Bell Tolls: Don DeLillo's *Americana*   71
    David Cowart

Consuming Narratives: Don DeLillo
and the 'Lethal' Reading   89
    Christian Moraru

Romanticism and the Postmodern Novel: Three
Scenes from Don DeLillo's *White Noise*   107
    Lou F. Caton

Don DeLillo's Postmodern Pastoral   117
    Dana Phillips

Afterthoughts on Don DeLillo's *Underworld*   129
    Tony Tanner

"What About a Problem That Doesn't Have
    a Solution?": Stone's *A Flag for Sunrise*, DeLillo's
    Mao II, and the Politics of Political Fiction   149
    Jeoffrey S. Bull

Chronology   167

Contributors   169

Bibliography   171

Acknowledgments   175

Index   177

Editor's Note

My Introduction centers upon the opening and closing sections of *Underworld*, and is a response to the brilliant "afterthoughts," on that novel, of the late Tony Tanner, reprinted as the penultimate essay in this volume.

Michael Oriard, in an overview of DeLillo's first five novels, commends them for asking the right questions, while Robert Nadeau finds in DeLillo the metaphysics of the New Physics.

DeLillo's vision of America is interpreted by Bruce Bawer as being excessively reductive, after which Greg Tate considers *Libra*, particularly praising the novelist's conception of Oswald's mother.

White Noise is regarded by Gregory Salyer as an instance, together with the novels of Leslie Silko, of an original religious stance towards our culture. Visionary experience in DeLillo is also the subject of Paul Maltby, who emphasizes the survival of the Romantic epiphany.

David Cowart returns us to DeLillo's first novel, *Americana*, and centers upon the theme of our Oedipal violation of the land, while Christian Moraru broods on issues of authorship and readership throughout DeLillo.

The Romantic epiphanies of *White Noise* are judged by Lou F. Caton to defy Post-Modernist critiques of meaning, after which Dana Phillips also sees that novel as a defense of "nature" against our still-current cultural commissars.

In the major essay reprinted in this book, the distinguished critic Tony Tanner, an admirer of DeLillo's work, indicates what he takes to be some of the weaknesses of *Underworld*.

Jeoffrey S. Bull, in the final essay, compares *Mao II* and Robert Stone's *A Flag for Sunrise*, finding in each the difficulty of writing contemporary political fiction.

Introduction

One can venture that the major American novelists now at work are Thomas Pynchon, Don DeLillo, Philip Roth, and Cormac McCarthy. They write the Style of our Age, and each has composed canonical works. For DeLillo, I would name these as *White Noise*, *Libra*, and *Underworld*, certainly his principal book up to this time. Roth, immensely prolific, wrote his masterpiece in the scabrous *Sabbath's Theater*, while his tetralogy, *Zuckerman Bound*, and *American Pastoral* are equally likely to survive our era. McCarthy's *Blood Meridian* continues to overwhelm me: *Suttree* before it, *All the Pretty Horses* more recently, also should be permanent. Pynchon, named by Tony Tanner as DeLillo's precursor, is as central to our narrative fiction now as John Ashbery is to our poetry. *The Crying of Lot 49* and *Gravity's Rainbow* have defined our culture—to call it that—and *Mason & Dixon* is even more remarkable, a work of amazing geniality and a kind of hopeless hope.

If just four recent fictions are to be selected for the United States in the early years of the twenty-first century, then name them as *Blood Meridian*, *Sabbath's Theater*, *Mason & Dixon*, and *Underworld*. All of DeLillo is in *Underworld*, and so is New York City 1951-1996. He has not written the epic of the city; perhaps Hart Crane did that forever, with *The Bridge* (1930). But DeLillo's sense of America, in the second half of the twentieth century, is achieved perfectly in *Underworld*.

DeLillo, a wisdom writer, makes no Hemingwayesque attempt to challenge Shakespeare and Tolstoy. Nor does he desire any contest with Pynchon, though Tony Tanner shrewdly implies that this was unavoidable. Pynchon's cosmos of paranoia, indispensable waste, plastic consumerism is the literary context of *Underworld*. DeLillo is highly aware of his own belatedness, yet his resources are extraordinary, and he so subsumes Pynchon so as to achieve a distinguished triumph over any anguish of contamination that might have impeded *Underworld*. By the time the vast

1

book concludes, DeLillo's relation to Pynchon is like Pynchon's own relation to *The Recognitions* of William Gaddis and to Borges. The Pynchon-DeLillo implicit contest becomes akin to *Blood Meridian*'s struggle with Melville and Faulkner or Roth's permanent status as Franz Kafka's grand-nephew (as it were).

Tanner, disappointed with *Underworld*, argued otherwise, and sometimes cannot be refuted. I wince when Tanner observes: "And, crucially, *Underworld* has no Tristero." Tristero remains the greatest of Pynchonian inventions: *The Crying of Lot 49*'s sublimely mad, subversive alternative to the United States Postal Service is not matched by *Gravity's Rainbow*'s interplay between the System and the Zone. Nor, as Tanner insists, does *Underworld* have so persuasive a universal connection to justify its declarations that everything is linked and connected. But again, DeLillo knows this and makes of his supposed weakness a radical strength.

Tanner is again accurate when he observes that Nick Shay, DeLillo's surrogate, as a character is just not there at all, nor does Shay want to be. The only character with a consciousness before Mason and Dixon, anywhere in Pynchon, is Oedipa Maas, and she is there only in the closing moments of the novella. The only consciousness in DeLillo is DeLillo; despite his supposed Post-Modernism, he is a High Romantic Transcendentalist determined not to be out of his time. If there is religiosity in *Underworld*, it is not DeLillo's and is portrayed as part of the waste. And yet there is something more profound than mere nostalgia in DeLillo's Romanticism. His authentic masters are Emerson, Thoreau, Whitman, and his visions, flashing out against the noise and the waste, are enduring illuminations.

At the opening of "Self-Reliance," Emerson gave us a superb irony:

In every work of genius we recognize our own rejected thoughts: they come back to us with a certain alienated majesty.

DeLillo lovingly parodies this in Nick Shay's final meditation:

Maybe we feel a reverence for waste, for the redemptive qualities of the things we use and discard. Look how they come back to us, alight with a kind of brave aging.

Tanner was anxious about the epiphanies of DeLillo's urban transcendentalism, and wondered if they were only evidences of a decayed Catholicism. And yet, DeLillo's vibrant Emersonianism seems to me clear enough. *Underworld*, which Tanner says is totally reliant on history, actually is self-reliant and like Emerson is adversarial to history. Old Bronx boy and baseball fan that I am (like DeLillo, addicted to the Yankees), I thrill to the Prologue of *Underworld*, which I wish had kept its title of "Pafko at the Wall," Though you *could* say that DeLillo is following baseball history in his vision of Bobby Thomson's Shot Heard Round the World in October 1951, I myself have strong memories of that moment at the old Polo Grounds, and what I recall is mere history, and "it is all falling indelibly into the past." Romantic vision of the high mode, whether in *Song of Myself* or *Underworld*, is precisely what does not fall.

MICHAEL ORIARD

Don DeLillo's Search for Walden Pond

While Thoreau was able to shape his months on Walden Pond into an instructive lesson for his future life, and into a ritual rebirth as critics have named it, DeLillo's characters are invariably left at the end of the novels still groping, or, at best, tentatively embarking on a course of possible rebirth but uncertain outcome.

[DeLillo's] fifth novel, *Players* (1977), shares many of the major thematic and technical qualities of the first four, but in a most fundamental way it breaks the pattern. From *Americana* to *End Zone* to *Great Jones Street* to *Ratner's Star* DeLillo traces a single search for the source of life's meaning. By the end of *Ratner's Star* the quest has been literally turned inside out; the path from chaos to knowledge becomes a Moebius strip that brings the seeker back to chaos. The main characters in *Players* are not sustained by the illusion that answers to cosmic questions can be found; they seek meaning in their lives, but meaning of a tentative and minimal nature. The novels before *Players* create a quartet, a four-volume sequence that DeLillo's [next] novel does not directly extend.

DeLillo's first four novels, then, are segments of a single proto-novel. Certainly the casts of characters in all the novels share common traits. Whether they be media executives, college football players, rock musicians,

From *Critique: Studies in Modern Fiction*, Vol. XX, No. 1, 1978, pp. 5–24.

or mathematicians, characters who populate DeLillo's fictional worlds speak as learned metaphysicians.

DeLillo is concerned less with creating verisimilitude than with allowing his characters' deepest being to speak directly to the reader. DeLillo's novels are also characterized by wacky off-beat humor, by verbal virtuosity that startles and delights and often puzzles, and by multiple digressions into realms of quirky erudition or profound wisdom. The novels are a little like jigsaw puzzles assembled on a card table that is bumped—the pieces are all there but they do not seem to fit neatly together. Such is their author's intention; in the concluding novel of the quartet, *Ratner's Star*, a character speaks about some imagined contemporary writers:

> There's a whole class of writers who don't want their books to be read. This to some extent explains their crazed prose. To express what is expressible isn't why you write if you're in this class of writers. To be understood is faintly embarrassing. What you want to express is the violence of your desire not to be read. The friction of audiences is what drives writers crazy. These people are going to read what you write. The more they understand, the crazier you get. You can't let them know what you're writing about. Once they know, you're finished. If you're in this class, what you have to do is either not publish or make absolutely sure your work leaves readers strewn along the margins.

DeLillo, of course, is teasing his audience here, but the reader, occasionally baffled by a particularly abstract excursion into seemingly irrelevant metaphysics, senses that the author is also at times purposely evasive—the center of the novels is not always clearly defined, but a lot of fun and wisdom is to be found along the margins.

The quest of the soul for meaning that was begun in *Americana*, continued in *End Zone* and *Great Jones Street*, and seemingly concluded in *Ratner's Star* is not a once-only progression on a linear course from confusion to enlightenment, but one completion of the cycle of human seeking. DeLillo offers no final answers; the importance to him is not the completion of the cycle, but the vision of reality which the process reveals.

The basic plot in each of DeLillo's four books is simple and spare; it is in the tangential excursions that his main ideas emerge, and the novels show remarkable unanimity in their primary concerns. The settings of the four novels is their first similarity, typified by Gary Harkness's description of the landscape in *End Zone*:

We were in the middle of the middle of nowhere, that terrain so flat and bare, suggestive of the end of recorded time, a splendid sense of remoteness firing my soul. It was easy to feel that back up there, where men spoke the name of civilization in wistful tones, I was wanted for some terrible crime....

The end zone of [DeLillo's second novel] is thus the setting of the novel and of the other novels, too: not only the goal of the running back in a football game, but the human condition at the outer extremity of existence, a place where the world is on the verge of disintegration, and the characters teeter between genius and madness.

In this region of end zones that DeLillo describes, characters struggle for order and meaning as their world moves inexorably toward chaos. DeLillo's men and women fight the natural law of entropy, while human violence hastens its inevitable consequences.

The characters in all four novels ... perceive the world about them rushing toward oblivion, see order, rationality, and meaning increasingly elusive, and recognize their only hope to retard such disintegration in Thoreau's advice to simplify. David Bell observes that visionaries confront the large madness with purity of intention and simplicity; the rest face only complexity. But simplicity has its varieties: for the dropouts David encounters on the Indian reservation simplicity means conformity and obliteration of individual consciousness; for Americans, in general, it means the destruction of everything distinctive—forests, big red barns, colonial inns, snug little railroad depots—and their replacement with tasteless, identical structures. Even in a perverse drive toward uniformity, however, lies the possibility of regeneration, which DeLillo calls our American asceticism, for asceticism too can be a ritual preparation for action. Gary Harkness embraces football because it is primitive, it harks back to ancient warriorship, it is built on pain and discipline, and it epitomizes simplicity: "Existence without anxiety. Happiness. Know your body. Understanding the real needs of man...." His intention is not to obliterate uniqueness but to reestablish contact with the basic human values and virtues that are threatened by a violent and over-technologized society. Bucky Wunderlick's goal is similar when he says, "Least is best;" he attempts to minimize, and to retreat to his room to test the depths of silence. Robert Pirsig observes that insight comes when monotony and boredom are accepted; this commitment Bucky makes as he awaits the inspiration to act. In *Ratner's Star*, too, Chester Greylag Dent chooses to live on the bottom of the ocean, in the quietest place on earth, because, as he says, True greatness always involves a period of complete withdrawal.... The appeal of mathematics itself is its simplicity; in a world of complexity, mathematics makes sense...."

The importance of mathematics is that it is a language without the ambiguities, imprecision, and distortions of verbal language, and it is thus considered in *Ratner's Star* as a possible solution to perhaps the most prominent issue in all four of the novels—the necessity of remaking language. The dislocation of characters from an ordered and meaningful center is consistently expressed in terms of the failure of language.

Final solutions, ultimate meanings are ... not available to mankind, and the realization of this inescapable fact lies behind DeLillo's dominant attitude towards life. Life is a game, as Hemingway said, and writing fiction is a particular game within that larger game. Game is a broad category, and many kinds of games occur in DeLillo's fiction. Sexual play is described in *Americana* as true public sport, a contest in which spectacle eclipsed outcome, winner gave nothing.... In the same novel playing a game is equated with consciously confusing others with teasing, unfathomable remarks. Games can also be profoundly serious: David Bell's father describes the advertising business as a crap game in an alley for six million bucks; the losers of the game can lose everything. David himself played dangerous sports in college—with sports cars, motorcycles, and motorboats—in which the closeness of death provided the satisfaction, and after college he plays tennis to assert his superiority over his opponents.

Besides the games characters play—for amusement, for domination, for self-fulfillment, or for their own sake—DeLillo's fiction is also suffused with a spirit of play itself or game-consciousness that similarly characterizes the fiction of John Barth and Robert Coover. In *Ratner's Star* Robert Softly introduces his colleagues to a game called halfball similar to baseball except that runs, hits, and errors all count in the final score. A team can add to its total by committing errors, but those same errors can also contribute to the other team's score: The errormaker must balance the gains he is making in his error column against the gains he is allowing the other player to make in the run column.... With slight alterations, the rules of halfball can describe DeLillo's fictional technique, for he tests limits and must weigh consequences, too. No errormaker, DeLillo challenges his readers with copious digressions and excursions along the tangents of his topics. The pleasures of his novels lie largely in those digressions, but if the reader becomes completely disoriented, the author has digressed too far, and the gain is negated by a greater loss. To risk nothing is unsatisfying *Great Jones Street* is the least impressive of the novels, the least risky, and the least game-like. To risk too much is serf-defeating, however *Ratner's Star* occasionally leaves the reader grasping for a center that eludes his outstretched mine. The most successful of the novels is *End Zone*, for reasons closely tied to the subject of the book, football.

[*End Zone* is] representative of the [other novels] in its concerns for simplicity, language, and violence. To consider DeLillo's major themes and his skill in handling them, one must fully observe them in the context of a single novel.... [The characters] live their daily existence at the extreme limit of human experience, psychologically and intellectually as well as physically. In this end zone of the mind, life is simplified; the characters confront the basic determinants of their existence in an effort to prevent their own surrender to chaos.

End Zone is, above all else, a novel about language, the center of man's striving for, and deflection from, order and meaning.

That the novel is explicitly about language is hinted on the very first page when DeLillo playfully warns the reader, double metaphor coming up. Like his contemporaries William Gass, Robert Coover, and John Barth, he may be termed a metafictionist; like these writers, he is strongly aware of the nature of language and makes language itself, and the process of using language, his themes. DeLillo's consciousness of the reality of words as things is obvious at every stage in the novel....

A distinct play element is evident in DeLillo's use of language. Many words are spoken for their own sake, for their feel in the mouth of the speaker, for the harmony of their sounds, and for their originality. The book is filled with splendid vulgarity....

But playfulness and the imaginative pleasures of language are not its only function in the novel. Words often bear great power in and of themselves. The name of the football team at Logos College is changed from Cactus Wrens to Screaming Eagles to the obvious improvement of its hostile image. Players have their private sounds, their huh huh huh or awright, awright, awright, or we hit, we hit that become magic incantations producing high emotional intensity. Words like queer, relationship, and all i-z-e words are weighted with great significance for the characters, even when not specifically associated with any object or event.

DeLillo's primary intention, however, moves beyond his assertion of the creative power of the word to a judgment of language as an inadequate basis for our relationship to the objective world. Philosophers of language have taken two approaches to the limitations of language: some feel that language itself is inadequate by reason of its vagueness, unexplicitness, ambiguity, context-dependence, and misleadingness; and others hold that ordinary language is perfectly suitable, and that the mischief lies in deviating from ordinary language without providing any way of attaching sense to the deviation. DeLillo shares both skepticisms. The failure of ordinary language is manifested by the clichés that proliferate throughout the novel. The author's use of them is adroit and always with a purpose: he satirizes the cliché, exploits its meaninglessness, contrasts it to vital and significant language, revitalizes it with a skillful twist, or demonstrates how it cheapens experience and can lead to fraudulent action. The world of football is wonderfully appropriate as an arena for dissecting clichés, for no language is so fraught with them as sports jargon. DeLillo proves that even in sports reporting such overused terminology can be avoided by a sufficiently fertile imagination. Part Two of the novel, for instance, contains a stunning description of a football game and has more vitality than any such account in other literature or journalism. In details throughout the rest of the novel the author is equally original; for example, when Gary says of one of his teammates, "He's the defensive captain." He captains the defense, he turns an innocuous but essentially unresonant phrase into a metaphor for the defensive team as ship or military unit. He does not change the connotations of defensive captain but rather restores its original meaning. DeLillo's comic touch is nearly perfect in his undercutting of clichés. When Gary, for example, complains of the ambiguity of the whole business, he could not possibly be more ambiguous himself.

If language is desensitized by overuse, attempts to recreate language are often equally inadequate. The primary examples DeLillo uses for the abuse of language are the various jargons that dominate a technological society. The terminologies of business, electrical engineering, game theory, abstract philosophy, militarization, and space technology are no more intelligible to the mass of mankind than is the complex jargon of football.... One of the novel's characters includes in his list of barriers to communication that of multiple definitions and that of terminologies which are untranslatable. Both of these failures are demonstrated on the football field where the players themselves do not understand the jargon, where one coach talks of a planning procedures approach whereby we neutralize the defense, and another only screams, "I want you to bust ass out there today." Neither coach communicates to his players how the job is actually to be done.

Many writers have emphasized the destructive violence of football; DeLillo has more insightfully recognized the truer meaning of the sport. Football celebrates the ability of men to transcend the essential violence of existence, to create beauty where none seems possible.... Football in *End Zone* is the metaphor for positive violence, the kind of violence needed to recreate language and thus a new perception of life. Such a regeneration is to be achieved by simplifying existence and harking back to primitive origins in order to recover the primal uses of language. The metaphor for the negative violence that overwhelms such possibility is war.

Football is an illusion that order is possible, and language has sustained the same illusion. To change history and correct the illusion, one must first change language. DeLillo attempts to make the change on a small scale in his novel, but writers conscious of the need for a new language face a paradoxical problem. If language patterns inherited at birth dictate the patterns of a man's actions, how can a writer change those patterns through the medium of his inherited language? As Tony Tanner observes:

> Any writer has to struggle with existing language which is perpetually tending to rigidify in old formulations and he must constantly assert his own patterning powers without at the same time becoming imprisoned in them.

That DeLillo is conscious of the problem is clear in the novel's ambiguous conclusion. The final paragraph reads:

> In my room at five o'clock the next morning I drank half a cup of lukewarm water. It was the last of food or drink I would take for many days. High fevers burned a thin straight channel through my brain. In the end they had to carry me to the infirmary and feed me through plastic tubes....

The ending can be viewed as a vision of defeat—admission that the course of history is impossible to alter because the course of language is too firmly imbedded in our being. We are doomed to remain a nation devoted to human xerography. The concluding incident can also be seen as a retreat into the most extreme simplicity of existence, to a complete voiding of old forms, to an asceticism from which Gary can begin to generate something new. It can be a Phoenix image of positive regenerative violence.

DeLillo does not attempt to solve the paradox with an easy answer.... [His] failure to finish his story indicates his own lack of clear solutions, but he has made the reader aware throughout the novel of the primacy of language and the need for using it in an original manner. His novel itself is at least a tentative step toward reconstructing language into a truer description of reality.

After *End Zone* DeLillo has continued the quest for a new language and an ultimate understanding of life's meaning. Although the ending of *Ratner's Star* brought the search to confirmed inconclusion, if so paradoxical a term can be used, it marked not a deadend for the writer but a culmination of one four-part exploration. *Players* does not so much mark out new territory as retrace some early side paths and emphasize one in particular—the game-quality of life. The novel's model protagonists, Lyle and Pammy Wynant, create at least the illusion of order in their lives by playing inconsequential solo games—from Pammy's tap dancing to Lyle's arranging the contents of his pockets on his dresser in a systematic manner. Their attempts to play more meaningful games with other people lead only to complications and confusion, and to the eventual suicide of a sexually troubled friend. At the end Pammy sees that despite her efforts to live a contributive life, her fate (as well as that of Lyle, last seen waiting forlornly in a motel room) is expressed in the single word on a flophouse marquee: TRANSIENTS. The novel acknowledges no source nor even a specific quest, but portrays only disengaged people attempting to make life more than random interactions—and failing.

Players is as thoroughly game-centered as *End Zone* and is DeLillo's most self-conscious fiction. The novel's two parts, which recount first the Wynants' separate lives viewed on a split screen and then their attempts to alter them, are bracketed by a sort of Prologue and Epilogue that explicitly establish the artificiality of DeLillo's fictional creation. In his first four novels DeLillo chronicled the modern American's futile search for the mystery of existence. In *Players* he observes the attempts of a representative couple to create minimal order and meaningfulness in a world in which that mystery is hopelessly elusive. Whether *Players* signals the game-filled mode and interest of DeLillo's novels to come is impossible to predict, but we can say with certainty that his first five novels, though failing to answer the riddles of the cosmos, honestly and wittily ask the right questions, and in doing so establish Don DeLillo as an important original voice in contemporary fiction.

ROBERT NADEAU

Preface and Don DeLillo

Not only are metaphysical assumptions ... just as important and primary in the creative work of scientists as we have long known them to be in humanistic endeavors, [but also] the implications of new scientific theories ... have often had unexpected impact upon those assumptions. It is ... conceivable, although there is no precedent for it, that a radically new scientific paradigm, like that of the new physics, could prove so inconsistent with received metaphysical assumptions as to occasion a massive revolution in thought, out of which an alternate metaphysic would emerge. This is, I am convinced, our present situation. Not long after the publication of Einstein's special theory of relativity in 1905, many of the architects of what was fast becoming a revolution in scientific thought began to realize that they were not simply in the process of redefining concepts in a discipline, but were raising some formidable questions about the character of reality itself. They perceived, in short, that the revolution in physics seemed to be leading inexorably to a revolution in metaphysics, that a full acceptance of this new scientific view of the nature of things necessitated some profound changes in the conceptual machinery upon which an entire cosmos had been constructed.

Once we perceive that the common-sense assumptions in [classical and Newtonian] science are not a priori truths, but rather a consequence of the

From Readings from the *New Book on Nature: Physics and Metaphysics in the Modern Novel*, University of Massachusetts Press, 1981, pp. 1–16, 161–82.

experience of man in [a] particular culture, we should be better prepared to digest the concepts from the new physics that appear to undermine them. We should then be in a position to explore the mythopoeic function of this new science as it is now manifesting itself in the contemporary novel. Although most of the concepts from physics that have had an impact upon the novelists studied here can be traced to theoretical advances in physics made in the 1920s and '30s, we will also briefly review more recent controversies in quantum physics. Some of the novelists, like Pynchon and DeLillo, appear to have followed these developments rather closely, but the principal benefit of reviewing them is, I think, that they reveal a good deal about the fundamental organizing principles in the symbolic universe of Western man.

Although Don DeLillo's [first] six ... novels are considerably more limited in scope of reference and range of implications than the three novels of Thomas Pynchon, there is remarkable similarity between these novelists' individual conceptions of the contemporary human dilemma. Both assume that the tendency of Western man to construct reality in terms of closed systems and symbolics is not only without epistemological foundation, but also functions as program and guide for the fragmentation of individual identity and the possible extinction of the entire race of man. They also share the conviction that the continued survival of human civilization is dependent upon a fundamental restructuring of the dynamics of our world-conceiving minds, and each favors a return to a more primal sense of being that allows for an enlarged awareness of self as manifestation of one unified process. Although DeLillo, like Pynchon, is preoccupied with exposing the [Aristotelian] principle of the either-or as the most invidious dynamic in the construction of closed systems and symbolics, the purging from consciousness of abstract systems definitions of reality is normally accompanied in his fiction by a renewed awareness of the denotative aspect of language. DeLillo apparently feels, more strongly than Pynchon, that by detaching ourselves from the word as Logos, and placing greater emphasis upon the function of the word as concrete referent, we would be better able to construct an alternate reality more consistent with the metaphysics implied in the new physics.

The system under investigation in *Americana* is the electronic communications network, and the aspect of that system that receives the most careful scrutiny is the filmic image. David Bell, the youthful and thoroughly American protagonist, discovers in his work as a network producer that words and meaning were at odds. Words did not say what was being said or even the reverse. This child of Godard and Coca-Cola ... whose father and grandfather were both legends in the advertising industry, conceives of himself and others as little more than a compilation of images derived from a lifetime of exposure to movies and television programming. There is a tendency in this culture, speculates David early in the narrative, to regard the lens of the motion picture camera as history. What the machine accepts is verifiably existent; all else is unborn or worse.... His belief that conceptions of self are increasingly the projections of identity marketed by commercial films and television leads to the conclusion that the authentic or unique self is being trivialized out of existence.

Since the architects of this truth are the media managers who fashion images of the idealized self for the purpose of marketing products, the American dream, previously thought to be a function of received political and religious ideologies configuring in the lived experience of our cultural forebears, becomes increasingly the province of advertising. As David sees it, this new American dream made no allowance for the truth beneath the symbols, for the interlinear notes, the presence of something black (and somehow very funny) at the mirror of one's awareness. Bombarded all of his life with the institutional messages, the psalms and placards, the pictures, the words of the advertising industry, he senses that all the impulses of the media were fed into the circuitry of my dreams, and that he has become, finally, an image made in the image and likeness of images....

Exposure to media entices Americans, suggests DeLillo, to view gratification of impulse in terms of the likeness or image of self that appears in advertising to have the most access to scarce commodities.... What is finally merchandised, [explains David, through his home movie on American identity,] is the prospect of altering the image of the self for purposes of consumption, as opposed to refashioning, or reconstructing, the environ-ment to create larger possibilities for growth and satisfaction. This segment of David's film also includes the comment: Advertising discovered the value of the third person but the consumer invented him. The country itself invented him.... What this invention cannot represent, in that it reduces self to a set of single, composite, unidimensional images, is the richness and variety of experience in a diversified culture replete with contrasting life-styles and traditions. In the absence of extensive associations with the deep structure of received traditions and communal ethos that communicates the truth beneath the symbols, the individual ceases to be highly individuated and also suffers the loss of any profound sense of relation to that which is other.

The reasons that this [film] is not likely to be successful are best understood by [the sculptor named] Sullivan. Like so many of DeLillo's characters, David is fascinated with numbers, assumes that numbers have power, and also that the whole country runs on numbers.... The attempt to recover an authentic self in the film is wrong-headed in Sullivan's view because it mirrors self through numeration, or through a vast accumulation of static frames of film. This obsession with numbers is, she tells David, somewhat less than Euclidean in its sweep and purity; that one of my main faults was a tendency to get blinded by the neon of an idea, never reaching truly inside it; that to follow a number to infinity was not necessarily to arrive at God....

The collage of images that records the activities that represent, in David's perception, the life the culture deconstructs not into essences of identity, but rather into an ultimate cleavage between oppositions void of all signification.

[And yet the] movie actually succeeds in the sense that it demonstrates, like the novel itself, the impossibility of imposing closed systems or symbolics, constructed in terms of the either-or, upon the essentially fluid and indeterminate life process. This is not, however, as DeLillo suggests in the conclusion of the narrative, a widely accepted truth in American culture. Ten minutes after David Bell, image and product of the third-person singular, boards an aircraft to return to the mecca of the advertising industry in New York, a woman asks for his autograph....

In *End Zone* DeLillo is not, as some of the earlier reviewers presumed, drawing a simple-minded comparison between American football and modern warfare. What he has done in this narrative, with admirable ingenuity, is draw extensive parallels between the game as exemplar of all closed systems used in the construction of human reality, and the nuclear defense system. He then deconstructs the former in order to expose the latter as our most terrifying manifestation of the same habits of mind. Like Barth and Pynchon, who also dare to think the unthinkable in confronting the very real prospect of nuclear holocaust, the culprit for DeLillo is not the irremediable organization of our instinctual life, but the structure of our arbitrarily developed and potentially malleable symbolic universe.

Gary Harkness, the star running-back whose two major intellectual interests are the special character and appeal of football and the technology of nuclear war, attends four major universities before being recruited to play football for Logos College. The college, founded by a deaf mute, has undertaken an ambitious new football program under the direction of head coach Emmett Creed whose own illustrious career had been virtually destroyed when he broke the jaw of a second-string quarterback two years earlier at another university. The suggestion in the choice of names for coach and college that the game functions as emblem for systems definitions of reality is reinforced throughout the remainder of the narrative. Creed, famous for bringing order out of chaos, conceives of football as a complex of systems which ideally interlock in some final harmony....

[Gary's] deconstruction of the game reveals increasing resemblances between this system and the dramatically more lethal system of nuclear technology.... When the essential structure of football is bracketed out in the pick-up game in the snow through the elimination of huddles, customary gestures and postures, and even plays and opposing lines of players, what remains is the fundamental opposition between man with ball battling others to keep possession of ball. The either-or as fundamental feature in the construction of systems is inescapable in football just as it is in all other systems and double consciousness ..., as Gary's metaphysically minded fellow-player Bing points out, is just as inescapable here as it is elsewhere. Another player on this remarkable team, Ted Joost, even dreams about closure of the entire system of football with the use of a computer broadcasting signals to receivers in the helmets of every player in every game then being played....

Gary's intense fascination with the possibilities of nuclear war begins with his exposure to a book assigned in a course on disaster technology at the University of Miami.... Even in the face of serious depression over his seemingly perverse interest in the subject, Gary is irresistibly drawn to this display of the rationality of irrationality, in which tens of millions die and entire cities are destroyed.... Following a graphic description of the effects of nuclear blasts on cities and people, [Major Stanley, an AFROTC instructor,] comments that war is a test of opposing technologies configuring on such a high level of abstraction that nobody has to feel any guilt. Responsibility is distributed too thinly for that.... It is, as Gary comes to view it, the underlying systems organization of the arsenal that sustains its growth, mitigates responsibility for its existence, and which may, as the mind that creates it hungers for closure, eventually lead us to the apocalypse. This last prospect begins to seem even more likely to Gary when the major, in another private conversation later in the narrative, tells him that the big problem with war games, whether they were being played at the Pentagon, at Norad or Fort Belvoir, at a university or think tank, was the obvious awareness on the part of the participants that this wasn't the real thing.... The nuclear defense system becomes real, or ceases to function as simply an abstract schema of the possible, when, the major suggests, it is put into use. Closure in this system requires, in other words, the wedding of the ethereal war game, or war as unrealized possibility, with the war itself.

Although DeLillo in *Ratner's Star* is definitely exercising poetic license in suggesting that human civilization originated at a much earlier date than can be supported by scientific evidence, we discover in this narrative not only an impressive acquaintance with concepts from the new physics but also the manner in which these concepts inform his artistic vision.... After discovering at an early age an extraordinary ability to conduct this internal dialogue in mathematical codes, Billy [Twillig, fourteen-year-old Nobel laureate in mathematics,] learns to take pleasure in inhabiting that lonely place in his mind where he is free from subjection to reality, free to impose his ideas and designs on his own test environment.... This ardent disciple of the Pythagorean mathematical idea leaves his research post at The Center for the Refinement of Ideational Structures ... to journey to a vast, internationally funded scientific laboratory and think tank called Field Experiment Number One. It is the hope of the highly unorthodox directors of this project that Billy will succeed where others have failed in decoding radio messages emanating in space from the vicinity of the body known in astronomy as Ratner's star.

Billy, who reasons so thoroughly in the realm of the mathematical that he conceives of himself as having two existences, right and left in terms of an equation, and who also fears that the mathematical side might overwhelm the other, leaving him behind, a name and shape ..., functions in the narrative primarily as a vehicle through which DeLillo discourses upon the inability of closed scientific paradigms to fully contain or define natural process. Mathematical reasoning, with its claim to necessary conclusions; its pursuit of connective patterns and significant form ..., is premised upon assumptions, as Billy's mentor Softly points out in a work in progress, that are a product of an outmoded cosmology.

Late in the novel DeLillo, as omniscient narrator, deals directly and at some length with the metaphysical implications of the new physics and draws some fairly definite conclusions.... The prospect that the mathematical coordinates can provide a direct transcription of self is doubtful, he notes, because in the wave-guide manipulation of light and our nosings into the choreography of protons, we implicate ourselves in endless uncertainty. DeLillo then asserts that this is the ethic you've rejected. Inside our desolation, however, you come upon the reinforcing grid of works and minds that extend themselves against whatever lonely spaces account for our hollow moods, the woe incoming. Why are you here? To unsnarl us from our delimiting senses?... This compulsion to define the essence of our being as mathematical or scientific entity will eventually, he concludes, make us hypothetical, a creature of our own pretending, as are you....

DeLillo, like Pynchon, is definitely not advocating an end to scientific investigation, nor does he mean to belittle the enterprise in the least. He is using present scientific knowledge to make the case that closed systems of abstractions that tend toward closure are not only invalidated by this knowledge, but provide a virtual guarantee that the entire human experiment will come to an abrupt halt in nuclear war. Although this is precisely what takes place at the conclusion of *Ratner's Star*, DeLillo is far more explicit here than in his other narratives in delineating those features of language, or those terms in the construction of the symbolic universe, that have driven us, in his view, to this absurd predicament.

The closure of economic and political systems that brings on the holocaust appears, first of all, to be the consequence of the effort by a bizarre business tycoon named Troxl to establish complete control over the international money market.... As the cartel [of which Troxl is part], renamed significantly ACRONYM ..., begins to establish a monopoly over all model building organizations ..., including Field Experiment Number One, it becomes increasingly more effective in moving the international monetary exchange system toward closure. As this movement occurs, global tensions increase proportionally.

The same compulsion to transform human reality into an idée fixe by containing it within abstract systems definitions is also at work in the effort to develop in the Logicon project a universal language that would facilitate communication with extraterrestrial beings like those initially thought to be transmitting the radio message. As Lester Bolin, who is most involved in the project, explains, this metalanguage cannot be spoken by a computer until they figure out how to separate the language as system of meaningless signs from the language about language.... The problem, as the anthropologist Wu realizes, is that such a metalanguage cannot mirror the world because it involves the impossible attempt to free reality from the structures it must possess as long as there are humans to breed it.... Like any closed scientific paradigm that seeks to contain the open-ended, essentially indeterminate processes of nature, that which is finally mirrored is not the world but subjectively based human constructs. Since this mode of defining or explaining does not take into account the role of the observer in the participatory universe of the new physics, it communicates only itself.

The spokesman for the alternate metaphysics consistent with the new physics in this narrative is Shazar Lazarus Ratner, the impossibly aged and decrepit physicist after whom the star was named, who remains alive, ironically to be sure, only by virtue of an elaborate artificial life-support system. Ratner, like Whitehead, conceives of God, whom he refers to in the manner of orthodox Jews as G-dash-d, as identical with the endless process of becoming that is the life the universe.... Underlying the perceived world is, he says, the hidden. The that-which-is-not-there.... The inability to perceive, in normal states of consciousness, our proper relation to the ontological ground of Being is, suggests Ratner, largely due to the fact that everything in the universe works on the theory of opposites ..., including language. The lesson learned in quantum physics that all things are present in all things. Each in its opposite ..., has meaning, implies Ratner, only when we allow ourselves to go into mystical states and pass beyond the opposites of the world and experience only the union of opposites in a radiant burst of energy.... Although transcendence of oppositions in language systems is a precondition for apprehending our actual condition in metaphysical terms, this does not, as Ratner sees it, diminish the power or importance of language.... The point of Ratner's somewhat rambling discourse is that although oppositions are both useful and necessary in the construction of our knowledge of the cosmos, and have real existence in the life of the cosmos itself, we must balance this understanding against the recognition that they are manifestations of one fundamental unity, and are, therefore, not absolute.

When the scientists working on the Logicon project begin to sense that nuclear war is inevitable, they summon a woman from the slums who supposedly has unexplained insight into the future.... After struggling through a series of violent contortions, Skia Mantikos, whose name means shadow prophet ..., manages to utter a single, and from our perspective, very significant word: Pythagoras.... It is important, of course, that the scientists, including Billy, who are privileged to hear this prophetic word do not have the first clue as to what it might mean. All of which serves to communicate DeLillo's fear that because language systems, particularly the mathematical, are assumed capable of revealing the immalleable essence of the real in an ordered, predictable, and closed totality the Western intellectual tradition might well be incapable of even questioning the validity of that assumption.

BRUCE BAWER

Don DeLillo's America

Most of Don DeLillo's novels are born out of a preoccupation with a single theme: namely, that contemporary American society is the worst enemy that the cause of human individuality and self-realization has ever had. In one semi-surrealist opus after another, DeLillo has told the story of a conspicuously successful American who jumps off the assembly line and, in one way or another, tries to well find himself. *End Zone* (1972), for instance, is the story of Gary Harkness, a college football player who is revolted by the doctrine of team spirit; America, he says, is becoming a nation devoted to human xerography, and he wants to be more than a photocopy. So he leaves a promising gridiron career at Penn State and ends up playing ball at an obscure college in west Texas. *Great Jones Street* (1973) is about a rock star, Bucky Wunderlick, who, convinced his fans are not responding to him as individuals anymore but simply as a mob, drops out of his band in the middle of a successful tour and moves into a seedy East Village flat, where he becomes the focus of a bizarre drug plot straight out of Thomas Pynchon's *The Crying of Lot 49*. In *Players* (1977), a young stockbroker named Lyle Wynant leaves Yuppiedom behind when his fascination with a murder at the Stock Exchange leads him to become involved with terrorists. In *The Names* (1982), James Axton, an international businessman disenchanted with the life of a corporate jet-setter, is intrigued by an unusual series of cult murders in

From *The New Criterion*, Vol. III, No. 8, April, 1985, pp. 34-42.

Greece and the Mideast; like Wynant, he becomes increasingly obsessed and, ultimately, involved with the killers.

One thing that these novels all share, aside from the goodbye-American-dream motif, is a stunning implausibility. Representation of reality is not DeLillo's strong suit. It's hard to accept most of his characters as living, breathing human beings, or to conjure up a clear picture of Logos College in *End Zone* or the huge, futuristic scientific institute called Field Experiment Number One in *Ratner's Star* (1976), or to believe in the existence of all these cliques, clans, and cabals .... (pp. 34-5)

But then, these novels are not meant to be true-to-life tales. They are tracts, designed to batter us, again and again, with a single idea: that life in America today is boring, benumbing, dehumanized. Not only has the American system robbed us of our individuality; the era's despicable technological innovations have afflicted us all with a dreadful condition known as sensory overload a term introduced by a character in *Great Jones Street*:

> A man in Missouri spent a hundred and sixty-one days in a deep cavern.... He ate canned food, he drank water, he burned over nine hundred candles. He said it's the first time in his life he wasn't bored. Sensory overload. People are withdrawing from sensory overload. Technology. Whenever there's too much technology, people return to primitive feats ....

Return to primitivism: this, in different ways and to varying degrees, is what the protagonists do in most of DeLillo's novels. Harkness's tiny Texas college, Wunderlick's East Village flat, Wynant's terrorists, and Axton's cult are all versions of the Missourian's cave they are places to escape to, refuges from a technologically overdeveloped society whose major achievement, DeLillo would have us believe, is to have dragged us further and further away from our true selves.

And what are our true selves? DeLillo's answer to that question is clear. To DeLillo, to be human means to be, at heart, a primitive beast; those of us who live in high-tech America are, therefore, more out of touch with our humanness than any humans who have ever lived. To find oneself one must, like the Missouri caveman, return to primitivism; and in the world according to DeLillo, returning to primitivism means, in essence, entering into a community, conspiracy, or subculture governed largely by primitive violence. In DeLillo's overly diagrammatic world, savagery is the only alternative to depersonalization by means of sensory overload; only through a pure, brute physicality can one reclaim one's selfhood.... At the heart of each of DeLillo's novels is the assumption that, deep down, all human beings long to wreak havoc, to run wild, to kill.... [To] DeLillo, art in present-day America, anyway has got to confront the primitive yearning, deep inside every human soul, to kill, maim, and destroy.

Why? Because if you don't, you're denying your humanness. It's better, DeLillo seems to say in one novel after another, to be a marauding, murderous maniac and therefore a human than to sit still for America as it is, with its air-conditioners, assembly lines, television sets, supermarkets, synthetic fabrics, and credit cards. At least when you're living a life of primitive violence, you're closer to the mystery at the heart of it all. That's what life is to DeLillo: a mystery, an enigma. His books are full of codes, ciphers, secret names and places and organizations. Most of the books take the form of suspense stories (why is the cult murdering these people in *The Names*? what do the conspirators want with Wunderlick in *Great Jones Street*? what's the meaning of the interplanetary radio signal in *Ratner's Star*?) but significantly the clues never add up to much of anything. By the end of the typical DeLillo novel, in fact, things are hovering pretty near the point of utter incomprehensibility. What is always clear, however, is that one is supposed to come away from these novels convinced that life is a teleological puzzle that no novelist (or scientist, for that matter) is ever going to piece together a mystery that technological advances can only serve to distance us from.

White Noise represents yet another go at these rapidly aging nihilistic clichés. This time around, the passenger on the Primitivism Express is Jack Gladney, professor of (like it or not) Hitler Studies at a large Eastern college. Though, like all DeLillo heroes, Jack is a connoisseur of destruction, and though he starts making gibes about our stifling assembly-line culture on the first page of the book, it takes an airborne toxic event in his hometown to make him truly frantic about his mortality and the unrelieved emptiness of his life. It doesn't help any, either, when he discovers that his wife Babette, a teacher of posture, has slept with another man, a quack doctor who claims to have developed a drug that eradicates the fear of death. Though it is less surrealist than any of his previous novels, *White Noise* as is par for the course with DeLillo grows steadily darker, more fantastic, its direction less and less clear. Jack, like Axton in *The Names*, grows obsessive, loses touch with his family, breaks out of his structured existence. He learns from his colleague Murray that there are two kinds of people in the world. Killers and diers. Most of us are diers (mainly, it seems, because we don't have the guts to be killers). Violence, Murray explains, is a form of rebirth, murder a means of self-liberation. Jack decides he is a killer. He starts carrying a gun with him to school; eventually he steals the neighbors' car and, rod in tow, seeks out the quack doctor.

There should be profound emotions at work here, but *White Noise* is, like its predecessors, so masterfully contrived a piece of argumentation that believable human feelings and actions are few and far between. There is hardly a natural moment in the whole book. Characters do not think, they cogitate; they do not talk, they engage in dialectic and deliver endless monologues about the novel's major themes. It is often difficult to tell them apart when reading a stretch of dialogue, because they all sound exactly alike. Indeed, with rare exceptions, they all think exactly alike. When they are not pondering the significance of one contemporary American phenomenon or another (e.g., supermarkets, TV commercials, the *National Enquirer*), they are contemplating life, death, and the cosmos. And when their mouths open, they produce clipped, ironic, self-consciously clever sentences full of offbeat metaphors and quaint descriptive details.

Life itself, that queer entity that Flaubert and Tolstoy and Thomas Mann somehow never grew tired of describing does not interest DeLillo at all; for him, life seems to exist so that we can theorize about it. He never leaves anything alone and just lets it be. His narrator and characters, in *White Noise* as elsewhere, are always knee-jerk generalizers. The introductory description of Babette, for instance (Babette is tall and fairly ample .... Her hair is a fanatical blond mop), turns within a couple of sentences into a broad, seemingly frivolous general statement, the only apparent purpose of which could be to reduce Babette to a stereotype: If she were a petite woman, the hair would be too cute, too mischievous and contrived. Ample women do not plan such things. They lack the guile for conspiracies of the body. Later in the novel, Jack observes that his teenage son's hairline is receding, wonders guiltily whether he might be at fault (Have I raised him, unwittingly, in the vicinity of a chemical dump site ...?), and before you know it has happily found himself a suitable generality: Man's guilt in history and in the tides of his own blood has been complicated by technology, the daily seeping falsehearted death. DeLillo's, quite clearly, is a mind that lets itself be violated by any old idea that happens along.

If you like your novels studded with these kinds of Philosophy McNuggets, you'll love *White Noise*. Lead a character in this novel into a supermarket, bank, or kitchen, and presto! he launches, unbidden, into an impromptu interpretive essay, the thrust of which is that deep beneath the surface of our plastic culture lurk the manifold mysteries of human existence.

Of course, supermarkets and banks and kitchens can hold symbolic meanings for people. But why, pray tell, must those meanings be talked about endlessly, with such awesome banality and at such tiresome, unrevealing length? DeLillo's purpose in having his characters carry on about supermarkets and banks, of course, is chiefly ironic: to him, such phenomena are paramount signs of the dehumanization of America. He is, as might be expected, especially devoted to the tiredest of all contemporary clichés, the one about the tyranny of television. In *White Noise*, as in *Players* (at the beginning of which Lyle Wynant is a cathode-ray addict of psychotic proportions), DeLillo portrays the American mind, high and low, as being haunted constantly by sounds and images from the tube. At times, to be sure, he comes close to a perceptive characterization of the role that commercial slogans, jingles, and brand names play in some TV-centered American households, interpolating, for instance, stray sentences from the Gladney family's television set into the stream of dialogue. But DeLillo defeats any hope of verisimilitude by going way overboard. During the airborne toxic event, he has Jack describe the huge black cloud of poisonous Nyodene gas (the novel's major symbol) as resembl[ing] a national promotion for death, a multimillion-dollar campaign backed by radio spots, heavy print and billboard, TV saturation. This description does not help the reader to see the cloud, or serve to consolidate its symbolic pre-eminence in the book; it tends, rather, to diminish it. It is inconceivable that a man whose family was threatened by a cloud of toxic gas would describe it in such a way. The simile is an utterly contrived one, dictated not by the author's intuitive gift for imagery but by his polemical motives, his obsession with commercialism. The only image it fixes in the mind is one of DeLillo himself, sitting at his typewriter, mechanically tapping out his book.

DeLillo's people don't talk about things, if they can help it; they talk about the nature of things. Jack's smug, brainy fourteen-year-old son Heinrich (the successor of obnoxiously brilliant adolescents in *The Names* and *Ratner's Star*) likes to expatiate upon the nature of modern knowledge: "What good is knowledge if it just floats through the air? It goes from computer to computer. It changes and grows every second of every day. But nobody actually knows anything." Murray, for his part, discourses pretentiously about the nature of modern death: "It has a life independent of us. It is growing in prestige and dimension ...." We can take cross-section pictures of it, tape its tremors and waves .... But it continues to grow, to acquire breadth and scope, new outlets, new passages and means. The more we learn, the more it grows. The less DeLillo's characters have to say, the more they talk.

Perhaps the most disturbing aspect of *White Noise* is Jack's fascination with Hitler. The dictator is the subject not only of his professional research but of his private obsessions. He has hitched his wagon to Hitler because, as Murray tells him, You thought [Hitler] would protect you. Jack admits as much when he explains why he named his son Heinrich: "I thought it had an authority that might cling to him. I thought it was forceful and impressive and I still do. I wanted to shield him, make him unafraid." He tells his daughter Denise:

> There's something about German names, the German language, German things. I don't know what it is exactly. It's just there. In the middle of it all is Hitler, of course.
>
> He was on again last night.
>
> He's always on. We couldn't have television without him.
>
> They lost the war, she said. How great could they be?
>
> A valid point. But it's not a question of greatness.
>
> It's not a question of good and evil. I don't know what it is. Look at it this way. Some people always wear a favorite color. Some people carry a gun. Some people put on a uniform and feel bigger, stronger, safer. It's in this area that my obsessions dwell.

Keep in mind that this is DeLillo's idea of a sympathetic character. Indeed, we are clearly meant to see Jack as the archetypal twentieth-century victim—a victim whose sense of helplessness is so profound that he cannot help but succumb to the temptation, shocking but psychologically understandable, to identify with the aggressor; and since Jack is the archetypal twentieth-century victim, whom else could DeLillo have him identify with but the century's premier aggressor, Adolf Hitler?

White Noise is not, as it happens, the first DeLillo novel in which Hitler has made an appearance. Quite the contrary. Germany, Nazism, Hitler haunt DeLillo's novels the way Maud Gonne haunts the poetry of Yeats. The reason is obvious: Hitler is the ultimate example of twentieth-century man reverting to primitivism. If the nature of humanity is essentially a dark mystery, Hitler is the murderous monster at the heart of that darkness. He is (so DeLillo seems to feel) all of us writ large. This, presumably, is why there is a rock group in *Great Jones Street* named Schicklgruber and, in *End Zone*, a character named Hauptfuhrer; it is why, in the latter novel, there is a student who wants to get my hair dyed blond so everybody will think I' m one of those small blondie boys with that faraway look in their eyes who used to be so big on the Himmelplatz three or four decades ago. It's why the putative pornographic film at the thematic center of *Running Dog* turns out to be not pornography at all but a film of Hitler, in derby, wing collar, baggy pants, and boutonniere, doing an imitation of Charlie Chaplin. It's why, in *White Noise*, Jack and Murray compare notes on their respective scholarly subjects, Hitler and Elvis, and discover that the two men were really very much alike. DeLillo's point, throughout, is unmistakable: Hitler was just like us. We are all Hitler.

Am I alone in finding this whole business extremely offensive? DeLillo's offense, to my mind, is that he refuses to make distinctions. To him, as to Jack Gladney, the question of Hitler is simply not a question of good and evil. Nor, it is clear, do moral considerations enter into his appraisal of any human act. A craving for primitive destructiveness dwells deep in all our hearts, DeLillo's books insist; it is what makes us human. But is DeLillo honestly interested in what makes us human? I submit that he is not. His characters are little more than authorial mouthpieces, all but interchangeable with one another. And what makes human beings fascinating, and worth writing novels about, is their differences. Real people talk differently and think differently and have different interests and tastes and fears. None of this is reflected in DeLillo's novels. It is impossible, in the end, to accept his characters as human beings, or to take his novels seriously as representations of reality. All they amount to, really, is documents in the history of nihilistic chic.

But it is probably declasse of me to try to discuss DeLillo's novels as representations of reality. Surely, I can hear DeLillo's devotees saying, you realize his true subject is not 'real life' at all, or even ideas about life, but words, words, words—language, codes of every kind, the whole question of signification? Very well, it's true: DeLillo's narrators and characters are constantly talking about language. Football, Harkness tells us in *End Zone*, is the one sport guided by language, by the word signal, the snap number, the color code, the play name. The murders in *The Names* are likewise guided by language: Axton's cult chooses its victims by their initials. DeLillo's characters are, as a rule, unusually sensitive to words, often worrying, in casual conversation with friends and family, about whether they've used le mot juste.

Words the very sound or look of them, utterly divorced from their meanings alternately hurt and comfort these people. (p. 41)

Though DeLillo's philosophy of language is not perfectly coherent or consistent, it is clear that his preoccupation is not with language as a means of communicating sophisticated ideas and complicated feelings, but with language as ritual. The ultimate purpose of language, DeLillo seems to feel, is not to convey meaning but simply to affirm one's existence. Language, especially language freed of the rhetorical trappings of civilization and the illusion that scientific progress leads to greater understanding, is, simply, the cry of human identity. This idea dominates the end of *The Names*, when James Axton, at the Parthenon, is surrounded by people speaking a variety of tongues and realizes that [t]his is what we bring to the temple, not prayer or chant or slaughtered rams. Our offering is language. The fundamental importance of language as a ritual of identity is likewise suggested toward the end of *White Noise*, when Jack wonders: "Is there something so innocent in the recitation of names that God is pleased?"

One cannot deny that all this is at least theoretically interesting. And it is certainly conceivable that a compelling novel of ideas might be built on an intellectual foundation much like the one I have outlined. DeLillo, however, has yet to write it. Though his preoccupation with the philosophy of language occasionally yields thought-provoking, or at least memorably expressed, observations (e.g., Mathematics is what the world is when we subtract our own perceptions), it generally results in little more than one discouraging battery after another of pointless, pretentious rhetoric. He does not develop ideas so much as juggle jargon.

What makes the case of Don DeLillo especially unfortunate is that he does have real talent. He has always had a flair for humor—dark humor, naturally, of the Vonnegut-Heller sort—and that gift, in particular, is demonstrated in *White Noise* more abundantly than in any of DeLillo's previous books. But his continuing lack of interest in developing his characters and ideas, and his stubborn adherence to a stylish, schematic view of modern America as a great big xerox machine, continue to cripple DeLillo as an imaginative writer. It's ironic. While those of us who live in the real America carry on with our richly varied, emotionally tumultuous lives, DeLillo (as *White Noise* amply demonstrates) continues, in effect, to write the same lifeless novel over and over again—a novel constructed upon a simpleminded political cliché, populated by epigram-slinging, epistemology-happy robots, and packed with words that have very little to say to us about our world, our century, or ourselves. If anyone is guilty of turning modern Americans into xerox copies, it is Don DeLillo.

GREG TATE

White Magic: Don DeLillo's Intelligence Networks

It seemed inevitable that DeLillo would one day write *Libra*, his new novel about Lee Harvey Oswald and the CIA. Not just because he's fascinated with the conspiratorial bent of the human species, but because in DeLillo's fiction Everyman is as culpable for the state of things as the monstrous secret agencies of power. DeLillo's books don't read like moral fiction; he doesn't write moralizing prose. But his fictional worldview has always implied a moral taxonomy unblinking enough to lump the sins of the lowly in with those of the Feds....

For DeLillo's small-time operators, history is a wilderness waiting to be conquered by sheer force of personality. The construction of a false persona—which looks like their shot at immortality—instead becomes the arena for a bumrush on insignificance. Hot in pursuit of the neuroses of lost souls, DeLillo subjects their ethical blind sides to the same condemnation he puts down on the powerful. Condemnation, however, is too inelegant a word for the way ethical lessons are handed out in DeLillo's books—mainly in one scintillating sentence after another. The epigrammatic rush of his sentences suggests a prose ménage a trois of Chandler, Sartre, and Barthes. Surgical and shamanistic, a DeLillo sentence mixes existentialism and deconstruction in a style charged with the cool vernacular zing that Crane, Twain, and

From *VLS*, No. 68, October, 1988, pp. 39-41.

Hemingway brought into the language and that Chandler made sing like guttertalk.

Like Chandler, DeLillo loves an epiphany as much as he loves a mystery, and in Oswald and the CIA he's latched on to subject matter that allows him to toss some combination lallapaloozas. While other DeLillo novels have read like metafiction whodunits, *Libra* shrewdly involves us more with the mystery of Oswald's being than with why Kennedy was assassinated. On the sly, *Libra* performs a service to popular history by putting to rest the notion of Oswald as a lone gunman who popped out of nowhere.

The weight of facts supporting the argument that Oswald was a pawn or creation of U.S. intelligence—at the very least well known to them long before November 22, 1963 is overwhelming. In Oswald, after all, we have a Marine who defects to Russia after receiving security clearance at a U2 spy-plane base in Japan, goes to the American embassy in Moscow and throws down his passport, belligerently declaring himself a Marxist. He leaves Russia married to the niece of a Russian colonel. Upon his return to the U.S., he's visited by FBI and CIA operatives and pumped for information; soon he's seen passing out pro-Castro literature in Miami.

As DeLillo runs his version, the assassination plot is hatched by the CIA masterminds Kennedy betrayed when he refused air support for their anti-Castro operatives during the Bay of Pigs. In planning an assassination attempt they hope to blame on Castro, these agents concoct an imaginary assassin. The joke is that if Oswald hadn't existed, the CIA would have invented him.

Libra reaches fuguish complexity in floating every possible source for a Kennedy assassination plot you've ever heard—Oswald as lone gunman, Mafia, pro-Castro and anti-Castro operatives, Russians—while clearly settling on a CIA conspiracy. Through narrative legerdemain and a sense of detail bordering on the cartographic, DeLillo doesn't close the door on any of the suspects, even as he's narrowing it down to his chosen ones....

Libra stretches credulity with a string of coincidences that can make even synchronicity diehards beg for relief. Were DeLillo not such a spooky writer, the novel might collapse beneath its parallel narrative shafts and converging plot lines. DeLillo doesn't just invent characters; he possesses them, inhabiting their personas, like a vampire or psychotherapist. His social range, always vast, has never seemed so preternaturally knowledgeable. When he takes you inside the head of Jack Ruby or a Russian intelligence man or Oswald's mama, you feel like a telepathic and unrepentant voyeur— or a gatherer of covert information. Same difference, and another metafictional effect: DeLillo replicates the very thing he's deconstructing.

Geographically and structurally, the novel roams with Oswald all over space and time: Texas, the Bronx, Dallas, Miami, Japan, Russia. It also takes place in the present: Nicholas Branch, a retired CIA historian, has been assigned the fool's task of writing an account of the assassination.

Libra is most obsessed with the Spook Mind, the psyche of the secret police set loose upon the world by the powerful. The bulk of the book's characters are spies—Ivy League spooks and aristocratic émigré operatives, anti-Castro spooks and spies who moonlight with the John Birch Society, Russian intelligence men and Japanese double agents, U2 pilot Francis Gary Powers. The cult of secret intelligence is rendered as a faith, the men in it driven less by purpose than by fear of being left out in the cold. Behind the freebooting adventurism is the anxiety of being turned out of the warm womb of the national intelligence apparatus.

While the Kennedy assassination has been seen as the harbinger of things to come in the '60s U.S. of A., prelude to an era of shocking political violence, through DeLillo we come to see the Bay of Pigs and the many failed plots against Castro as the era's true preview—the first inkling that the American imperialist monster might not be such hot shit after all. The CIA cowboys who had to live with the Bay of Pigs disaster had failed the macho credo of the patriarchy. In *Libra*, we come to sense that the defeat embarrassed their culture, and they decided to place the blame on Kennedy's head.

Oswald and the renegade spooks become, in DeLillo's hands, case studies of the white supremacist male as Other, as a species flailing against the reality that history is moving so fast their only hope for survival is going undercover—plotting and scheming against the world because subversion has become the last refuge of their dying doctrine. As with all DeLillo novels, *Libra* is also fiction about the making of fiction, and about those fictionalized versions of the facts that we call history. DeLillo's reconstruction of Oswald from the data that has his CIA historian Branch in a tizzy is a satirical celebration of the freedom of fiction makers to play around with the facts.

The most poignant reward of DeLillo's fiction is being seduced by the pity and compassion he showers on the coldblooded monsters among his characters. I'm thinking of a scene involving the most ruthless of DeLillo's CIA cowboys, T-Jay Mackey—though dozens of other close-ups on the domestic lives of spies in *Libra* illustrate the same point....

It's DeLillo's portrayal of Oswald, though, that nearly makes you want to cry. Oswald comes on the set star-crossed, fucked from birth. His daddy dies of a heart attack before he's born, and he and his mother spend most of his childhood living at the poor-house gate. The relationship between

Oswald and his mom is claustrophobic, spiteful, and unrooted. In Texas, to which he will one day return on his mission, his Bronx accent gets him figured for a geek. Oswald is no nerd—he's just consumed by the belief that he's destined for something more than routine white-boydom.

Like several other DeLillo protagonists, Oswald has a problem with language and verbal communication, possibly in the form of dyslexia.

Always the pain, the chaos of composition. He could not find order in the little field of symbols.... [T]he language tricked him with its inconsistencies. He watched sentences deteriorate, powerless to make them right. The nature of things was to be elusive. Things slipped through his perceptions. He could not get a grip on the runaway world. Limits everywhere. In every direction he came up against his own incompleteness. Cramped, fumbling, deficient. He knew things. It wasn't that he didn't know.

DeLillo might well be alluding to his own tortured creative process—to the burden of needing infinite knowledge to write his kind of books. Not only does he need to know Oswald; he needs to know the Oswald others know. In the metafiction that is *Libra*, every other character seems to be creating a fictitious Oswald, preying on Oswald's impassioned sense of self-destiny and limited self-knowledge—even Oswald, who endlessly invents and reinvents his own myth. But in a sense he remains an enigma to himself. The voice that lays claim to knowing the real Oswald belongs to Oswald's mother, who throughout his life is forever negotiating to get him a better deal from fate. She may be the most berserk stage mother ever encountered in literature. As Oswald stumbles toward his destiny, she's always one step behind, attempting to explain the plot that's been in effect against her son's life from birth. And in seeking some plot, any plot, she scrambles and rambles out a first-person history as overbaked with irrationality as the Official Story.

Against DeLillo's observation that all plots, and hence all narratives, inevitably end in death, Oswald's mother's narrative is the unhinged and chaotic narrative of life, the force that goes on and on beyond the power of the machinations of men to contain it, control it, silence it, deny it, and ultimately to historicize it. DeLillo makes us remember that even Lee Harvey Oswald had a mother and, therefore, once upon a time, an innocence. Through Marguerite Oswald's arguments, DeLillo demonstrates that the God-novelist not only has the power to peek into his neighbors'skulls and pass judgment, but to listen intimately, to record the fragility and folly of that absolving mechanism figuratively known as the human heart....

GREGORY SALYER

Myth, Magic and Dread: Reading Culture Religiously

I have been asked to reflect upon the values and assumptions that inform my teaching and writing as a professor working in the area of religion and literature. My first response is to thank David Jasper and the contributors to this issue for even raising the question. All too often those of us who are trained to analyze texts and arguments are the most blind to the assumptions that pervade our own work as individuals and scholars working within the academy. I am not going to make the argument that we can unpack our assumptions, lay them out on the table, and then consider our self-reflective work to be finished. My point is, rather, that we tend to turn our critical lenses outwardly much more eagerly and vigorously than we do inwardly. While any assumptions that we deign to expose will always be informed by deeper, antecedent assumptions, the process of looking inward is valuable, even necessary I would argue, if we are to be critics in the fullest sense of the word. The special issue of the *Journal of the American Academy of Religion* entitled 'Settled Issues and Neglected Questions in the Study of Religion' (Winter 1994) is a step in this direction. The initial discussion that gave rise to the present issue began at the annual meeting of the American Academy of Religion in Washington DC in 1993. The conversation, however, took place not in a session but in a Thai restaurant somewhere in the city. We must have made quite a sight: several people engaged in an intense discussion

From *Literature and Theology: An International Journal of Theory, Criticism and Culture*, Vol. 9, No. 3, September, 1995, pp. 261-77.

of theology, religion, and literature over curried chicken and wine. That the conversation took place outside the formal confines of the conference is a shame; that it took place at all indicates to me that many of us do want to create a context for self-reflective discussions of what we do, how we do it, and why.

Gayatri Spivak has noted that scholars are the disc jockeys of culture, spinning hits like Shakespeare, Milton, and Toni Morrison to which our students and other audiences are supposed to dance. She is partly right of course, but we are also much more. We are interpreters of culture in all of its expressions and dynamics. We are critics who constantly pull apart the threads in the fabric of culture. We point out the tears and even attempt to patch the holes. As scholars of religion and literature we occupy a privileged position in this analysis because we concern ourselves with the construction and interpretation of meaning and value. We observe and participate in the processes of meaning-making, and we both supervise and lament the passing of meaning as it flickers and dies. We also ask about the meaning of meaning of meaning and interrogate the products of culture through discourses such as religion and literature.

To help focus my discussion, I will use three novels by two different writers: Leslie Marmon Silko's *Ceremony* and *Almanac of the Dead* and Don DeLillo's *White Noise*. *Ceremony* is one of the most acclaimed American novels of this century and is one of a quartet of Native American novels (along with N. Scott Momaday's *House Made of Dawn*, James Welch's *Winter in the Blood*, and Louise Erdrich's *Tracks*) that defines the Native American 'renaissance' of the last half of this century. *Almanac* is Silko's tour de force and presents her vision of the future and of the past in an historiographic rumination on the end of white history and the reconstitution of native peoples on the land that bore them. DeLillo's *White Noise* is in my view the best articulation of the American mythos in the late twentieth century. It is a sustained yet fragmented meditation upon plots, technology, death, and other cultural phenomena. These three novels represent well the issues that I seek to engage as a religious reader of American culture. *White Noise* offers a world that calls for iconoclasm and for the realization of the motives behind interpretation as language approaches myth and technology approaches magic. Silko's two novels offer a very different picture of how myth and magic can overcome the dread that pervades *White Noise*. What emerges from these readings are diverse strategies for doing the work of a religion and literature critic, and these strategies all focus on the processes and products of meaning.

Early in the novel *White Noise* we are introduced to The Most Photographed Barn in America, a tourist attraction somewhere in New England that draws amateur and professional photographers from around the country. After some contemplation of the scene surrounding the most photographed barn in America, Murray, a wacked-out semiotician and cultural critic, observes cryptically, 'No one sees the barn.' He explains by noting that 'Once you've seen the signs about the barn, it becomes impossible to see the barn'[1]. A marvellous example of poststructuralist theory in action, this scene in *White Noise* depicts more than the tyranny of the sign and the illusions of presence. For me it presents the challenges of cultural criticism: the opportunity to see behind the masks of our cultural icons, the opportunity to resist the built-in interpretation of ideas and images that are manufactured for public consumption, and the opportunity to observe the dynamics of interpretation that flow in, around, and through the hermeneutic material of culture. As cultural critics we offer strategies of resistance to the pre-packaged interpretations that are delivered to us in the guises of what is valuable, meaningful, and true. In being iconoclasts we open new channels of interpretation of the sacred. We are negative theologians: negative in our iconoclasm, theological in our exploration of the sacred.

The most photographed barn in America is lost beneath the palimpsest of signs that precede and announce it. Murray the critic is able to peel off these layers and gaze upon the emptiness beneath. Murray is a self-conscious interpreter and thus knows that even he is the product of strategies, assumptions, and beliefs that are themselves palimpsests and open to critical interpretation. Like Murray, religious readers know that they are always participants in the process of interpretation. This process creates a conversation; it keeps knowledge fluctuating and moving; it empowers interpreters while promising nothing. There is little or no conversation among the tourists who gaze upon the (non-) spectacle of the barn because the image has contained within it a monologic stop that resists interpretation and demands only to be seen. We know better than to accept this presentation. Murray dissolves the power of the image by deconstructing its inherent interpretation and by speculating upon its source. 'We're not here to capture an image,' he notes, 'we're here to maintain one' (12). The search for origins, Derrida has taught us, is ultimately fruitless in terms of finding an original presence. The result of that search, however, is a deconstructive process that opens up the 'text' and invades our individual interpretive space by challenging us to view our own creations born of hermeneutic naiveté.

The religious reader of culture asks why we fall for the illusion of capturing something when it can be shown that we are creating and maintaining it in the process. This need for hermeneutic stasis speaks to our incessant desire for a meaning which will stand still and be analyzed. But any meaning that stands still for an interpreter is not sacred, though sacredness is precisely the rhetoric that is used to sell meaning to a public all too willing to surrender to it. Even Murray knows that the barn scene calls for a religious reading. He remarks, 'Being here is a kind of spiritual surrender. We see only what the others see ... A religious experience in a way, like all tourism' (12). Cultural critics resist that surrender while imaginatively participating in it. Herein lies the age-old dilemma of studying religion and/or any sort of cultural signifying system. One needs to be inside to appreciate the experience and yet outside to escape the seductive power of the text or image. Frank Kermode's observation in The Genesis of Secrecy is appropriate here. We are all both insiders and outsiders, and being inside an event or text is simply a more elaborate way of being outside[2]. As cultural critics and interpreters, we centre our work on the nothingness of the sacred that lies just on the other side of language. While language is both mythical and magical, the hollow centre that we seek evokes dread. In Western culture at least, language was thought to stand between us and the world. In the late twentieth century, we know that language creates the world. That knowledge, or that crucial fiction at least, does not satisfy our thirst for meaning any more than the other theories of language do. We desire more than mirrors and windows; we seek meaning outside the prison-house of language. As Thomas Altizer explains, we seek nothingness, and our search is a religious one: 'Is religious studies now truly assuming its ultimately priestly role, a role of deeply sanctioning our nothingness, and sanctioning it by knowing it as reality itself, and not only as reality, but as an ultimate reality, and an ultimate reality which is sanctioned by way of bestowing upon it the aura of religion itself?'[3] Religious interpretation is an exercise in nihilism, an attempt to peel off the layers of language in order to discover the nothing beneath.

The protagonist in White Noise, Jack Gladney, observes, 'What we are reluctant to touch often seems the very fabric of our salvation' (31). We are always outsiders to our own salvation, but the desire for meaning keeps us searching. As the Buddha explained, desire causes suffering, and our desire for meaning creates many problems. Among these are distance and difference. Cultural icons like the most photographed barn in America create distance and otherness under the illusion of narrative cohesiveness and communitas. As cultural critics in general and as religion and literature critics in particular, we can offer interpretive strategies that dissolve the otherness that cultural icons create as we criticize the very desire to construct mass-produced and advertised pseudo-communities that empower the generators of the idols while fragmenting the culture as a whole.

The failure to find community does not hamper the search for it. Myth, magic, and ritual persist despite (or perhaps because of) the hole in the centre of existence that draws us in but stops us from entering. We tell stories in order to mythicize our experiences, to make them community property, and thereby to make some connection to the world and to those who live in it. Our stories appear more frequently now and with less depth and breadth, but they all centre on absence or loss. 'Storytelling is always after the fact, and it is always constructed over a loss' notes J. Hillis Miller in Fiction and Repetition. Stories hover around the absences that we call the sacred; they weave themselves around the hole in an effort to achieve wholeness. They do not stick but are sloughed off as newer and possibly more meaningful stories appear. I think especially of how the Vietnam War is uninterpretable for thinking Americans to this day. We consistently fail to tell the story in a satisfactory way, and so we keep telling stories that attempt to weave themselves around the event, to bring its many strands together in a meaningful way. We want a coherent story, not necessarily a story with a happy ending, but at least a story that provides some orientation, even if it is temporary. What we need is myth, and there are few to be found and none that last.

What happens when the icons of mass culture are demythologized or undermythologized is that the common and everyday becomes the stuff of the imagination and is elevated to the status of mythic material. As Jack Gladney says in White Noise. 'The world is full of abandoned meanings. In the commonplace I find unexpected themes and intensities' (184). Because his interpretive acumen has revealed the paucity of traditional mythical and magical material, he turns to other elements of the world to find meaning. Like many of us, Jack Gladney was 'ready to search anywhere for signs and hints, intimations of odd comfort.' His search takes place literally under the cloud of the Airborne Toxic Event, a mysterium tremendum et fascinans in the form of a plume that erupts from a punctured tanker car. The cloud produces what Jack describes as 'a sense of awe that bordered on the religious.' The nearby town is evacuated, and Jack has the opportunity to reflect upon a new situation that offers new data to analyze and another attempt to find a story or some magical formula that will produce a meaningful experience. He finds it. As the huddled evacuees sleep, Jack pulls up a chair to observe his children and hears Steffie muttering something. Jack is convinced that she is revealing something important from the recesses of the collective unconscious, 'fitting together units of stable meaning ...

words that seemed to have a ritual meaning, part of a verbal spell or ecstatic chant.' The words that he finally understands Steffie to be mumbling are Toyota Celica. The truth of the cliché only amazed him more. He discovers a moment of 'splendid transcendence' in his daughter's unconscious repetition of an advertisement. Jack discovers his meaning, his experience of the sacred in an apotheosis of the profane. White noise has been elevated to the level of myth and magic.

For Gladney meaning appears in unexpected connections between disparate things (magic) and in the construction of meaning around these events through language (myth). 'It was these secondary levels of life, these extrasensory flashes and floating nuances of being, these pockets of rapport forming unexpectedly, that made me believe we were a magic act, adults and children together, sharing unaccountable things' (34). The secondary levels of life are mined for meaning because the primary levels are exhausted by interpretation. Like the barn, they are layers of programmed responses around a core of nothing.

Our cultural critic/semiotician Murray is the best example of such searching for meaning in the commonplace. He is the sniffer of grocery items, the one open to letting waves and radiation flow through him in hopes of discerning some pattern. One of Murray's favourite fetishes is of course television. He speaks of it as the channel to the sacred.

You have to learn how to look. You have to open yourself to the data. TV offers incredible amounts of psychic data. It opens ancient memories of world birth, it welcomes us into the grid, the network of little buzzing dots that make up the picture pattern ... The medium practically overflows with sacred formulas if we can remember how to respond innocently and get past our irritation, weariness and disgust. (51)

The data is there; all that is lacking is an interpretative strategy that will make it come alive. So the question of finding meaning in a world exhausted by interpretation and commodification centres on the will to interpretation and on the availability of viable hermeneutic modes, an inexhaustible supply of which exists in *White Noise*.

To Murray's list of hindrances to seeing the psychic data, I would add one other—dread. We dread interpretation precisely because it is an exercise of working toward absence, which produces the ultimate sense of being outside. The temptation we all face is to interpret passively by accepting the commodified meaning of things. Active interpretation is hard work and leads ultimately to absence. It is much better, we seem to think, to live with the illusions of presence and with our inside/outside dualities than to face the faceless countenance of nothing. How much easier and even rewarding it is to let interpretation happen to us. In doing so we help to maintain the images that are static, commodified, and empty of meaning, like that of the most photographed barn in America. Murray sees this idea evident in the psychic data that presents itself in the grocery store, which for him is a version of heaven.

Everything is concealed in symbolism, hidden by veils of mystery and layers of cultural material. But it is psychic data, absolutely. The large doors slide open, they close unbidden. Energy waves, incident radiation. All the letters and numbers are here, all the colors of the spectrum, all the voices and sounds, all the code words and ceremonial phrases. It is just a question of deciphering, rearranging, peeling off the layers of unspeakability. Not that we would want to, not that any useful purpose would be served. This is not Tibet. Even Tibet is not Tibet anymore. (38)

Murray, while calling for active interpretation, nonetheless promises nothing. The key phrase here is Murray's disclaimer 'not that we would want to, not that any useful purpose would be served.' Active interpretation gets you nowhere; it serves no useful purpose. There is no end to interpretation just as there is no Tibet. And yet we interpret anyway, deciphering, rearranging, making meaning if we can. It is a necessary and futile endeavour. 'All plots tend to move deathward. This is nature of plots ...We edge nearer death every time we plot. It is like a contract that all must sign, the plotters as well as those who are the targets of the plot' (26). So says Jack Gladney in one of his lectures on Hitler. Plotting is structuring events through language; it is the first stage of myth-making, and it leads towards death.

Technology itself creates difference and disorientation. It is our Frankenstein, a creation turning on its creators and living a life of its own. It evokes both life and death. Like plotting, which we learn is movement of life toward death, technology promises immortality and extinction in the same breath.

You could put your faith in technology. It got you here, it can get you out. This is the whole point of technology. It creates an appetite for immortality on the one hand. It threatens universal extinction on the other. Technology is lust removed from nature. (285)

Lust removed from nature, meaning removed from experience, the sacred expelled from the profane, the insiders placed outside: all these ideas are connected and all move toward the same end, which is death. While technology, like the cultural icon, appears to offer immortality and hope, it also extracts not only lust from nature but also responsibility from history. Military technology turns murder into a video game while other technologies consume the world around us as they substitute a plethora of virtual worlds. As Gladney remarks, 'Man's guilt in history and in the tides of his own blood has been complicated by technology, the daily seeping falsehearted death' (22). And difference is there too, wedging itself between humans and their experiences, the ultimate sort of fall that derives from the desire to 'be like God.' Jack notices at his doctor's office that 'A network of symbols has been introduced, an entire awesome technology wrested from the gods. It makes you feel like a stranger in your own dying' (142).

This incredible sense of bifurcation and disorientation produced by technology has to do with the mimetic qualities of magic and myth. The magic of technology and the mythic dimensions of language pretend to show us something beyond us when in fact they are only reflecting each other. Roland Barthes, in one of the most underutilized discussions of myth, shows that myth transforms history into nature by stealing language from one context then restoring it in another so that it appears like something 'wrested from the gods' when in fact it is simply recycled language.

What the world supplies to myth is an historical reality, defined ... by the way in which men have produced or used it; and what myth gives in return is a natural image of this reality ... [I]n [myth] things lose the memory that they once were made ... A conjuring trick has taken place; it has turned reality inside out, it has emptied it of history and has filled it with nature, it has removed from things their human meaning so as to make them signify a human insignificance. The function of myth is to empty reality; it is, literally, a ceaseless flowing out, a hemorrhage, or perhaps an evaporation, in short a perceptible absence[4].

The corollary of Barthes' axiom that myth transforms history into nature is that nature is simply the layering on of myth. Derrida writes that there is nothing outside the text; Barthes' version is that there is no nature on the other side of myth. The natural is simply a function of the prevailing myth, if there is one. If there is not one, then the natural is undecidable and distance and alienation take its place.

The most moving example of the result of technological mimesis, the mirroring of myth and nature, occurs when Babette, Jack Gladney's wife, appears on television while the rest of the family is watching. The family has not expected to see her on television, and the response is 'a silence as wary and deep as an animal growl. Confusion, fear, astonishment spilled from our faces. What did it mean?' (104). Jack attempts to come to grips with the fact that representation has invaded reality and this suggests to him that Babette is 'a walker in the mists of the dead.' He considers that if she is not dead, then he is. Wilder, the secret protagonist of the novel and the Gladney's youngest child, a toddler, is the only one who sees life in the image. He mumbles to his mother, or to the image of his mother, approaches the set, and touches her 'leaving a handprint on the dusty surface of the screen.' Technology places a wedge of distance and difference between ourselves that interpretation has difficulty overcoming. Our attempts to get outside of language are like Wilder's handprint on the television screen. In our search for meaning we simply leave traces on the margins of our existence.

I am learning that there are other ways to employ myth and magic or language and technology without producing the dread that dominates the characters in *White Noise*. I am learning these things from a Laguna Pueblo writer named Leslie Marmon Silko. Silko does not believe that myth is an endless deferral of sacred meaning, nor that the magic of technology has to be ultimately fragmenting and disorienting. For Silko the centre that we seek is the very earth that is both womb and tomb for humanity. Storytelling can spin webs around otherness and loss in ways that are creative, meaningful, and ultimately healing. Both otherness and narration are processes and thus are always in flux, always shifting. But storytelling works to dissolve the difference that otherness entails. Storytelling is grandmother spider spinning her web, encompassing otherness into the larger creation of the story.

One of the ways Silko portrays otherness is through an alienated male named Tayo in her most acclaimed novel *Ceremony*. Tayo is a man who is deeply ill both physically and spiritually. His constant vomiting and urinating seem to be attempts to purge from his body the experiences that soldiering, displacement, and death in World War II have given him. While a prisoner of war and while walking the Bataan Death March, Tayo curses the jungle rain, the rain that turns the skin green and that poured down upon the body of his dear cousin Rocky after a Japanese soldier smashed Rocky's skull with the butt of his rifle. Tayo's curse has produced a drought back in Laguna, New Mexico, a drought that not only serves to write Tayo's spiritual desiccation on the broadest canvas but also threatens Laguna communal life and represents mother earth's disfavour with her children who are engaged in a world war. For Tayo the ritual use of language releases tremendous power that can work toward creation or destruction.

Tayo's problem does not centre on assimilation into the white demarcations of difference and a loss of native understandings of wholeness as we might expect. Rather, Tayo's sickness comes from being unable to forget that wholeness when then world demands that he follow the dictates of otherness. When Tayo is ordered to shoot Japanese soldiers, he is unable to follow this command because he sees his beloved Uncle Josiah's face in the place of the Japanese soldiers' faces. Even after Rocky turns over a Japanese corpse and forces Tayo to look into the eyes, all he can see is his uncle lying dead. For Tayo there is no difference between the soldiers and his uncle, and that lack of difference prevents Tayo from carrying out the orders he receives. Tayo is haunted by connections and relationships that no one else seems to see.

Later Tayo understands just why he could not appropriate the interpretation that was required to kill the soldiers. Betonie, a Navajo healer who uses contemporary repositories of information like telephone books and calendars, tells Tayo that he saw the Japanese for what they are, namely, relatives of Native Americans. He remarks, 'Thirty thousand years ago they were not strangers. You saw what the evil had done: you saw the witchery ranging as wide as this world.'[5] Difference is the result of witchery; wholeness is the way things are.

The Army psychiatrist who treats Tayo immediately after his return seeks to reinforce Tayo's individuality through difference. Tayo considers himself to be invisible, white smoke. The doctor sees Tayo's condition as pathological, but for Tayo his invisibility is a desperate attempt to integrate himself into the world of white culture. For Tayo, '... [W]hite smoke had no consciousness of itself. It faded into the white world of their bed sheets and walls' (14). Tayo's psychiatric treatment is enforced by the introduction of difference to the degree that Tayo becomes separated from himself. The doctor's relentless questions batter him until the split is achieved and Tayo hears himself speaking to the doctor in the third person saying, 'He can't talk to you. He is invisible. His words are formed with an invisible tongue, they have no sound' (15). Tayo ends this exchange between himself and the doctor by vomiting, a persistent symptom of his illness, and by proclaiming to the doctor, 'Goddamn you, look what you have done' (16). What he has done is forced Tayo into distinctions of otherness and made those distinctions definitive. It is the same sentiment that Jack Gladney feels when he remarks that he feels like a stranger in his own dying. What the doctor has not done is to provide Tayo with a story that can envelope those distinctions and hold them coherently so that the distinctions are not definitive or ultimate but fade in the larger perspective of the story. Such stories, writes Silko, have the strength and fragility of a spider's web. Tayo needs a ceremony of integration, not a dissertation on otherness and difference.

Old Ku'oosh, the Laguna healer, knows about ceremonies and about the strength and fragility of stories. When he first comes to Tayo, his instruction is on the nature of language. The medicine man speaks softly and with a dialect 'full of sentences that were involuted with explanations of their own origins, as if nothing the old man said were his own but all had been said before and he was only there to repeat it' (34). The old man tells Tayo bluntly that this world is fragile. And here I want to quote at length what is perhaps the most often quoted passage from *Ceremony*.

The word he chose to express 'fragile' was filled with the intricacies of a continuing process, and with a strength inherent in spider webs woven across paths through sand hills where early in the morning the sun becomes entangled in each filament of web. It took a long time to explain the fragility and intricacy because no word exists alone, and the reason for choosing each word had to be explained with a story about why it must be said this certain way. That was the responsibility that went with being human, old Ku'oosh said, the story behind each word must be told so there could be no mistake in the meaning of what had been said; and this demanded great patience and love. (35-6).

Words are filaments in the web of stories, and all the stories are connected. This is their strength and their weakness, the strength and fragility of a spider web. Ku'oosh reminds Tayo that it takes only one person to tear away the delicate strands for the world to be injured. And Betonie confirms this idea for Tayo during his ceremony and reminds him that the ceremony is for the fragile world, not just for him.

Other men in *Ceremony*, notably Tayo's friends who have also returned from the war, do not have Tayo's problem. They are able to maintain the interpretative strategies that were taught to them through white culture and thereby forget the wholeness narrated through Laguna legends. While the war itself shifted the terms of otherness toward the Japanese on a national scale, life after the war finds the men in search of other differences through which to channel their power. These men view women as an extension of World War II, the war that suddenly made them equal with their white comrades. White women are the ultimate conquest for Emo, Harley, and Leroy, and their stories of conquest at one point appropriate the form of the Laguna legends that Silko weaves into the novel in verse form. She even has these men banging beer bottles like drums as they tell these stories, as if they were sacred chants. It is as if to say that stories of conquest turn upon women in the post-war life of these men. While the stories become the myths they live by, they only enrage Tayo and make him sicker. In fact he ends up disrupting one of these stories by stabbing Emo with a broken beer bottle. Tayo seems to know that he cannot be healed by continued conquest, that is, by the extension of otherness into different areas; what he needs instead is to bring some coherence to the many shards of his existence. Difference creates the possibility of conquest; storytelling creates the possibility of coherence.

A significant aspect of Tayo's cure concerns his ability to overcome the gender differences that his friends perpetuate. While Tayo is not like them in terms of their need to make women an extension of the war, neither is he inhabiting any sense of narrative wholeness with regard to women. His mother deserted him when he was young and left him with his Aunt who treated him like an outcast. One element of the ceremony that Betonie discerns for Tayo has to do with simply 'a woman.' While Tayo encounters several women in his ceremony, it is clear that they are all in a mythological sense one woman, and she is the earth.

The Night Swan appears before Tayo goes off to war but serves to foreshadow the ceremony he will need afterwards. The Night Swan is a lover of Tayo's beloved Uncle Josiah, and she mysteriously appears in Cubero, at the foot of Mt. Taylor, and disappears after Josiah's death. Tayo goes to meet her to inform her that Josiah cannot make their appointment, and there and then she introduces him to mysteries of rain and love. The Night Swan is associated with the blue of Mt. Taylor, which in Laguna is called Tse pi'na or Woman Veiled in Rain Clouds. She is the blue of the mountain and synechdocally the blue of the west, of rain and wind. The rain envelopes them as they make love, and the text reads, 'She moved under him, her rhythm merging into the sound of the rain in the tree. And he was lost somewhere, deep beneath the surface of his own body and consciousness, swimming away from all his life before that hour' (99). They part in the midst of the smell of damp earth, and she says to Tayo, 'You don't have to understand what is happening. But remember this day. You will recognize it later. You are a part of it now' (100). Grandmother spider is beginning to spin her web.

Tayo does recognize this day later when he meets Ts'eh, a woman who lives on Mt. Taylor. She is surrounded by the colour yellow and thus is connected to the corn mother, pollen, and the Yellow Woman stories of Laguna mythology and lore that involves sacred and sexual abduction. Tayo is not physically abducted but does feel powerfully drawn to her. She feeds him corn the night before he rises to meet a dawn 'spreading across the sky like yellow wings' (189). Like Yellow Woman, Ts'eh is both lover and mother, and is mother earth as well. When Tayo dreams of making love with Ts'eh, the description indicates that he is being absorbed into the earth: 'He felt the warm sand on his toes and knees; he felt her body, and it was warm as the sand, and he couldn't feel where her body ended and the sand began' (232). Tayo's healing involve ritualized union with female expressions of mother earth.

The evil and the witchery at work in Tayo and in the world function by separation, the placement of cultural, ideological, and historical space between people. That space, moreover, is negatively charged; it is the site of an exercise of power. The delineation of otherness carries an implicit hegemony and hierarchy. As Simone de Beauvoir notes in *The Second Sex*:

> No subject will readily volunteer to become the object, the inessential; it is not the Other who, in defining himself as the Other, establishes the One. The Other is posed as such by the One in defining himself as the One. But if the Other is not to regain the status of being the One, he must be submissive enough to accept this alien point of view.[6]

De Beauvoir's depiction of otherness is relevant to Silko's presentation of it in her work. But de Beauvoir did not have the benefit of Silko's native understanding of otherness, and thus we also read in The Second Sex that Otherness is a fundamental category of human thought as primordial as consciousness itself and found even in the most 'primitive' of societies. While we certainly find otherness in DeLillo's virtual world, Silko encounters this notion throughout her fiction.

For Silko there are two ways of being in the world. In one humans are at odds with themselves, their creations, and their environment separated by fragmenting and disorienting interpretations. In another human beings are centered in a multiplying reflection of the cosmos whose focus is not the individual but the dynamic relationship of all things connected by stories. The former are called destroyers, and the latter are creators. Both destroyers and creators use technology. For the destroyers their tools exist outside themselves and are simply means to a particular disingenuous end. For the creators technology is integrated into the very fabric of existence itself and serves to enhance and extend life.

In Silko's most recent novel, the labyrinthine and copious *Almanac of the Dead* (763 pages), each understanding of technology mirrors the other as the plot, which is history itself, works its way to a semi-apocalyptic end. This novel offers a different version of technological mimesis. Where creators see connections; destroyers see differences. Images of blood dominate the novel and serve to depict the Native concept of networking, which is countered on the Euro-American side by electricity and of course computer networks. For Native people all over the world, the earth spirits communicate through the blood of their children. Damballah, Quetzalcoatl, and Spider Woman all speak to those who are connected by blood and stories and instruct them in the coming revolution. Those who do not get the message are technophiles of various kinds consumed by such things as gunrunning, the sale of body parts taken from homeless people, torture videotapes, an array of sexual experimentation including a Tucson Judge and his favorite basset hound, and—almost anticlimatically—drugs.

Almanac of the Dead works to dissolve the differences wrought by Euro-American technology through a narration that encompasses both types of technology in a story about the end of white culture and the reconstitution of the earth and her native peoples. The mirroring of Native and Western uses and abuses of technology is especially telling in the setting of Tuxtla, Mexico. In Tuxtla Tacho is a native person who serves as a chauffeur for Menardo, an effete Mexican who has garnered his wealth by providing security services for the rich and powerful in Tuxtla, read CIA. Tacho is privy to special information in his ability to gamble and to interpret Menardo's dreams, but he never gives Menardo the complete story. He cannot do so because Menardo is an assassination target of local Marxists who have placed Tacho there in order to gather intelligence on Menardo and his clients until the appropriate time for the assassination. Menardo, in the meantime, has become obsessed with security technology, in particular one bullet-proof vest that one of his American Mafia clients has given to him. Ultimately, the vest becomes a fetish for him, and he prefers reading the technical information about the vest to the presence of his wife. Menardo eventually comes to wear the vest constantly, even during sex and sleep. Now thoroughly obsessed, Menardo devises a scheme to exhibit the power of his new fetish. He arranges to have Tacho fire a 9mm pistol at him just as his CIA friends arrive at the club. Menardo will pull off a marvellous practical joke, which is a notorious rite of passage for this group, and will also demonstrate how the man in charge of security is the most secure person in the elite group. As the men arrive, Menardo loudly commands Tacho to fire so that all may hear, and, of course, the vest fails. The assassination is effected by Menardo himself, and Tacho's innocence is guaranteed. Unlike the Mexican blankets that are woven so tight that water beads up on them in the rain, the bullet-proof vest proves to be woven too loosely. This scene enacts a powerful ironic reversal of the massacre at Wounded Knee in 1890 where Ghost Dance shirts worn by the Lakota failed to protect them from the soldiers' bullets as they assumed. The technology of the destroyers becomes the tool of their own destruction as the negative force of otherness begins to implode. In *Almanac of the Dead*, Euro-American culture is unravelling thread by thread in both its spirituality and its technology. In Native cultures, on the other hand, technology is used both to thwart the otherness of Euro-

American culture and to spin a web of stories that offers Native peoples all over the world a way to see how land, history, and technology all cohere into a reconstituted world where Native people take back their lands from Alaska to Chile.

The technology portrayed in *Almanac of the Dead* is tied to the revisionist history that Silko offers. It is a history with a future, and that future includes the restoration of all tribal lands to native people from Alaska to Chile. Silko is not reticent about announcing this agenda and neither are the Native Americans who continue to work toward this end. In a coffee-table book titled *A Circle of Nations* that includes photographs and writings from prominent Native American artists, Silko writes the following in her preface titled 'The Indian with A Camera':

> The Indian with a camera is an omen of a time in the future that all Euro-Americans unconsciously dread: the time when the indigenous people of the Americas will retake their land.[7]

The opening pages of *Almanac of the Dead* are not text but a map with Tucson at the centre. Boxes of information on the map function as interpretive guides. In one of these boxes we read the following statement:

> Sixty million Native Americans died between 1500 and 1600. The defiance and resistance to things European continue unabated. The Indian Wars have never ended in the Americas. Native Americans seek nothing less than the return of all tribal lands. (17)

Leslie Marmon Silko is neither shy nor cryptic regarding the future or the past. She relentlessly details the diverse crimes, whether legal or cultural, committed against Native Americans and the Laguna Pueblo to this day. And she does so with the calm persistence of a person who knows her past and her future as well as her place and mission in the present. Native Americans will take back their lands; the process is already underway. And that process is driven by storytelling, by narrating otherness out of a dominant position in the ideology of the invaders and replacing it with a narrative cohesion that is both strong and fragile.

An Alaskan medicine woman in *Almanac of the Dead* represents well how storytelling and technology or myth and magic weave a web that overcomes witchery and dread. A satellite television is installed in her Yupik village, and most of the villagers ignore it or fall asleep in front of it. A pelt made of fur and hair is sacred to the old woman and becomes the channel she uses to lock in on the spirits of the ancestors. The television enhances the power of the pelt by the appropriation of the satellite signals. Silko writes:

> The old woman had gathered great surges of energy out of the atmosphere, by summoning spirit beings through the recitations of the stories that were also indictments of the greedy destroyers of the land. With the stories the old woman was able to assemble powerful forces flowing from the spirits of the ancestors.[8]

The old Yupik woman uses her pelt, her stories, and a weather map on the television screen successfully to crash an airplane that is carrying surveyors and equipment from American oil companies. When the insurance adjustor arrives and someone suggests that the number of airplane crashes in the area could be explained by the same forces at work in the Bermuda Triangle, he replies, 'None of that stuff is true. It can all be explained' (160).

Indeed it can, and that is the problem of history and of the future as Silko paints them. Americans have been developing the capacity for explanation for so long that they have been hypnotized by their own accounts and measurements and can no longer see anything else. Like the most photographed barn in America, commodified meaning creates a lack of vision, an inability to see larger relationships, the larger story. Blind and greedy officials lead blind and greedy citizens into the end of history in *Almanac of the Dead*.

Meanwhile, Native people are reconstituting themselves through the ancient connection of blood and stories and are slowly but surely beginning the process of taking back the land.

Almanac of the Dead ends on just this note. Sterling, one of the main characters, returns to his Laguna home where he walks out to the uranium mine and surveys the destruction. Silko writes:

> Ahead all he could see were mounds of tailings thirty feet high, uranium waste blowing in the breeze, carried by the rain to springs and rivers. Here was the new work of the Destroyers; here was the destruction and poison. Here was where life ended. (760)

Or where it would end if there were no creators in the world. In recent years a stone formation has emerged in the shape of a great snake. Only the traditionals can see this snake, and to most whites it is completely undetectable. But for Sterling it is a sign of life among the ruins of white culture. And while it remains invisible to that dominant culture, it nonetheless arises from the rubble, solid and secure. Further, the great stone snake points the way to the future, which is in the south and from which will come a horde of Native people led by the heroic twins of myth and legend. The history of blood and earth is the history that will survive, while the destroyers are already passing away.

Silko's fiction works to show a deeper technology than that which continually enchants Western culture, especially in the late twentieth century. The earth has always been networked, she argues, through the energies of blood and spirits and through human beings who seek not to destroy but to create. The witchery of the Destroyers always turns upon itself while the creators wait patiently in the web of the earth. In fact Silko herself is a creator since she employs the technology of writing and the publishing industry in order to disseminate the stories that will energize the reclamation of the land.

What emerges from Silko's narration is that storytelling is not only a process of dissolving the rigid differences upon which Euro-American culture depends, it is also a process of decolonization. While pre-contact storytelling knit the tribe together under shifting conditions, post-contact and contemporary narration functions as the web and as the spider, and the spider is also known for her bite. For Silko storytelling encompasses difference by spinning its web around the holes of otherness causing us to focus instead on the interconnections: the network of words, land, and life.

I have read *White Noise* against *Ceremony* and *Almanac of the Dead* in the hope that different ways of reading culture religiously will appear. In *White Noise* we saw the implications for interpretation in a culture that has painted itself into a corner philosophically and religiously. With Silko's work we can see a consistent use of storytelling and ritual that seeks to overcome the difference and dread that is occasioned by interpreting toward nothingness. Two characters seem to encompass these ideas in provocative ways.

White Noise ends with Wilder riding his tricycle across several lanes of expressway traffic as adults watch helplessly. He survives, and it becomes another moment of splendid transcendence in Jack Gladney's life. Yet Wilder represents something that none of the other characters in the novel can have—innocence. Wilder's innocence is a result of his inability to speak. His piercing and seemingly unending cry earlier in the novel is the only real expression he is able to evoke. As Nietzsche observed, language and consciousness are concurrent, and Wilder's lack of language makes him the embodiment of the unconscious spaces where the sacred is dimly perceived, but never really found. He is the silence that exists at the center of interpretation. His innocence is prelapsarian and beyond the reach of the adults. Wilder is on the other side of interpretation.

Contrasted with Wilder's innocence is Tayo's experience. Tayo's fall comes about through the introduction of white ideas of language and truth that create difference and fragmentation in Tayo's life. By living out the stories from Laguna mythology and by participating in the magic of the ceremony, Tayo experiences both convergence and emergence. The patterns of the constellation that Betonie reveals, the woman on Mount Taylor, and the experiences of war all converge through the ceremony so that Tayo emerges whole at the end. The stories spin the webs that hold the interpretation together.

What we have, then, are two ways of reading religiously. Both employ myth, magic, and dread but with very different results. The person who learns to read religiously is attuned to both otherness and wholeness, both fragmentation and coherence, both myth and magic in their constantly shifting manifestations.

NOTES

1. Don DeLillo, *White Noise* (New York: Penguin, 1984), p. 12.

2. Frank Kermode, *The Genesis of Secrecy* (Cambridge, Mass: Harvard UP, 1979), p. 27.

3. Thomas J.J. Altizer, 'The Challenge of Nihilism.' *JAAR*. LXII (Winter 1994) 1021.

4. Roland Barthes, *Mythologies*. Trans. Annette Lavers (New York: Hill and Wang, 1957), pp. 142-3.

5. Leslie Marmon Silko, *Ceremony* (New York, Penguin), p. 124.

6. Simone de Beauvoir, *The Second Sex*, in Bowie, Michael and Solomon, eds *Twenty Questions: An Introduction to Philosophy*. 2nd Ed. (New York, Harcourt, Brace, Jovanovich, 1992), p. 562.

7. Leslie Marmon Silko, 'Forward: The Indian with a Camera,' in John Gattuse, ed. *A Circle of Nations: Voices and Visions of American Indians*. (Hillsboro, Oregon: Beyond Words Publishing, 1993), p. 6.

8. Leslie Marmon Silko, *Almanac of the Dead* (New York: Penguin, 1991), p. 156.

PAUL MALTBY

The Romantic Metaphysics
of Don DeLillo

W hat is the postmodern response to the truth claims traditionally made
on behalf of visionary moments? By "visionary moment," I mean that flash
of insight or sudden revelation which critically raises the level of spiritual or
self-awareness of a fictional character. It is a mode of cognition typically
represented as bypassing rational thought processes and attaining a "higher"
or redemptive order of knowledge (gnosis). There are, conceivably, three
types of postmodern response which merit attention here.

First, in recognition of the special role literature itself has played in
establishing the credibility of visionary moments, postmodern writers might
draw on the resources of metafiction to parodically "lay bare" the essentially
literary nature of such moments. Baldly stated, the visionary moment could
be exposed as a literary convention, that is, a concept that owes more to the
practice of organizing narratives around a sudden illumination (as in, say, the
narratives of Wordsworth's *Prelude* or Joyce's *Dubliners*) than to real-life
experience. Thomas Pynchon's *The Crying of Lot 49* is premised on this
assumption. Pynchon's sleuthlike protagonist, Oedipa Maas, finds herself in
a situation in which clues—contrary to the resolution of the standard
detective story—proliferate uncontrollably, thereby impeding the emergence
of a final enlightenment or "stelliferous Meaning" (82). It is a situation that
not only frustrates Oedipa, who is continually tantalized by the sense that "a

From *Contemporary Literature*, Vol. XXXVII, No. 2, Summer, 1996, pp. 258-77.

revelation ... trembled just past the threshold of her understanding" (24), but which also mocks the reader's expectation of a revelation that will close the narrative.

A second postmodern response might be to assess the credibility of the visionary moment in the light of poststructuralist theory. Hence the representation of a visionary moment as if it embodied a final, fast-frozen truth, one forever beyond the perpetually unstable relationship of signifier to signified, would be open to the charge of "logocentrism" (where the transient "meaning effects" generated by the endless disseminations of language are mistaken for immutable meanings). Moreover, implied here is the subject's transcendent vantage point in relation to the visionary moment. For the knowledge that the "moment" conveys is always apprehended in its totality; there is no current of its meaning that escapes or exceeds this implicitly omnipotent consciousness. As if beyond the instabilities and surplus significations of language, the subject is assumed to be the sole legislator of meaning. (All of which is to say nothing of any unconscious investment in the meaning of the visionary moment.)

A third postmodern response might deny the very conditions of possibility for a visionary moment in contemporary culture. The communication revolution, seen by sociologists like Baudrillard to be the key constitutive feature of our age, has aggrandized the media to the point where signs have displaced their referents, where images of the Real have usurped the authority of the Real, whence the subject is engulfed by simulacra. In the space of simulation, the difference between "true" and "false," "actual" and "imaginary," has imploded. Hence Romantic and modernist conceptions of visionary moments—typically premised on metaphysical assumptions of supernal truth—are rendered obsolete in a culture suffused with simulacra; for under these "hyperreal" conditions, the visionary moment can only reproduce the packaged messages of the mass media.

What these three responses to the truth claims of the visionary moment share is a radically antimetaphysical stance. We see the visionary moment, with all its pretensions to truth and transcendence, exposed as (1) a literary convention, (2) a logocentric illusion, and (3) a hyperreal construct. In short, the metaphysical foundations of traditional conceptions of the visionary moment cannot survive the deconstructive thrust of postmodern thinking.

This essay will examine the status of the visionary moment in particular, and of visionary experience in general, in three of Don DeLillo's novels, namely, *White Noise* (1985), *The Names* (1982), and *Libra* (1988).

DeLillo has been widely hailed as an exemplar of postmodernist writing. Typically, this assessment rests on readings that focus on his accounts of the postmodern experience of living in a hyperreality.[1] But to postmodernize DeLillo is to risk losing sight of the (conspicuously unpostmodern) metaphysical impulse that animates his work. Indeed, the terms in which he identifies visionary experience in his fiction will be seen to align him so closely with a Romantic sensibility that they must radically qualify any reading of him as a postmodern writer.

In part 2 of *White Noise*, the Gladney family shelters at a local barracks from the toxic cloud of a chemical spill. As Jack Gladney observes his children sleeping, he recounts a visionary moment. It begins as follows:

> Steffie ... muttered something in her sleep. It seemed important that I know what it was. In my current state, bearing the death impression of the Nyodene cloud, I was ready to search anywhere for signs and hints, intimations of odd comfort.... Moments later she spoke again.... but a language not quite of this world. I struggled to understand. I was convinced she was saying something, fitting together units of stable meaning. I watched her face, waited.... She uttered two clearly audible words, familiar and elusive at the same time, words that seemed to have a ritual meaning, part of a verbal spell or ecstatic chant.
> Toyota Celica. (154-55)

Before I continue the quotation, consider the following issues. Up to this point, DeLillo has manipulated his readers' expectations; what we expect from Gladney's daughter, Steffie, is a profound, revelatory utterance. Instead, we are surprised by (what appears to be) a banality: "Toyota Celica." Here it looks as if DeLillo is mocking the traditional faith in visionary moments or, more precisely, ironically questioning the very possibility of such moments in a postmodern culture. After all, a prominent feature of that culture is the prodigious, media-powered expansion of marketing and public relations campaigns to the point where their catchwords and sound bites colonize not just the public sphere but also, it seems, the individual unconscious. Henceforth, even the most personal visionary experience appears to be constituted by the promotional discourses of a consumer society. However, the irony of this apparently postmodern account of a visionary moment proves to be short-lived as Gladney immediately recounts his response to Steffie's words:

A long moment passed before I realized this was the name of an automobile. The truth only amazed me more. The utterance was beautiful and mysterious, gold-shot with looming wonder. It was like the name of an ancient power in the sky, tablet-carved in cuneiform. It made me feel that something hovered. But how could this be? A simple brand name, an ordinary car. How could these near-nonsense words, murmured in a child's restless sleep, make me sense a meaning, a presence? She was only repeating some TV voice....Whatever its source, the utterance struck me with the impact of a moment of splendid transcendence. (155)

The tenor of this passage is not parodic; the reader is prompted by the analytical cast and searching tone of Gladney's narration to listen in earnest. Gladney's words are not to be dismissed as delusional, nor are they to be depreciated as those of "a modernist displaced in a postmodern world" (Wilcox 348). The passage is typical of DeLillo's tendency to seek out transcendent moments in our postmodern lives that hint at possibilities for cultural regeneration. Clearly, the principal point of the passage is not that "Toyota Celica" is the signifier of a commodity (and as such has only illusory significance as a visionary utterance), but that as a name it has a mystical resonance and potency: "It was like the name of an ancient power in the sky," a name that is felt to be "part of a verbal spell or ecstatic chant." For what is revealed to Gladney in this visionary moment is that names embody a formidable power. And this idea is itself the expansive theme, explored in its metaphysical implications, of *The Names*, the novel that immediately preceded *White Noise*. Indeed, when read in conjunction with *The Names*, the metaphysical issues of *White Noise* can be brought into sharper relief.

The Names addresses the question of the mystical power of names: secret names (210, 294), place names (102-3, 239-40), divine names (92, 272).[2] For DeLillo wants to remind us that names are often invested with a significance that exceeds their immediate, practical function. Names are enchanted; they enable insight and revelation. As one character explains: "We approach nameforms warily. Such secret power. When the name is itself secret, the power and influence are magnified. A secret name is a way of escaping the world. It is an opening into the self" (210).

Consider the remarkable ending of *The Names*—an extract from the manuscript of a novel by Tap, the narrator's (James Axton's) nine-year-old son, replete with misspellings. In Tap's novel, a boy, unable to participate in the speaking in tongues at a Pentecostal service, panics and flees the church:

"Tongue tied! His fait was signed. He ran into the rainy distance, smaller and smaller. This was worse than a retched nightmare. It was the nightmare of real things, the fallen wonder of the world" (339). These lines conclude both Tap's novel and *The Names* itself. "The fallen wonder of the world" connotes the failure of language, in its (assumed) postlapsarian state, to invest the world with some order of deep and abiding meaning, to illuminate existence. More specifically, the language that has "fallen" is the language of name, the kind of pure nomenclature implied in Genesis where words stand in a necessary, rather than arbitrary, relationship to their referents.[3] The novel follows the lives of characters who seek to recover this utopian condition of language. For example, people calling themselves "abecedarians" (210) form a murder cult whose strategy is to match the initials of their victims' names to those of the place names where the murders occur—all in a (misguided) effort to restore a sense of the intrinsic or self-revealing significance of names. And note Axton's response to the misspellings in his son's manuscript:

> I found these mangled words exhilarating. He'd made them new again, made me see how they worked, what they really were. They were ancient things, secret, reshapable.
> ... The spoken poetry in those words.... His ... misrenderings ... seemed to contain curious perceptions about the words themselves, second and deeper meanings, original meanings. (313)

The novel suggests that the visionary power of language will only be restored when we "tap" into its primal or pristine forms, the forms that can regenerate perception, that can reveal human existence in significant ways. Hence the novel's inquiry into "original meanings," the concern with remembering "the prototype" (112-13), whence "[i]t was necessary to remember, to dream the pristine earth" (307). The "gift of tongues" is also understood as a primal, and hence visionary, language—"talk as from the womb, as from the sweet soul before birth" (306)—and, as such, it is revered as "the whole language of the spirit" (338), the language by which "[n]ormal understanding is surpassed" (307). (And far from DeLillo keeping an ironic distance from such mystical views of glossolalia, he has endorsed them in interviews.)[4] Moreover, one can hardly miss the novel's overall insistence on the spoken word—especially on talk at the familiar, everyday, pre-abstract level of communication—as the purest expression of primal, visionary language:

We talked awhile about her nephews and nieces, other family matters, commonplaces, a cousin taking trumpet lessons, a death in Winnipeg.... The subject of family makes conversation almost tactile. I think of hands, food, hoisted children. There's a close-up contact warmth in the names and images. Everydayness....

This talk we were having about familiar things was itself ordinary and familiar. It seemed to yield up the mystery that is part of such things, the nameless way in which we sometimes feel our connections to the physical world. Being here.... Our senses are collecting at the primal edge.... I felt I was in an early stage of teenage drunkenness, lightheaded, brilliantly happy and stupid, knowing the real meaning of every word.[5] (31-32)

The affirmation of a primal, visionary level of language which, moreover, finds its purest expression in "talk" (glossolalia, conversation) is vulnerable to postmodern critique on the grounds that it is premised on a belief in original and pure meanings. Suffice it to say here, such meanings are assumed to exist (as in some transcendent realm) outside the space of intertextuality, or beyond the "logic of supplementarity" whereby, according to Derrida, "the origin ... was never constituted except reciprocally by a nonorigin" (Of Grammatology 61).

The idea that language has "fallen" or grown remote from some pure and semantically rich primal state is characteristically (though not exclusively) Romantic, and most reminiscent of views held by, among others, Rousseau and Wordsworth. In his "Essay on the Origins of Languages" and Confessions, Rousseau identified speech, as opposed to writing, as the natural condition of language because it "owes its form to natural causes alone" ("Essay" 5). In the face of a culture that conferred greater authority on writing than on speech, he affirmed the priority of the latter on the grounds that "Languages are made to be spoken, writing serves only as a supplement to speech" (qtd. in Derrida 144). While writing "substitut[es] exactitude for expressiveness" ("Essay" 21), the bias of speech is toward passionate and figurative expression which can "penetrate to the very depths of the heart" (9). Indeed, "As man's first motives for speaking were of the passions, his first expressions were tropes.... [Hence] [a]t first only poetry was spoken; there was no hint of reasoning until much later" (12). Moreover, it was "primitive," face-to-face speech—as opposed to the sophistications of writing, and especially the tyranny made possible by the codification of laws—that, according to Rousseau's anthropology, once bound humans together naturally in an organic, egalitarian community. And recall that in his

"Preface" to the Lyrical Ballads, Wordsworth deplored the "arbitrary and capricious habits of expression" of poets who, following urbane conventions of writing, had lost touch with the elemental language of rustics. The latter, by virtue of their "rural occupations" (that is, their regular intercourse with nature) are "such men [who] hourly communicate with the best objects from which the best part of language is originally derived" (emphasis added). Furthermore, this is "a far more philosophical language" than that used by poets (735). Of course, all this is not to suggest that DeLillo would necessarily endorse Rousseau's or Wordsworth's specific claims. But what all three share in is that familiar Romantic myth of some primal, pre-abstract level of language which is naturally endowed with greater insight, a pristine order of meaning that enables unmediated understanding, community, and spiritual communion with the world around.

If we return to Jack Gladney's visionary moment, we should note that while "Toyota Celica" may be a brand name, Gladney perceives it as having an elemental, incantatory power that conveys, at a deeper level, another order of meaning. He invokes a range of terms in an effort to communicate this alternative meaning: "ritual," "spell," "ecstatic," "mysterious," "wonder," "ancient" (155). Similarly, for Murray Siskind, Gladney's friend and media theorist, the recurring jingle "Coke is it, Coke is it" evokes comparisons with "mantras." Siskind elaborates: "The medium [that is, television] practically overflows with sacred formulas if we can remember how to respond innocently" (51). DeLillo highlights the paradox that while so much language, in the media society, has degenerated into mere prattle and clichés, brand names not only flourish but convey a magic and mystical significance. Hence they are often chanted like incantations: "Toyota Corolla, Toyota Celica, Toyota Cressida" (155); "Tegrin, Denorex, Selsun Blue" (289); "Dacron, Orlon, Lycra Spandex" (52).

Earlier passages in *White Noise* derive their meaning from the same Romantic metaphysics of language as Gladney's "moment of splendid transcendence." First, consider Gladney's response to the crying of his baby, Wilder (and note, by the way, the typically Romantic impression of the mystique of desolate spaces, and the appeal to "the mingled reverence and wonder" of the Romantic sublime):

> He was crying out, saying nameless things in a way that touched me with its depth and richness. This was an ancient dirge.... I began to think he had disappeared inside this wailing noise and if I could join him in his lost and suspended place we might together perform some reckless wonder of intelligibility....

... Nearly seven straight hours of serious crying. It was as though he'd just returned from a period of wandering in some remote and holy place, in sand barrens or snowy ranges—a place where things are said, sights are seen, distances reached which we in our ordinary toil can only regard with the mingled reverence and wonder we hold in reserve for feats of the most sublime and difficult dimensions. (78-79)

And, for Siskind, "Supermarkets this large and clean and modern are a revelation to me"; after all, "Everything is concealed in symbolism, hidden by veils of mystery and layers of cultural material. But it is psychic data, absolutely.... All the letters and numbers are here, ... all the code words and ceremonial phrases" (38, 37-38). Evidently, for DeLillo, language operates on two levels: a practical, denotative level, that is, a mode of language oriented toward business, information, and technology, and a "deeper," primal level which is the ground of visionary experience—the "second, deeper meanings, original meanings" that Axton finds in Tap's childishly misspelled words; the "ancient dirge" that Gladney hears in Wilder's wailing; the "language not quite of this world" that he hears in Steffie's sleep-talk; the "psychic data" that Siskind finds beneath white noise.

In communications theory, "white noise" describes a random mix of frequencies over a wide spectrum that renders signals unintelligible. DeLillo applies the metaphor of a circumambient white noise to suggest, on the one hand, the entropic state of postmodern culture where in general communications are degraded by triviality and irrelevance—the culture of "infotainment," factoids, and junk mail, where the commodity logic of late capitalism has extended to the point that cognition is mediated by its profane and quotidian forms. Yet, on the other hand, DeLillo suggests that within that incoherent mix of frequencies there is, as it were, a low wavelength that carries a flow of spiritually charged meaning. This flow of meaning is barely discernible, but, in the novel, it is figured in the recurring phrase "waves and radiation" (1, 38, 51, 104, 326)—an undercurrent of invisible forces or "nameless energies" (12) that have regenerative powers. And how do we "tune in" to this wavelength? Siskind says of his students, who feel alienated from the dreck of popular television, "they have to learn to look as children again" (50), that is to say, to perceive like Gladney's daughter, Steffie, or Axton's son, Tap, are said to perceive. In an interview, DeLillo has observed, "I think we feel, perhaps superstitiously, that children have a direct route to, have direct contact to the kind of natural truth that eludes us as adults" ("Outsider" 302). The boy protagonist of *Ratner's Star* (1976) is considered, by virtue of his minority, more likely than adults to access the "primal dream" experience of "racial history," of "pure fable, myth, archetype"; as one character tells him, "you haven't had time to drift away from your psychic origins" (264-65). And here it must be remarked that this faith in the insightfulness of childhood perception is a defining feature of (but, of course, not exclusive to) that current of Romantic writing which runs from Rousseau's *Emile* (1762), through the writings of Blake and Wordsworth, to De Quincey's *Suspiria de Profundis* (1845). For Coleridge, "To carry on the feelings of childhood into the powers of manhood; to combine the child's sense of wonder and novelty with the appearances which every day for perhaps forty years had rendered familiar ... this is the character and privilege of genius" (49). And recall, especially, the familiar lines from Wordsworth's "Intimations of Immortality" which lament the (adult's) loss of the child's "visionary gleam," that "master-light of all our seeing"; which celebrate the child as a "Seer blest! / On whom those truths do rest, / Which we [adults] are toiling all our lives to find, / In darkness lost" (460-61). In *The Prelude*, Wordsworth also argued that adult visionary experience is derived from childhood consciousness, the "seedtime [of] my soul," a consciousness that persists into adulthood as a source of "creative sensibility," illuminating the world with its "auxiliar light" (498, 507).

The Romantic notion of infant insight, of the child as gifted with an intuitive perception of truth, sets DeLillo's writing apart from postmodern trends. For, of all modes of fiction, it is postmodernism that is least hospitable to concepts like insight and intuition. Its metafictional and antimetaphysical polemic has collapsed the "depth model" of the subject (implied by the concept of inner seeing) and, audaciously, substituted a model of subjectivity as the construct of chains of signifiers. In such fiction as Robert Coover's *Pricksongs and Descants*, Walter Abish's *In the Future Perfect*, and Donald Barthelme's *Snow White*, for example, we find subjectivity reconceived as the conflux of fragments of texts—mythical narratives, dictionaries and catalogues, media clichés and stereotypes.

In an interview, DeLillo has said of *White Noise* that "Perhaps the supermarket tabloids are ... closest to the spirit of the book" ("I Never Set Out" 31). What one might expect from any critique of postmodern culture is a satirical assault on the tabloids as a debased and commodified form of communication. Yet the frequency with which DeLillo cites tabloid news stories—their accounts of UFOs, reincarnation, and supernatural occurrences (see, for example, *White Noise* 142-46)—suggests that there is more at issue than simply mocking their absurd, fabricated claims. For he recognizes our need for a "weekly dose of cult mysteries" (5), and that, by means of tabloid discourse, "Out of some persistent sense of large-scale ruin, we kept inventing hope" (146-47). In *White Noise*, the tabloids are seen to function as a concealed form of religious expression, where extraterrestrials are substituted for messiahs and freakish happenings for miracles. In short, on a wavelength of which we are virtually unconscious, the tabloids gratify our impulses toward the transcendental; "They ask profoundly important questions about death, the afterlife, God, worlds and space, yet they exist in an almost Pop Art atmosphere" ("I Never Set Out" 31).

White Noise abounds with extensive discussions about death and the afterlife (38, 99, 196-200, 282-92, and elsewhere), a concern of the book that is surely symptomatic of a nostalgia for a mode of experience that lies beyond the stereotyping and banalizing powers of the media, a mode of experience not subject to simulation. In a culture marked by an implosive de-differentiation of the image and its referent, where "Once you've seen the signs about the barn, it becomes impossible to see the barn" (12), the nonfigurability of death seems like a guarantee of a domain of human experience that can transcend hyperreality.

In another visionary experience, Gladney has mystical insight into the force—a huge, floating cloud of toxic chemicals—that threatens his life:

> It was a terrible thing to see, so close, so low.... But it was also spectacular, part of the grandness of a sweeping event.... Our fear was accompanied by a sense of awe that bordered on the religious. It is surely possible to be awed by the thing that threatens your life, to see it as a cosmic force, so much larger than yourself, more powerful, created by elemental and willful rhythms. (127)

This "awed," "religious" perception of a powerful force, which seems in its immensity capable of overwhelming the onlooker, is characteristic of that order of experience explored by the Romantics under the name of "the Sublime." The concept of the sublime has had a long and complex evolution since Longinus's famous treatise on the subject, and here it must suffice to note just one key statement that has served as a foundation for the notion of the Romantic sublime. In his *Philosophical Enquiry into the Origin of Our Ideas of the Sublime and the Beautiful* (1757), Edmund Burke advanced the following definition: "Whatever is fitted in any sort to excite the ideas of pain, and danger, that is to say, whatever is in any sort terrible, or is conversant about terrible objects, or operates in a manner analogous to terror, is a source of the sublime; that is, it is productive of the strongest emotion which the mind is capable of feeling" (39). Burke identified the sources of "terrifying" sublimity in such attributes as "power," "vastness," "infinity," and "magnificence," and among the effects of the experience of the sublime, he identified "terror," "awe," "reverence," and "admiration." It is remarkable that Gladney's experience of the sublime yields almost identical terms: "terrible," "grandness," "awed," "religious," "cosmic," "powerful." Moreover, such terms are familiar to us from descriptions of sublime experience in Romantic literature. For example, in *The Prelude*, in such accounts as his epiphany at the Simplon Pass and the ascent of Mount Snowdon (535-36, 583-85), Wordsworth frequently invokes impressions of the "awful," the "majestic," "infinity," and "transcendent power" to convey his sense of the terrifying grandeur of nature. In the violent, turbulent landscape of the Alps, he perceived "Characters of the great Apocalypse, / The types and symbols of Eternity, / Of first, and last, and midst, and without end" (536). Wordsworth's invocation of "Apocalypse," like the sense, in *White Noise*, of a life-threatening "cosmic force," reveals a defining property of the experience of the sublime: the subject's anxious intimation of a dissolution of the self, of extinction, in the face of such overwhelming power. "[T]he emotion you feel," says Burke of such "prodigious" power, is that it might "be employed to the purposes of ... destruction. That power derives all its sublimity from the terror with which it is generally accompanied" (65). And here it should be added that the experience is all the more disturbing because such immense power defies representation or rational comprehension (hence the recourse of Wordsworth, DeLillo, and others to hyperbole—"cosmic," "infinite," "eternal," and so on).[6]

The Romantic-metaphysical character of DeLillo's rendering of sublime experience is evident in the pivotal place he gives to the feeling of "awe." Not only is the term repeated in Gladney's description of his feelings toward the toxic cloud, but it is used three times, along with the kindred terms "dread" and "wonder," in a later account of that characteristically Romantic experience of the sublime, namely, gazing at a sunset:[7]

> The sky takes on content, feeling, an exalted narrative life....
> There are turreted skies, light storms.... Certainly there is awe, it
> is all awe, it transcends previous categories of awe, but we don't
> know whether we are watching in wonder or dread.... (324)

Given the Romantics' valorization of "I-centered" experience (in respect of which, *The Prelude* stands as a preeminent example), the feeling of awe has received special attention in their literature. After all, that overwhelming feeling of spellbound reverence would seem like cogent testimony to the innermost life of the psyche, an expression of what Wordsworth, in "Tintern Abbey" and *The Prelude*, called the "purer mind" (164, 506). However, that deep-rooted, plenitudinous I-centered subject of awe is a far cry from postmodern conceptions of the self as, typically, the tenuous construct of intersecting cultural codes. As noted earlier, this is the model of the self we find in the quintessentially postmodern fiction of Abish, Barthelme, and Coover, among others. It is a model which accords with Roland Barthes's view of the "I" that "is already itself a plurality of other texts, of codes which are infinite.... [Whence] subjectivity has ultimately the generality of stereotypes" (10). Evidently, DeLillo's awestruck subjects contradict the postmodern norm.[8] Finally, why create such subjects at all? Perhaps they may be regarded as an instance of DeLillo's endeavor to affirm the integrity and spiritual energy of the psyche in the face of (what the novel suggests is) late capitalism's disposition to disperse or thin out the self into so many consumer subject positions (48, 50, 83-84). In short, we might say that sublimity is invoked to recuperate psychic wholeness.

Studies of *Libra*, which identify it as a postmodernist text, typically stress its rendering of Lee Harvey Oswald as the construct of media discourses and its focus on the loss of the (historical) referent and the constraints of textuality.[9] And yet for all its evident postmodern concerns, there is a current of thinking in the novel that is highly resistant to any postmodernizing account of it. Consider, for example, this observation by David Ferrie, one of the book's anti-Castro militants:

> Think of two parallel lines.... One is the life of Lee H. Oswald. One is the conspiracy to kill the President. What bridges the space between them? What makes a connection inevitable? There is a third line. It comes out of dreams, visions, intuitions, prayers, out of the deepest levels of the self. It's not generated by cause and effect like the other two lines. It's a line that cuts across causality, cuts across time. It has no history that we can recognize or understand. But it forces a connection. It puts a man on the path of his destiny. (339)

Observations of this type abound in *Libra*: elsewhere we read of "patterns [that] emerge outside the bounds of cause and effect" (44); "secret symmetries" (78); "a world inside the world" (13, 47, 277); "A pattern outside experience. Something that jerks you out of the spin of history" (384). Clearly, repeated invocations of invisible, transhistorical forces which shape human affairs do not amount to a postmodern rejection of empiricist historiography. Rather, this is the stuff of metaphysics, not to say the occult. Indeed, in a discussion of *Libra*, published in *South Atlantic Quarterly*, DeLillo seriously speculates on supernatural interventions in human history:

> But Oswald's attempt on Kennedy was more complicated. I think it was based on elements outside politics and, as someone in the novel says, outside history—things like dreams and coincidences and even the movement or the configuration of the stars, which is one reason the book is called *Libra*....
>
> ... When I hit upon this notion of coincidence and dream and intuition and the possible impact of astrology on the way men act, I thought that *Libra*, being Oswald's sign, would be the one title that summarized what's inside the book. ("Outsider" 289, 293-94; emphasis added)

I also cite this interview as evidence that DeLillo is more likely to endorse his characters' beliefs in transcendent realities than to dismiss them as, in the words of one commentator, a "fantasy of secret knowledge, of a world beyond marginalization that would provide a center that would be immune to the play of signification" (Carmichael 209).

Libra appeals to the truth and sovereignty of "the deepest levels of the self," that is, the levels of "dreams, visions, intuitions" (339). Indeed, alongside those readings of the novel that point to its postmodern rendering of the subject without psychic density—"an effect of the codes out of which he is articulated" (Carmichael 206); "a contemporary production" (Lentricchia, "*Libra*" 441)—we must reckon with the book's insistent focus on "another level, ... a deeper kind of truth" (260), on that which "[w]e know ... on some deeper plane" (330), on that which "speaks to something deep inside [one].... the life-insight" (28). Such appeals to insight or intuition are common in Romantic literature and conform with Romanticism's depth model of subjectivity. That model is premised on the belief that truth lies "furthest in," that is, in the domain of the "heart" or "purer mind"; the belief that truth can only be accessed by the "inner faculties" (Wordsworth), by "inward sight" (Shelley), or, recalling the American Romantics, by "intuition." "[W]here," Emerson rhetorically inquired, "but in the intuitions which are vouchsafed us from within, shall we learn the Truth?" (182).[10] The comparisons may be schematic but, still, are close enough to indicate that the mindset of *Libra* is neither consistently nor unequivocally post-modern. No less emphatic than the book's evidence for a model of mind as an unstable "effect" of media codes is the evidence for a model of it as self-sufficient and self-authenticating, as an interior source of insight or vision.

What are the ideological implications of DeLillo's Romantic metaphysics? A common reading of Romanticism understands its introspective orientation in terms of a "politics of vision."[11] This is to say that, first, Romantic introspection may be seen as an attempt to claim the "inner faculties" as an inviolable, sacrosanct space beyond the domain of industrialization and the expanding marketplace. Second, the persistent appeal to the visionary "faculty" of "insight" or "intuition" or "Imagination" supplied Wordsworth, Blake, and others with a vantage point from which to critique the utilitarian and positivist ethos of capitalist development. But the crucial component of the "politics of vision" is the concept of what M.H. Abrams has called "the redemptive imagination" (117-22). Abrams notes how Blake repeatedly asserts that the "Imagination ... is the Divine Body of the Lord Jesus" (qtd. in Abrams 121) and quotes from The Prelude to emphasize that Wordsworth also substituted Imagination for the Redeemer:

> Here must thou be, O Man!
>
> Strength to thyself; no Helper hast thou here;
> .....
>
> The prime and vital principle is thine
>
> In the recesses of thy nature, far
>
> From any reach of outward fellowship[.]
> (qtd. in Abrams 120)

What needs to be added here is that this faith in the "redemptive imagination" is premised on an idealist assumption that personal salvation can be achieved primarily, if not exclusively, at the level of the individual psyche. Indeed, this focus on salvation as chiefly a private, spiritual affair tends to obscure or diminish the role of change at the institutional level of economic and political practice as a precondition for the regeneration of the subject.[12] And it is a similar "politics of vision" that informs DeLillo's writing and that invites the same conclusion. DeLillo's appeals to the visionary serve to affirm an autonomous realm of experience and to provide a standard by which to judge the spiritually atrophied culture of late capitalism. Thus against the impoverishments and distortions of communication in a culture colonized by factoids, sound bites, PR hype, and propaganda, DeLillo endeavors to preserve the credibility of visionary experience and, in particular, to validate the visionary moment as the sign of a redemptive order of meaning. He has remarked, "The novelist can try to leap across the barrier of fact, and the reader is willing to take that leap with him as long as there's a kind of redemptive truth waiting on the other side" ("Outsider" 294). Yet, as we have already seen, that "leap" is into the realm of the transhistorical, where "redemptive truth" is chiefly a spiritual, visionary matter. And it is in this respect that his fiction betrays a conservative tendency; his response to the adverse cultural effects of late capitalism reproduces a Romantic politics of vision, that is, it is a response that obscures, if not undervalues, the need for radical change at the level of the material infrastructure.

The fact that DeLillo writes so incisively of the textures of postmodern experience, of daily life in the midst of images, commodities, and conspiracies, does not make him a postmodern writer. His Romantic appeals to a primal language of vision, to the child's psyche as a medium of precious insight, to the sublime contravene the antimetaphysical norms of postmodern theory. Moreover, while there is, to be sure, a significant strain of irony that runs through his fiction, it does not finally undercut his metaphysics. As Tom LeClair has noted in a discussion of *White Noise*, "DeLillo presses beyond the ironic, extracting from his initially satiric materials a sense of wonderment or mystery" (214). "Wonder" and "mystery," to say nothing of "extrasensory flashes" (*White Noise* 34), are frequently invoked in DeLillo's writing as signifiers of a mystical order of cognition, an affirmation that the near-global culture of late capitalism cannot exhaust the possibilities of human experience. But it is precisely this metaphysical cast of thinking that separates DeLillo's fiction from the thoroughgoing postmodernism of, say, Walter Abish or Robert Coover, and that should prompt us to qualify radically our tendency to read him as an exemplary postmodern writer.

NOTES

1. See, for example, Lentricchia, "Tales" and "*Libra*"; Frow; Messmer; and Wilcox.

2. Perhaps the choice of title for the novel is, among other things, calculated to evoke that long tradition of Neo-Platonist and medieval mysticism which meditated on divine names. One might cite the writings of Pseudo-Dionysius, author of The Divine Names, or the Merkabah mystics,

early Kabbalists who speculated on the secret names of God and the angels. For such mystics, the way to revelation is through the knowledge of secret names.

3. This is precisely the theme of an early essay by Walter Benjamin, who, reflecting on the degeneration of language into "mere signs," observed: "In the Fall, since the eternal purity of names was violated, ... man abandoned immediacy in the communication of the concrete, name, and fell into the abyss of the mediateness of all communication, of the word as means, of the empty word, into the abyss of prattle" (120).

4. "I do wonder if there is something we haven't come across. Is there another, clearer language? Will we speak it and hear it when we die? Did we know it before we were born? ... Maybe this is why there's so much babbling in my books. Babbling can be ... a purer form, an alternate speech. I wrote a short story that ends with two babies babbling at each other in a car. This was something I'd seen and heard, and it was a dazzling and unforgettable scene. I felt these babies knew something. They were talking, they were listening, they were commenting.... Glossolalia is interesting because it suggests there's another way to speak, there's a very different language lurking somewhere in the brain" ("Interview" 83-84). And "Glossolalia or speaking in tongues ... could be viewed as a higher form of infantile babbling. It's babbling which seems to mean something" ("Outsider" 302). (Such comments help explain the significance of the crying of Baby Wilder in *White Noise* [78-79], an episode I shall discuss later.)

5. A little later we read: "People everywhere are absorbed in conversation.... Conversation is life, language is the deepest being" (52).

6. Kant formulated the following succinct definition: "We can describe the sublime in this way: it is an object (of nature) the representation of which determines the mind to think the unattainability of nature as a presentation of [reason's] ideas" (qtd. in Weiskel 22).

7. Recall these lines from Wordsworth's "Tintern Abbey": "a sense sublime / Of something far more deeply interfused, / Whose dwelling is the light of setting suns" (164). I am indebted to Lou Caton, of the University of Oregon, for drawing my attention to a possible Romantic context for the sunsets in *White Noise*.

8. Here, I anticipate two likely objections. First, the "airborne toxic event" may seem like an ironic postmodern version of the sublime object insofar as DeLillo substitutes a man-made source of power for a natural one. Yet Gladney's words emphasize that that power is experienced as a natural phenomenon: "This was a death made in the laboratory, defined and measurable, but we thought of it at the time in a simple and primitive way,

as some seasonal perversity of the earth like a flood or tornado" (127). Second, I disagree with Arthur Saltzman (118-19) and others who see postmodern irony in the account of the sunset insofar as (to be sure) (1) the sunset has been artificially enhanced by pollution and (2) most observers of the spectacle "don't know ... what it means." After all, the passage in question clearly insists on the sense of awe irrespective of these factors.

9. See, for example, Lentricchia, "*Libra*"; Carmichael; and Cain.

10. In his lecture "The Transcendentalist," Emerson asserted, "Although ... there is no pure transcendentalist, yet the tendency to respect the intuitions, and to give them, at least in our creed, all authority over our experience, has deeply colored the conversation and poetry of the present day" (207).

11. Jon Klancher notes that it was M. H. Abrams who tagged Romanticism as a "politics of vision." However, he argues that insofar as Romanticism is an uncircumscribable, historically variable category, one whose construction alters in response to "institutional crises and consolidations," its "politics of vision" can be, and has been, read as not only radical but also conservative (77-88).

12. It is often argued that social history gets repressed in Wordsworth's "extravagant lyricizing of the recovered self" and in his "'sense sublime'" (Klancher 80).

Works Cited

Abish, Walter. *In the Future Perfect*. New York: New Directions, 1975.

Abrams, M. H. *Natural Supernaturalism: Tradition and Revolution in Romantic Literature*. New York: Norton, 1971.

Barthelme, Donald. *Snow White*. New York: Atheneum, 1967.

Barthes, Roland. *S/Z*. Trans. Richard Miller. New York: Hill and Wang, 1974.

Benjamin, Walter. "On Language as Such and on the Language of Man." 1916. *One-Way Street and Other Writings*. Trans. E. Jephcott and Kingsley Shorter. London: Verso, 1985. 107-23.

Burke, Edmund. *A Philosophical Enquiry into the Origin of Our Ideas of the Sublime and the Beautiful*. 1757. Ed. J.T. Boulton. U of Notre Dame P, 1958.

Cain, William E. "Making Meaningful Worlds: Self and History in *Libra*." *Michigan Quarterly Review* 29 (1990): 275-87.

Carmichael, Thomas. "Lee Harvey Oswald and the Postmodern Subject:

History and Intertextuality in Don DeLillo's *Libra, The Names*, and *Mao II*." *Contemporary Literature* 34 (1993): 204-18.

Caton, Lou. "Setting Suns and Imaginative Failure in Don DeLillo's *White Noise*." Twentieth-Century Literature Conference. University of Louisville, Louisville, KY. 1995.

Coleridge, Samuel Taylor. *Biographia Literaria*. 1817, Ed. George Watson. London: Dent, 1975.

Coover, Robert. *Pricksongs and Descants*. New York: Plume, 1969.

DeLillo, Don. "I Never Set Out to Write an Apocalyptic Novel." Interview with Caryn James. *New York Times Book Review* 13 Jan. 1985: 31.

———. "An Interview with Don DeLillo." With Tom LeClair. *Anything Can Happen: Interviews with Contemporary American Novelists*. Ed. Tom LeClair and Larry McCaffery. Urbana: U of Illinois P, 1983. 79-90.

———. *Libra*. 1988. Harmondsworth, Eng.: Penguin, 1989.

———. *The Names*. 1982. New York: Vintage, 1989.

———. "An Outsider in This Society: An Interview with Don DeLillo." With Anthony DeCurtis. The Fiction of Don DeLillo. Ed. Frank Lentricchia. Spec. issue of *South Atlantic Quarterly* 89 (1990): 281-304.

———. *Ratner's Star*. 1976. New York: Vintage, 1989.

———. *White Noise*. 1985. Harmondsworth, Eng.: Penguin, 1986.

Derrida, Jacques. *Of Grammatology*. Trans. Gayatri Chakravorty Spivak. Baltimore: Johns Hopkins UP, 1976.

Emerson, Ralph Waldo. Nature, Addresses, and Lectures. Cambridge, MA: Belknap-Harvard UP, 1971. Vol. 1 of *The Collected Works of Ralph Waldo Emerson*. 4 vols. 1971-1987.

Frow, John. "The Last Things Before the Last: Notes on *White Noise*." The Fiction of Don DeLillo. Ed. Frank Lentricchia. Spec. issue of *South Atlantic Quarterly* 89 (1990): 413-29.

Klancher, Jon. "English Romanticism and Cultural Production." *The New Historicism*, Ed. H. Aram Veeser. New York: Routledge, 1989. 77-88.

LeClair, Tom. *In the Loop: Don DeLillo and the Systems Novel*. Urbana: U of Illinois P, 1987.

Lentricchia, Frank. "*Libra* as Postmodern Critique." The Fiction of Don DeLillo. Ed. Frank Lentricchia. Spec. issue of *South Atlantic Quarterly* 89 (1990): 431-53.

———. "Tales of the Electronic Tribe." New Essays on "*White Noise*." Ed. Frank Lentricchia. *The American Novel*. New York: Cambridge UP, 1991. 87-113.

Messmer, Michael W. "'Thinking It Through Completely': The

Interpretation of Nuclear Culture." *Centennial Review* 32 (1988): 397-413.

Pynchon, Thomas. *The Crying of Lot 49*, 1966. New York: Perennial-Harper, 1990.

Rousseau, Jean-Jacques. "Essay on the Origin of Languages." Trans. John H. Moran. *On the Origin of Language*. Ed. John H. Moran and Alexander Gode. Milestones of Thought, New York: Ungar, 1966. 5-74.

Saltzman, Arthur M. *Designs of Darkness in Contemporary American Fiction*. Penn Studies in Contemporary American Fiction. Philadelphia: U of Pennsylvania P, 1990.

Weiskel, Thomas. *The Romantic Sublime: Studies in the Structure and Psychology of Transendence*. Baltimore: Johns Hopkins UP, 1976.

Wilcox, Leonard. "Baudrillard, DeLillo's *White Noise*, and the End of Heroic Narrative." *Contemporary Literature* 32 (1991): 346-65.

Wordsworth, William. *Poetical Works*. Ed. Thomas Hutchinson. Rev. Ernest de Selincourt. Oxford: Oxford UP, 1978.

DAVID COWART

For Whom the Bell Tolls: Don DeLillo's Americana

D on DeLillo's 1971 novel *Americana*, his first, represents a rethinking of the identity or alienation theme that had figured with particular prominence in the quarter century after the close of World War II. The theme persists in DeLillo, but the self becomes even more provisional. The changing social conditions and imploding belief systems that alienate a Meursault, a Holden Caulfield, or a Binx Bolling do not constitute so absolute an epistemic rupture as the gathering recognition—backed up by post-Freudian psychology—that the old stable ego has become permanently unmoored. Whether or not he would embrace Lacanian formulations of psychological reality, DeLillo seems fully to recognize the tenuousness of all "subject positions." He knows that postmodern identity is not something temporarily eclipsed, something ultimately recoverable. DeLillo characters cannot, like Hemingway's Nick Adams, fish the Big Two-Hearted to put themselves back together. Thus David Bell, the narrator of *Americana* remains for the reader a slippery, insubstantial personality—even though he claims to be able to engage with his self whenever he looks in a mirror (13/11).[1] Bell in fact stumbles through life, waiting for some change, some new dispensation, to complete the displacement of the old order, in which the fiction of a knowable, stable identity enjoyed general credence.

From *Contemporary Literature*, Vol. XXXVII, No. 4, Winter, 1996, pp. 602-19.

In psychoanalytic theory, one's sense of self originates, at least in part, in the early relationship with the mother. DeLillo, like Freud or Lacan, extends this idea beyond individual psychology. He knows that Americans collectively define themselves with reference to a land their artists frequently represent, in metaphor, at least, as female. In *Americana* DeLillo represents this female land as maternal—a trope common enough in Europe (where nationalists often salute "the Motherland") but seldom encountered on this side of the Atlantic. The author thereby makes doubly compelling the theme of the land violated, for he presents not the familiar drama of rapacious Europeans despoiling a landscape represented as Pocahontas, but the more appalling tragedy of the American Oedipus and his unwitting violation of a landscape that the reader gradually recognizes as Jocasta.[2]

By means of these and other allegorizing identifications, DeLillo participates in and wields a certain amount of control over the profusion of images by which America represents itself. More than any other contemporary writer, DeLillo understands the extent to which images— from television, from film, from magazine journalism and photography, from advertising, sometimes even from books—determine what passes for reality in the American mind. Unanchored, uncentered, and radically two-dimensional, these images constitute the discourse by which Americans strive to know themselves. DeLillo's protagonist, a filmmaker and successful television executive, interacts with the world around him by converting it to images, straining it through the lens of his sixteen-millimeter camera. He attempts to recapture his own past by making it into a movie, and much of the book concerns this curious, Godardesque film in which, he eventually discloses, he has invested years. Thus one encounters—two years before the conceit structured Gravity's Rainbow—a fiction that insists on blurring the distinctions between reality and its representation on film. Film vies, moreover, with print, for readers must negotiate a curiously twinned narrative that seems to exist as both manuscript and "footage"—and refuses to stabilize as either. *Americana*, the novel one actually holds and reads, seems to be this same narrative at yet a third diagetic remove.

In his scrutiny of the mechanics of identity and representation in the written and filmed narratives of David Bell, especially as they record an oedipal search for the mother, DeLillo explores the America behind the *Americana*. What the author presents is a set of simulacra: manuscript and film and book mirroring a life and each other, words and images that pretend to mask a person named David Bell. But of course David Bell is himself a fictional character—and six years too young to be a stand-in for DeLillo (though one can recast the conundrum here as the attempt of this other subject—the author—to trick the simulacra into yielding up a modicum of insight into the mysteries of the ego's position within the Symbolic Order). DeLillo makes of his shadow play a postmodernist exemplar, a dazzling demonstration of the subject's inability to know a definitive version of itself. Thus Bell's film begins and ends with a shot of Austin Wakely, his surrogate, standing in front of a mirror that reflects the recording camera and its operator, the autobiographical subject of the film. A perfect piece of hermeticism, this shot announces an infinite circularity; it suggests that nothing in the rest of the film will manage to violate the endless circuit of the signifying chain. It suggests, too, the complexity—indeed, the impossibility—of determining the truly authentic subject among its own proliferating masks.

One can resolve some of the difficulties of DeLillo's first novel by searching for coherent elements amid the larger obscurity of its action and structure. The central events of the narrative evidently take place some time after the Kennedy assassination (the American century's climacteric) and before the Vietnam War had begun to wind down. Recollecting the second year of his brief marriage, terminated five years previously, Bell remarks that the conflict in Southeast Asia "was really just beginning" (38/35), and subsequently the war is a pervasive, malign presence in the narrative. Inasmuch as the hero is twenty-eight years old and apparently born in 1942 (his father in the film mentions that the birth occurred while he was overseas, shortly after his participation in the Bataan Death March), the story's present would seem to be 1970. Yet occasionally Bell intimates a much later vantage from which he addresses the reader. He seems, in fact, to be spinning this narrative at a considerable remove in time, for he refers at one point to "the magnet-grip of an impending century" (174/166). He is also remote in space: like another great egotist who embodied the best and worst of his nation, Bell seems to have ended up on an "island" (16/14, 137/129) off "the coast of Africa" (357/347).

DeLillo structures the novel as a first-person narrative divided into four parts. In the first of these Bell introduces himself as a jaded television executive in New York. Presently he collects three companions and sets out on a cross-country trip—ostensibly to meet a television film crew in the Southwest, but really to look in the nation's heartland for clues to himself and to the American reality he embodies. In part 2, through flashbacks, the reader learns about Bell's relations with his family (mother, father, two sisters) and about his past (childhood, prep school, college). In part 3, Bell stops over in Fort Curtis, a midwestern town, and begins shooting his autobiographical film with a cast composed of his traveling companions and various townspeople recruited more or less at random. This part of the story climaxes with a long-postponed sexual encounter with Sullivan, the woman sculptor he finds curiously compelling. Subsequently, in part 4, he abandons his friends and sets off alone on the second part of his journey: into the West.

Bell's "post-Kerouac pilgrimage," as Charles Champlin calls it (7), takes him from New York to Massachusetts to Maine, then westward to the sleepy town of Fort Curtis, in a state Bell vaguely surmises to be east (or perhaps south) of Iowa. After his stay in Fort Curtis he undertakes a "second journey, the great seeking leap into the depths of America," heading "westward to match the shadows of my image and my self" (352/341). A hitchhiker now, picked up "somewhere in Missouri" (358/348), he travels with the generous but sinister Clevenger, himself a remarkable piece of *Americana*, through Kansas, through "a corner-piece of southeastern Colorado," across New Mexico, and on into Arizona. Significantly, he never gets to Phoenix. Instead, he visits a commune in the Arizona desert before rejoining Clevenger and heading "east, south and east" (372/362), back across New Mexico to the west Texas town of Rooster (where DeLillo will locate Logos College in his next novel, *End Zone*). Parting with Clevenger for good, Bell hitchhikes to Midland, where he rents a car and drives northeast, overnight, to Dallas, honking as he traverses the ground of Kennedy's martyrdom. In Dallas he boards a flight back to New York.

In his end is his beginning. Seeking the foundational in self and culture, Bell travels in a great circle that is its own comment on essentialist expectations. His circular journey seems, in other words, to embody the signifying round, impervious to a reality beyond itself. In this circle, too, readers may recognize elements of a more attenuated symbolism. As an emblem of spiritual perfection, the circle suggests the New World promise that Fitzgerald and Faulkner meditate on. As an emblem of final nullity, it suggests America's bondage to historical process—the inexorable corsi and ricorsi described by Vico (whom Bell briefly mentions). DeLillo teases the reader, then, with the circle's multiple meanings: vacuity, spiritual completeness, inviolable link in the chain of signification, historical inevitability.

That history may be cyclical affords little comfort to those caught in a civilization's decline. Like his friend Warren Beasley, the Jeremiah of all-night radio, Bell knows intimately the collapse of America's ideal conception of itself. He speaks of "many visions in the land, all fragments of the exploded dream" (137/129). The once unitary American Dream, that is, has fallen into a kind of Blakean division; and DeLillo—through Bell—differentiates the fragments embraced by "generals and industrialists" from what remains for the individual citizen: a seemingly simple "dream of the good life."

> But this dream, or dream fragment, had its complexities, its edges
> of illusion and self-deception, an implication of serio-comic
> death. To achieve an existence almost totally symbolic is less
> simple than mining the buried metals of other countries or
> sending the pilots of your squadron to hang their bombs over
> some illiterate village. And so purity of intention, simplicity and
> all its harvests, these were with the mightiest of the visionaries,
> those strong enough to confront the larger madness. For the rest
> of us, the true sons of the dream, there was only complexity. The
> dream made no allowance for the truth beneath the symbols, for
> the interlinear notes, the presence of something black (and
> somehow very funny) at the mirror rim of one's awareness. This
> was difficult at times. But as a boy, and even later, quite a bit later,
> I believed all of it, the institutional messages, the psalms and
> placards, the pictures, the words. Better living through chemistry.
> The Sears, Roebuck catalog. Aunt Jemima. All the impulses of all
> the media were fed into the circuitry of my dreams. One thinks
> of echoes. One thinks of an image made in the image and likeness
> of images. It was that complex. (137-38/130)

This passage is an especially good example of the DeLillo style and the
DeLillo message. DeLillo's writing, like Thomas Pynchon's, is keyed to the
postmodern moment. Inasmuch as this is prose that strives to become as
uncentered and as shadow-driven as the peculiarly American psychological
and social reality under scrutiny, one glosses it only at the risk of violating
the author's studied indirection. But one can—again, without pretending to
exhaust its ambiguity and indeterminacy—hazard a modest commentary.

"Almost totally symbolic," the dream of the good life is subject to
"complexities" from which powerful ideologues are free. Focused, single-
minded, exempt from doubt, the military and industrial powerful confront
the "larger madness" of political life in the world (and especially in the
twentieth century) with a singleness of purpose that, however misguided, at
least enjoys the distinction, the "harvests," of "purity" and "simplicity." The
reader who would convert these abstractions into concrete terms need only
recall how for decades a Darwinian economic vision and a passionate hatred
of Communism made for an American foreign policy that was nothing if not
"simple." The irony, of course, is that simplicity is the last thing one should
expect of dealings between nations, especially when those dealings take the

form of war. But DeLillo evinces little interest in attacking the monomania of Lyndon Johnson and Robert McNamara or Richard Nixon and Melvin Laird. By 1971, their obtuseness had been exposed too often to afford latitude for anything fresh in a literary sense—and DeLillo has the good sense to know the fate of satiric ephemera like *MacBird!* (1966) and the contemporaneous *Our Gang* (1971). In *Americana*, by contrast, DeLillo explores the far-from-simple mechanics of life in a culture wholly given over to the image. The citizen of this culture, however seemingly innocent and uncomplicated, exists as the cortical nexus of a profoundly complex play of advertisements, media bombardments, and shadow realities that manage, somehow, always to avoid or postpone representation of the actual, the "something black ... at the mirror rim of one's awareness." DeLillo, then, chronicling this "existence almost totally symbolic," sees the American mass brain as "an image made in the image and likeness of images."

But the real lies in wait, says the author, whose thesis seems to complement Lacanian formulations of the subject position and its problematic continuity. The subject cannot know itself, and language, the Symbolic Order, discovers only its own play, its own energies, never the bedrock reality it supposedly names, glosses, gives expression to. Hence DeLillo actually echoes Lacan—not to mention Heidegger, Derrida, and others—in speaking of "interlinear notes" to the text of appearances, a presence at the edges of mirrors, a "truth beneath the symbols." *Americana* is the record of an attempt to break out of the endlessly circular signifying chain of images replicating and playing off each other to infinity. As such it is also the record of a growing awareness of the complexity with which a consumer culture imagines itself. For the author, this awareness extends to knowledge of the social reality beneath what Pynchon, in *The Crying of Lot 49*, characterizes as "the cheered land" (180).

Part of the agenda in the Pynchon novel, one recalls, is to bring to the surface of consciousness the disinherited or marginalized elements of the American polity. *The Crying of Lot 49* functions in part to remind readers that enormous numbers of Americans have been omitted from the version of the country sanctioned by the media and other public institutions, and that is one way to understand what DeLillo is doing when a reference to Aunt Jemima follows a cryptic remark about "the presence of something black (and somehow very funny) at the mirror rim of one's awareness." For years, one encountered no black faces in that cornucopia of middle-class consumerism, the Sears, Roebuck catalog, but the semiotics of breakfast-food merchandising could accommodate a black domestic like Aunt Jemima. The reference to a familiar and venerable commercial image affords a ready example of a reality that the sixties, in one of the decade's more positive achievements, had brought to consciousness—the reality of an American underclass that for years could be represented only as comic stereotype. Thus the reader who needs a concrete referent for what DeLillo is talking about here need go no further than a social reality that was, in 1970, just beginning to achieve visibility.

Aunt Jemima metonymically represents the world of advertising, a world dominated by that especially resourceful purveyor of the image, Bell's father (the familial relationship reifies the idea that television is the child of advertising). The father's pronouncements on his calling complement the book's themes of representational form and substance. He explains that advertising flourishes by catering to a desire on the part of consumers to think of themselves in the third person—to surrender, as it were, their already embattled positions as subjects. But the person who laments "living in the third person" (64/58) is his own son, this novel's narrating subject. "A successful television commercial," the father remarks, encourages in the viewer a desire "to change the way he lives" (281/270). This observation mocks and distorts the powerful idea Rilke expresses in his poem "Archäischer Torso Apollos": "Du musst dein Leben ändern (313).[3] The poet perceives this message—"You must change your life"—as he contemplates the ancient sculpture. He suggests that the work of art, in its power, its perfection, and (before the age of mechanical reproduction) its uniqueness, goads viewers out of their complacency. The artist—Rilke or DeLillo—confronts torpid, passionless humanity with the need to seek a more authentic life; the advertiser, by contrast, confronts this same humanity with a spurious, even meretricious need for change. The impulse behind this narrative, interestingly enough, is precisely that need to change a life one has come to see as empty—the need to return from the limbo of third-person exile, the need to recover, insofar as possible, a meaningful subjectivity.

Like the questers of old, then, Bell undertakes "a mysterious and sacramental journey" (214/204): he crosses a threshold with a supposedly faithful band of companions (Sullivan, Brand, Pike), travels many leagues, and descends into a Dantean underworld with the Texan, Clevenger, as cicerone. Indeed, the nine-mile circumference of Clevenger's speedway seems palpably to glance at the nine-fold circles of Dante's Hell (especially as Bell imagines, back in New York, a "file cabinet marked pending return of soul from limbo" (345/334)). When, from here, Bell puts in a call to Warren Beasley, who has "foresuffered almost all" (243/232), he modulates from Dante to Odysseus, who learns from Tiresias in the underworld that he must "lose all companions," as Pound says, before the completion of his quest.

Alone and empty-handed, without the boon that traditionally crowns such efforts, Bell is a postmodern Odysseus, returning not to triumph but to the spiritual emptiness of New York before ending up in solitude on a nameless island that would seem to have nothing but its remoteness in common with Ithaca. Indeed, announcing toward the end of his story that he will walk on his insular beach, "wearing white flannel trousers" (358/348), he dwindles finally to Prufrock, the ultimate hollow man.

In attempting to understand the reasons for Bell's failure, the reader engages with DeLillo's real subject: the insidious pathology of America itself, a nation unable, notwithstanding prodigies of self-representation, to achieve self-knowledge. The novelist must represent the self-representation of this vast image culture in such a way as to reveal whatever truth lies beneath its gleaming, shifting surfaces. But the rhetoric of surface and depth will not serve: America is a monument to the ontological authority of images. DeLillo seeks at once to represent American images and to sort them out, to discover the historical, social, and spiritual aberrations they embody or disguise.

DeLillo focuses his analysis on the character of David Bell, a confused seeker after the truth of his own tormented soul and its relation to the larger American reality. One makes an essential distinction between DeLillo's engagement with America and that of his character, who becomes the vehicle of insights he cannot share. Marooned among replicating images, Bell loses himself in the signifying chain, as doomed to "scattering" as Pynchon's Tyrone Slothrop. In his attempts to recover some cryptic truth about his family and in his manipulation of filmic and linguistic simulacra, Bell fails to see the extent to which he embodies an America guilty of the most abhorrent of violations—what the Tiresias-like Beasley calls the "national incest." David Bell's existential distress seems to have an important oedipal dimension, seen in his troubled memories of his mother and in his relations with other women in his life. I propose to look more closely, therefore, at just how the relationship between David Bell and his mother ramifies symbolically into the life of a nation.

The emphasis, in what follows, on the Freudian view of the Oedipus complex is not intended to imply an argument for its superiority to those post-Freudian (and especially Lacanian) views invoked elsewhere in this essay. When the subject is postmodern identity, one naturally opts for Lacan's refinements of Freudian thought, but insofar as Lacan took little interest in pathology per se, and insofar as DeLillo's emphasis is on a nation's sickness, the critic may legitimately gravitate to the older psychoanalytic economy and its lexicon. It is a mistake to think that entry into the Symbolic

Order precludes all further encounters with the Imaginary, and by the same token we err to view Freud's system as wholly displaced by that of his successor. Indeed, Lacan resembles somewhat the messiah who comes not to destroy the law but to fulfill it, and just as the theologian illustrates certain points more effectively out of the Old Testament than out of the New, so does the critic need at times to summon up the ideas of the Mosaic founder of psychoanalysis.

Throughout his narrative, Bell strives to come to terms with some fearsome thing having to do with his mother—something more insidious, even, than the cancer that takes her life. She grapples with a nameless anomie that becomes localized and explicable only momentarily, as in her account of being violated on the examining table by her physician, Dr. Weber (one recalls the similarly loathsome gynecologist in *The Handmaid's Tale*, Margaret Atwood's meditation on another rape of America). Neurasthenic and depressed, Bell's mother evidently lived with a spiritual desperation that her husband, her children, and her priest could not alleviate. Bell's recollections of his mother and his boyhood culminate as he thinks back to a party given by his parents, an occasion of comprehensive sterility that owes something to the gathering in Mike Nichols's 1968 film *The Graduate*, not to mention the moribund revels of "The Dead." The party ends with the mother spitting into the ice cubes; subsequently, the son encounters her in the pantry and has some kind of epiphany that he will later attempt to re-create on film. This epiphany concerns not only the mother's unhappiness but also the son's oedipal guilt, for Bell conflates the disturbing moments at the end of the party with his voyeuristic contemplation, moments earlier, of a slip-clad woman at her ironing board—a figure he promptly transforms, in "the hopelessness of lust" (117/109), into an icon of domestic sexuality: "She was of that age which incites fantasy to burn like a hook into young men on quiet streets on a summer night" (203).

Perhaps the remark of Bell's sister Mary, who becomes the family pariah when she takes up with a gangland hit man, offers a clue to this woman's misery: "there are different kinds of death," she says. "I prefer that kind, his kind, to the death I've been fighting all my life" (171/163). Another sister, Jane, embraces this death-in-life when she opts for Big Bob Davidson and suburbia. Bell's father completes the pattern: like the man he was forced to inter in the Philippines, he is "buried alive" (296/285). The death that his mother and sisters and father know in their different ways is also what David Bell, like Jack Gladney in *White Noise*, must come to terms with. The pervasive references to mortality reflect the characterization of death in the line from Saint Augustine that Warburton, the "Mad Memo-Writer," distributes: "And never can a man be more disastrously in death than when death itself shall be deathless" (23/21). Later, when Warburton glosses these words, he does not emphasize the spiritual imperative represented by death so much as the simple fact itself: "man shall remain forever in the state of death" because "death never dies" (108/101).

Bell's charm against death and social paresis may be his recurrent recollection of Akira Kurosawa's 1952 film *Ikiru*, especially the famous scene in which its protagonist, an old man dying of cancer, sits swinging in a nocturnal park amid drifting snowflakes.[4] Though he does not mention it, Bell must know that ikiru is Japanese for "living." Certainly he understands in the image something redemptive, something related to the fate of that other victim of cancer, his mother. In his own film he includes a sequence in which Sullivan, playing her, sits swinging like old Watanabe. In another, the amateur actor representing his father recalls that during his captivity in the Philippines the prisoners had filed by an old Japanese officer who sat in a swing and, moving to and fro, seemed to bless them with a circular motion of his hand. This detail may reflect only Bell's desire to graft certain intensely personal emblems onto the imagined recollections of his father, but he seems in any event curiously intent on weaving Kurosawa's parable into his own story of familial travail.

The submerged content of DeLillo's Kurosawa allusions suggests the larger meanings here. Kurosawa's character struggles within an enormous, implacable bureaucracy to drain a swamp (symbol of Japanese corruption and of his own part in it) and build a children's park. David Bell speaks of "the swamp of our own beings" (122), and, indeed, DeLillo's swamp and Kurosawa's represent the same discovery: that personal and national corruption prove coextensive. Like Kurosawa, too (or for that matter Saint Augustine), DeLillo understands that ikiru, living, can never be pursued outside the process of dying. The power of Kurosawa's conclusion, in which, dying, the protagonist sits in the swing, has to do with just how much his modest achievement has come to signify: it is what one can do with the life that gives the film its title. But this insight remains inchoate for Bell, who seems half-fatalistically to relish the knowledge that his own culture clears swamps only to achieve greater regularity—more straight lines, more utilitarian buildings—in a landscape progressively purged of graceful features that might please children. As an American, he knows that the clearing of "what was once a swamp" merely facilitates erection of some monument to transience and sterility: the "motel in the heart of every man" (268/257).

The reification of this place, a motel near the Chicago airport, provides the setting in which Bell and his ex-wife's cousin, Edwina, commit what she refers to as "some medieval form of incest" (273/261). This jocular reference contributes to a more substantial fantasy of incest at the heart of the book, a fantasy or obsession that figures in other fictions of the period, notably Louis Malle's witty and daring treatment of incestuous desire, *Un souffle au coeur* (1971), and the starker meditations on the subject in Norman Mailer's *An American Dream* (1965) and Roman Polanski's *Chinatown* (1974). If *Americana* had been written a generation later, at the height of controversy over repressed memory retrieval, it might, like Jane Smiley's *A Thousand Acres*, involve the revelation of literal incest. Bell, however, seems guilty of transgressing the most powerful of taboos only in spirit.

But he transgresses it over and over, nonetheless, for almost every woman he sleeps with turns out to be a version of his mother. In his relations with women he enacts an unconscious search for the one woman forbidden him, at once recapitulating and reversing the tragically imperfect oedipal model: as he was rejected, so will he reject successive candidates in what occasionally amounts to a literal orgy of philandering and promiscuity. Meanwhile he suffers the ancient oedipal betrayal at the hands of one surrogate mother after another. Thus when Carter Hemmings steals his date at a party, Bell spits in the ice cubes—a gesture that will make sense only later, when Bell describes his mother's similar (and perhaps similarly motivated) expression of disgust. Bell thinks Wendy, his college girlfriend, has slept with Simmons St. Jean, his teacher. Weede Denney, his boss, exercises a kind of seigneurial droit with Binky, Bell's secretary. And even Sullivan turns out to have been sleeping with Brand all along.

In Sullivan, at once mother and "mothercountry," Bell recognizes the most significant—and psychologically dangerous—of these surrogates. When she gives Brand a doll, she replicates a gesture made by Bell's mother on another occasion. To Bell himself she twice tells "a bedtime story" (332/320, 334/322). He characterizes three of her sculptures as "carefully handcrafted afterbirth" (114/106). Her studio, to which Bell retreats on the eve of his journey westward, was called the Cocoon by its former tenant; swathed in a "membranous chemical material" (116/108) that resembles sandwich wrap, it is the womb to which he craves a return. Here he curls up, goes to sleep, and awakens to the returning Sullivan: "A shape in the shape of my mother ... forming in the doorway" (118/110), "my mother's ghost in the room" (242/230). Bell's attraction to this central and definitive mother figure is so interdicted that it can only be described in negative terms; indeed, the climactic sexual encounter with Sullivan, a "black wish fulfilled"

(345/334), is remarkable for its sustained negative affect: "mothercountry. Optional spelling of third syllable" (345).—"Abomination" (331/319, 344/333), he keeps repeating, for symbolically he is committing incest.

Sullivan's narratives, the bedtime stories she tells the filial Bell, represent the twin centers of this novel's public meanings—the heart of a book otherwise wedded to superficies and resistant to formulations of psychological, sociological, or semiotic depth (here the play of simulacra retreats to an attenuated reflexivity: one story is told in Maine, the other about Maine). Sullivan's first story concerns an encounter with Black Knife, aboriginal American and veteran of the campaign against Custer; the other concerns the discovery of her patrilineage. The subject of these stories, encountering the Father, complements the larger narrative's account of coming to terms with the Mother.

Black Knife, one-hundred-year-old master ironist, describes the strange asceticism that drives Americans to clear their world of annoying, wasteful clutter: "We have been redesigning our landscape all these years to cut out unneeded objects such as trees, mountains, and all those buildings which do not make practical use of every inch of space." The idea behind this asceticism, he says, is to get away from useless beauty, to reduce everything to "[s]traight lines and right angles" (126/118), to go over wholly to the "Megamerica" of "Neon, fiber glass, plexiglass, polyurethane, Mylar, Acrylite" (127/119). Black Knife hopes that we will "come to terms with the false anger we so often display at the increasing signs of sterility and violence in our culture" (127/119)—that instead we will "set forth on the world's longest march of vulgarity, evil and decadence" (128/120). These imagined excesses would reify a vision like that of the Histriones in Jorge Luis Borges's story "The Theologians" or the Dolcinians of Umberto Eco's *The Name of the Rose*—heretics who seek to hasten the Apocalypse by committing as many sins as possible. Black Knife looks to the day when, "having set one foot into the mud, one foot and three toes," we will—just maybe—decide against surrendering to the swamp and pull back from our dreadful course, "shedding the ascetic curse, letting the buffalo run free, knowing everything a nation can know about itself and proceeding with the benefit of this knowledge and the awareness that we have chosen not to die. It's worth the risk ... for ... we would become, finally, the America that fulfills all of its possibilities. The America that belongs to the world. The America we thought we lived in when we were children. Small children. Very small children indeed" (128-29/120-21). We would, that is, repudiate the swamp in favor of an environment friendly to children—a park like the one created by that Japanese Black Knife, the Watanabe of Kurosawa's *Ikiru*.

The second bedtime story, which parallels the interview with Black Knife, concerns Sullivan's misguided attempt to recover her patrimony. In a sailing vessel off the coast of Maine, Sullivan and her Uncle Malcolm contemplate "God's world" (336/324), the land the Puritans found when they crossed the sea: America in its primal, unspoiled beauty. The voyage, however, becomes Sullivan's own night-sea journey into profound self-knowledge—knowledge, that is, of the intersection of self and nation. The vessel is the Marston Moor, named for the battle in which the Puritans added a triumph in the Old World to complement the success of their brethren in the New. The vessel's master is himself an avatar of American Puritanism, with roots in Ulster and Scotland. What Sullivan learns from her Uncle Malcolm immerses her—like Oedipus or Stephen Dedalus or Jay Gatsby or Jesus Christ—in what Freud calls the family romance. The child of a mystery parent, she must be about her father's business. She dramatizes the revelation that Uncle Malcolm is her real father in language that evokes by turns Epiphany and Pentecost and Apocalypse—the full spectrum of divine mystery and revelation.

The imagery here hints further at Sullivan's identification with the American land, for the heritage she discovers coincides with that of the nation. Described originally as some exotic ethnic blend and called, on one occasion, a "[d]aughter of Black Knife" (347/336), Sullivan proves also to be solidly Scotch-Irish, like so many of the immigrants who would compose the dominant American ethnic group. In that her spiritual father is a native American, her real father a north country Protestant, she discovers in herself the same mixture of innate innocence and passionately eschatological Puritanism that figures so powerfully in the historical identity of her country.

The perfervid descriptions of the wild Maine coast and the travail of the seafarers recall nothing so much as the evocations of spiritualized landscape in Eliot's Four Quartets (Sullivan is not so many leagues distant from the Dry Salvages, off Cape Ann). In the present scene, as in Eliot, the reader encounters a meditation on the way eternity subsumes the specific history of a place, a meditation in which deeply felt religious imagery intimates meanings that strain the very seams of language. Yet the mystery proves ultimately secular, and the only direct allusion to Eliot is from "Gerontion," one of his poems of spiritual aridity. Sullivan's shipmate, appalled at the absence of "Christ the tiger" (342/330) in the apocalyptic scene into which he has steered, also sees into the heart of things, and an unquoted line from the same poem may encapsulate both their thoughts: "After such knowledge, what forgiveness?"

The allusion to "Gerontion," like the other Eliot allusions in *Americana*, recalls the reader to an awareness of the spiritual problem of contemporary America that the book addresses. The climax of the sailing expedition occurs when a boy with a lantern appears on the shore: he is a sign, a vision at once numinous and secular. He disappoints Uncle Malcolm, who seems to have expected a vision more palpably divine. As Sullivan explains him, his shining countenance reveals certain truths of the human bondage to entropy—yet he also embodies an idea of innocence and the generative principle: "the force of all in all, or light lighting light" (342/330). He is, in short, the child that America has long since betrayed, the principle of innocence that sibylline Sullivan, glossing Black Knife's parable, suggests America may yet rediscover—and with it salvation.

DeLillo conceived *Americana* on a visit to Mount Desert Island, a place that moved him unexpectedly with its air of American innocence preserved.[5] Sullivan and her companion are off the island when the boy with the lantern appears. Though the moment bulks very small in the overall narrative, it will prove seminal as DeLillo recurs in subsequent novels to an idea of the redemptive innocence that survives, a vestige of Eden, in children. The boy with the lantern, an almost inchoate symbol here, will turn up again as the linguistically atavistic Tap in *The Names* and as Wilder on his tricycle in *White Noise*.

When Sullivan, in her valedictory, calls Bell "innocent" and "sick" (348/336), she describes the American paradox that he represents, but DeLillo defines the canker that rots the larger American innocence in terms considerably stronger. Bell's sister Mary, as played by Carol Deming in the film, remarks that "there are good wombs and bad wombs" (324/312), and the phrase recurs to Bell as he contemplates the southwestern landscape from Clevenger's speeding Cadillac (363/353). In other words, the mother he repeatedly violates is more than flesh and blood. DeLillo conflates and subverts a familiar icon of American nationalism: mother and country. In doing so he augments and transforms the traditional symbolism of the American land as the female victim of an ancient European violation. Fitzgerald, in *The Great Gatsby*, reflects on Dutch sailors and "the fresh green breast of the New World." Hart Crane, in *The Bridge*, and John Barth, in *The Sot-Weed Factor*, imagine the land specifically as Pocahontas. But DeLillo suggests that the real violation occurs in an oedipal drama of almost cosmic proportions: not in the encounter of European man with the tender breast of the American land but in the violation of that mother by their oedipal progeny. "We want to wallow," says Black Knife, "in the terrible gleaming mudcunt of Mother America" (127/119). Like Oedipus, then, Bell discovers in himself the source of the pestilence that has ravaged what Beasley calls "mamaland" (243/231). The American Oedipus, seeking to understand the malaise from which his country suffers, discovers its cause in his own manifold and hideous violations of the mother, the land that nurtures and sustains. Physical and spiritual, these violations take their place among the other *Americana* catalogued in DeLillo's extraordinary first novel.

NOTES

1. In preparing the 1989 Penguin edition of *Americana*, DeLillo made numerous small cuts in the text, and, generally speaking, the gains in economy improve the novel. For the most part, the author simply pares away minor instances of rhetorical overkill. For example, he deletes a gratuitously obscene remark about the spelling of "mothercountry," and he reduces the space devoted to the relationship of Bell and his ex-wife Meredith. Occasionally (as in the former instance), the author cuts a detail one has underlined in the 1971 edition, thereby affording the reader a glimpse into a gifted writer's maturing sense of decorum and understatement. Thus a minor motif like that of the woman ironing (it contributes to the reader's grasp of Bell's oedipal obsession) becomes a little less extravagant in the longer of the two passages in which it appears. Elsewhere, one applauds the excision of the syntactically tortured and the merely pretentious—for example, unsuccessful descriptions of film's epistemological and ontological properties. At no point, however, does DeLillo add material or alter the novel's original emphases— and I have only occasionally found it necessary or desirable to quote material that does not appear in both versions of the text. Except in these instances, I give page numbers for both editions—the 1971 Houghton Mifflin version first, the 1989 Penguin version second.

2. Though *Americana* remains the least discussed of DeLillo's major novels, an oedipal dimension has been noted by both Tom LeClair and Douglas Keesey, authors of the first two single-authored books on DeLillo. Neither, however, foregrounds this element. LeClair, in his magisterial chapter on this novel (which he names, along with *Ratner's Star* and *The Names*, as one of DeLillo's "primary achievements" [33]), represents the oedipal theme as largely ancillary to the proliferating "personal, cultural, and aesthetic ... schizophrenia" (34) that he sees as pervasive in the life of David Bell and in the culture of which he is a part. Thus LeClair explores the dynamics of what Gregory Bateson and R. D. Laing call "the double bind" in "the system of communications in Bell's family," which, "understood in

Bateson's terms, establishes the ground of Bell's character and presents a microcosm of the larger cultural problems manifested in *Americana*," (35-36). Keesey, by contrast, takes a feminist view of Bell's personality and life problems. Keesey is especially interesting on the oedipal relationship between Bell and his father, and on the idea that Bell, in his film, is striving unsuccessfully to recover the mother's "way of seeing" the world—a way lost to him when he embraced the values expressed in his father's "ads for sex and violence" (23).

3. Rilke's "Der Panther," by the same token, may lie behind the desire Bell's fellow traveler Pike expresses to encounter a mountain lion face to face.

4. The only substantial discussion of the Ikiru allusions is that of Mark Osteen, who acutely suggests that Bell sees himself in the film's moribund main character, Watanabe, and "fears his own living death" (463). The recurrent references to the scene on the swing represent "David's attempt to generate the kind of retrospective epiphany that Watanabe undergoes" (462-63).

5. In a Paris Review interview, DeLillo describes the genesis of this novel in a positive evocation of *Americana*:

> I was sailing in Maine with two friends, and we put into a small harbor on Mt. Desert Island. And I was sitting on a railroad tie waiting to take a shower, and I had a glimpse of a street maybe fifty yards away and a sense of beautiful old houses and rows of elms and maples and a stillness and wistfulness—the street seemed to carry its own built-in longing. And I felt something, a pause, something opening up before me. It would be a month or two before I started writing the book and two or three years before I came up with the title *Americana*, but in fact it was all implicit in that moment—a moment in which nothing happened, nothing ostensibly changed, a moment in which I didn't see anything I hadn't seen before. But there was a pause in time, and I knew I had to write about a man who comes to a street like this or lives on a street like this. And whatever roads the novel eventually followed, I believe I maintained the idea of that quiet street if only as counterpoint, as lost innocence. (279)

This recollection dictates not only the scene off Mount Desert Island but also and more clearly the scene in picturesque Millsgate, the little town on Penobscot Bay where the travelers pick up Brand. Here, at the end of part 1, Bell conceives the idea for his film—just as DeLillo, in a similar setting, conceived the idea of *Americana*.

WORKS CITED

Champlin, Charles. "The Heart Is a Lonely Craftsman." *Los Angeles Times Calendar* 29 July 1984: 7.

DeLillo, Don. *Americana*. New York: Houghton Mifflin, 1971.

———. *Americana*. Rev. ed. New York: Penguin, 1989.

———. "Don DeLillo: The Art of Fiction CXXXV." Interview. With Adam Begley. *Paris Review* 128 (1993): 274-306.

Keesey, Douglas. *Don DeLillo*. Twayne's United States Authors Series 625. New York: Twayne, 1993.

LeClair, Tom. *In the Loop: Don DeLillo and the Systems Novel*. Urbana: U of Illinois P, 1987.

Osteen, Mark. "Children of Godard and Coca-Cola: Cinema and Consumerism in Don DeLillo's Early Fiction." *Contemporary Literature* 37 (1996): 439-70.

Pynchon, Thomas. *The Crying of Lot 49*. Philadelphia: Lippincott, 1966.

Rilke, Rainer Maria. *Gesammelte Gedichte*. Frankfurt: Insel-Verlag, 1962.

CHRISTIAN MORARU

Consuming Narratives: Don DeLillo and the 'Lethal' Reading

He didn't really think he would have ended among the dead, injured or missing. He was already injured and missing. As for death, he no longer thought he would see it come from the muzzle of a gun or any other instrument designed to be lethal ... Shot by someone. Not a thief or deer hunter or highway sniper but some dedicated reader. (DeLillo, *Mao II* 196)

This excerpt from DeLillo's 1991 novel sets forth a poignant critique of the social response to narratives in an age that has integrated "aesthetic production" into "commodity production" (Jameson 4). Along with a whole series of contemporary writers from, say, Paul Auster to Mark Leyner, DeLillo trades upon the predicament of narrative representation, showing how cultural objects in general and stories in particular are fetishized in the public arena. The "fate of narrative" in our time, DeLillo suggests, reflects the "clumsy transposition of art into the sphere of consumption" (Horkheimer and Adorno 135), a displacement bound to give rise to a "system of non-culture" (128). However, it is not quite the "debasement" of "high culture" in the hands of "the culture industry" that DeLillo deplores; the entire culture as a collective apparatus of narrative misreading is here pinned down.

At the same time, even though his work does not necessarily advocate resistance to popular culture, it nonetheless unveils an uncanny resistance to

From *The Journal of Narrative Technique* 27, No. 2, Spring, 1997, pp. 190-206.

popularity. For DeLillo fame ranks among "mass delusion" phenomena, to recall Horkheimer and Adorno again. Insofar as it takes some kind of social performance, popularity is backfiring and treacherous, and creators should do their best to ward it off. For not only has the role of Baudelaire's "hypocritical" reader grown throughout modernity; the consumer of stories, DeLillo suggests, has become somewhat burdensome and menacing. S/he no longer is the honest co-author Rezeptionsästhetik took for granted. The audience, the media, and the publishing industry now make up a whole machinery of voracious consumption, an entire demonology of domestication, control, and alienation. Ironically enough, it is while striving to preclude this alienation that the author alienates, isolates himself or herself. More ironically perhaps, this resistance to popularity, which DeLillo himself has for a while practiced (Lentricchia, "*Libra* as Postmodern Critique"; DeLillo, "An Outsider"), the refusal to give interviews, appear on late shows, make speeches, and even publish, enhances the legend of the author, foregrounding the capacity of cultural systems to contain and profitably "recycle" artistic dissent.

This essay delves into DeLillo's imaginary of consumption, paying special attention to how his work thematizes the contemporary production as well as treatment of narratives. Following a closer look at *Mao II*'s model of fending off co-optation, I will specifically focus on instances of readerly reactions that characteristically garble, misuse and "abuse" stories. In doing so, these misreadings mount a "lethal" menace to cultural texts and their authors alike, eroding our inherited notions of textuality and authorship. Importantly, reading will here stand for a whole paradigm of cultural metabolism as nontextual narratives can be "read," too. Whether as a metaphor of domination through "plotting" and "perusing" of private lives (especially in *Libra* and *Running Dog*) or a paradoxical symbol of aesthetic insensitivity, reading stands out as a master motif in DeLillo. Again, it is the "wrong," "distorting," even "malefic" reading that I shall primarily deal with.

As my article's epigraph reveals, *Mao II* bestows a particular emphasis on such a "negative" response. Novelist Bill Gray's predicament is illuminating in this respect. A main character in *Mao II*, he vanished from society after publishing two acclaimed books. New editions of these volumes, however, as well as his reclusiveness itself have meanwhile enlarged Gray's mythic aura. There have also been rumors about his third book, whose publication he purposefully postpones by endless revisions. Now, for Gray revision is not a Flaubertian, ever incomplete and perpetually recommenced "smoothing" of the "style." As Charlie, Gray's publisher, suspects, Gray keeps "revising" and "rewriting" to defer publishing, that is, circulation and assimilation. Naive yet not pacific readers (he received a finger in the mail from one of them!), greedy publishing houses and inquisitive media assail his privacy, conspiring to turn him into a marketable icon.[1] It is true, Gray managed to "contain" the most diehard reader's endeavors to bring him into the open, "absorbing" Scott into his own recluse existence (Scott became Gray's "assistant"); he cannot withstand, however, his publisher's efforts to coax him into "reappearing."

Gray's "comeback" brings together key themes in DeLillo: the glamour of media iconography and the authorial "appearance" ("publication") it enforces, the ritual of reading, terror, and death, which is characteristically linked up with an intriguing notion of plot. Charlie tries to "upgrade" the novelist's myth by convincing him to read on TV French poems by Jean-Claude, a Swiss writer held as a hostage in Beirut. As we eventually come to understand, Gray is ultimately supposed to take Jean-Claude's place, which event should prepare the "market" for his third book. To secure Gray's involvement in this scenario and thereby to entangle him in what will turn out to be, by implication, the plot of the novelist's own death, Charlie suggests that Brita, a famous photographer, take the author's picture. Gray gives in at last, but for a different reason:

> Bill had his picture taken not because he wanted to come out of hiding but because he wanted to hide more deeply, he wanted to revise the terms of his seclusion, he needed the crisis of exposure to give him a powerful reason to intensify his concealment. Years ago there were stories that Bill was dead, Bill was in Manitoba, Bill was living under another name, Bill would never write another word. These were the world's oldest stories and they were not about Bill so much as people's need to make mysteries and legends. Now Bill was devising his own cycle of death and resurgence.... Bill's picture was a death notice. His image hadn't become public yet and he was already gone. This was the crucial turn he needed in order to disappear completely ... The picture would be a means of transformation. It would show him how he looked to the world and give him a fixed point from which to depart. Pictures with our likeness make us choose. We travel into or away from our photographs. (*Mao II* 140-41)

Gray's assistant realizes that the "master" employs the photographs "as a kind of simulated death" (140). "Mao," Scott reminds us, "used photographs to announce his return and demonstrate his vitality, to reinspire

revolution" (141). Gray, as a "second Mao," takes up the Chinese leader's
ploy, yet to effect the contrary: a complete "self-erasure." If his legend has
been paradoxically reinforced by his photo's absence from newspapers and
catalogues, the hundreds of photographs Brita shoots might "hide" him
completely, consecrate his disappearance. Gray hopes that absolute exposure,
the paroxysm of visibility, might provide a perfect hideaway. An allegory of
his innermost self, the still unpublished story is thus ideally camouflaged in
and through its author's photographic disclosure. As Scott owns, "the book
disappears into the image of the writer" (*Mao II* 71), indefinitely putting off
its consumption—its death in alien hands.

Another way of hinting at the private subject's "swallowing" by his or
her picture in *Mao II* is the insistent focus on photographed crowds. They set
off the "body common" (77), whose "millennial hysteria" foregrounds the
twilight of the private ego, now "immunized against the language of the self"
(8). The mass images featured in tabloids or on live TV speak to a tragic
immolation of the individual. From the dust jacket, which displays twenty-
four "photopaintings" from Andy Warhol's *Mao* series, to the large images of
Chinese and Iranian crowds reproduced or described throughout the book,
DeLillo's novel obsessively zeroes in on the masses. Hecatombs of privacy,
these cannot offer Gray a solution. Easily manipulable by official
iconography (see Mao's example), addicted to images and indiscriminate
consumption, crowds are in actuality exactly what the writer flees. On the
other hand, as the novelist himself anticipates, the attempted retreat through
photographic self-give-away proves a sheer illusion. Allowing his portrait to
be taken, Gray steps in the tragic world of plot, which means plotting his
own death. Struggling to avoid beheading on the scaffold of the "market," he
takes a fatal, downward—"deathward" (as *White Noise* puts it)—path, of
which he is not unaware:

> Something about the occasion [Gray tells Brita] makes me
> think I'm at my own wake. Sitting for a picture is morbid
> business. A portrait doesn't begin to mean anything until the
> subject is dead. This is the whole point....The deeper I pass into
> death, the more powerful my picture becomes. Isn't this why
> picture-taking is so ceremonial? It's like a wake. And I'm the actor
> made up for the laying-out.... It struck me just last night these
> pictures are the announcement of my dying. (*Mao II* 42-43)

Gray's analytic "development" of Brita's snapshots reaches even deeper.
It brings out the destructive meaning of "photographic execution," which

critics like Roland Barthes (6, passim) and Susan Sontag (64, passim) have also pointed up. "Everything around us," he contends, "tends to channel our lives toward some final reality in print or on film" (*Mao II* 43). We count only as virtual narratives, as "materials" for stories ("I've become someone's material.[2] Yours, Brita," Gray avows). We no longer stand as subjects, but solely "subject matter" awaiting its "heightened version": the cover story millions of readers will devour. In DeLillo's Baudrillardian universe indeed "nothing happens until it's consumed.... Nature has given away to aura. A man cuts himself shaving and someone is signed up to write the biography of the cut. All the material in every life is channeled into the glow" (44). The spectacular narrative "double" gains the upper hand over the "original" beings or facts. Actually, in striking accord with the self-referential logic of the media so cogently unearthed by critics from McLuhan to Baudrillard, there are no facts in this representational inferno, but merely events. The hostage's release in Beirut "is tied to the public announcement of his freedom. You can't have the first without the second" (129). "Vampirized" and literally "consumed" by its "double," the epic account, life has been converted into, "ingested" and abolished by, "the consumer event" (43). The latter symbolically feeds on the flesh of its subject while apparently "promoting" it by concocting and spreading its "story."

Fictive or less so, stories are ominous inasmuch as they expose their subject (the authorial self in *Mao II*) to a consuming, "viral" publicity. Failing to hide in the negative of his portraits, as it were, Gray gets "developed," exposed, woven into a "plot." As it "develops" itself, this plot brings the writer closer to death and thereby confirms the gloomy logic on which a book like *Libra* particularly dwells. Photographic and narrative exposure in the media triggers off a lethal "unveiling" that "monstrous" reading will complete. DeLillo deals with the whole process in terms that strikingly recall Robert Escarpit's etymological speculations on the "act of publication" as "brutal exposure" and subsequent "willful violence" done to the author and his/her work (45-46). There is no wonder why, as a character of DeLillo's *Ratner's Star* has it, "the friction of an audience ... drives writers crazy" (411). Fearing the "violence of reading," Gray ostensibly belongs to that "class of writers who don't want their books to be read," "express[ing]" in their works "the violence of [their] desire not to be read" (410). As Scott tells Brita, "for Bill, the only thing worse than writing is publishing. When the book comes out. When people buy it and read it. He feels totally and horribly exposed. They are taking the book home and turning pages. They are reading the actual words" (*Mao II* 53). Much like E. L. Doctorow's first-person narrator of *The Book of Daniel*, Gray dreads "the monstrous reader who goes on from one word to the next" (Doctorow 246).

It is essentially the "eventful story" that builds up the expectations of the "monstrous reader." Now, only very few writers can withstand this "sensationalist" narrative. As George, another intermediary between Gray and the terrorists, claims, "Beckett is the last writer to shape the way we think and see. After him, the major work involves midair explosions and crumbled buildings. This is the new tragic narrative" (*Mao II* 157). Remarkably, Beckett here designates the creator opposing cultural co-optation. After him, "the artist is absorbed, the madman in the street is absorbed and processed and incorporated" by the coins got in the street or by his or her being "put in a TV commercial" (157). Only the terrorist nowadays still remains "outside," for "the culture hasn't figured out how to assimilate him." And, surprisingly or not, the novelist is the only one who sees that terrorism, the rhetoric of absolute "eventfulness," speaks "precisely the language of being noticed, the only language the West understands" (157).

This strategy of holding back sociocultural incorporation lies, in various forms, at the core of DeLillo's entire work. One can distinguish it in earlier novels such as *Great Jones Street*, *End Zone*, *Ratner's Star* and *Running Dog*, or in later, more discussed texts like *White Noise* and *Libra*. In *Great Jones Street*, for instance, the artistic market becomes a major theme even more explicitly. It literally haunts the writers' imagination, casting a spell on their lives. In this respect, Fenig, a "two-time Laszlo Piatakoff Murder Mystery Award nominee"—whose ironic name points to financial interest— is an emblematic character. Introducing himself to Wunderlick, he unfolds a whole market mythology:

> I'm in my middle years but I'm going stronger than ever. I've been anthologized in hard cover, paperback and goddamn vellum. I know the writer's market like few people know it. The market is a strange thing, almost a living organism. It changes, it palpitates, it grows, it excretes, it sucks things and then spews them up. It's a living wheel that turns and crackles. The market accepts and rejects. It loves and kills.... The market's out there spinning like a big wheel, full of lights and colors and aromas. It's not waiting for me. It doesn't care about me. It ingests human arms and legs and it excretes vulture pus. (27)

Figures of cultural consumption as immolation and ingestion of the author abound in DeLillo. Here, the corporeal metaphors of predation and digestion represent the market as a bestial body whose metabolism, as Ratner's Star's obsession with feces also suggests, sets forward an entire scatological economy (324, passim). Fenig suspects that he has lately ignored what Charlie calls in *Mao II* the "launching power of our mass-market capabilities" (127). In fact, Fenig considers himself a victim of the predatory "big wheel." Failing to merchandise his new "brand of porno kid fiction" despite its "Aristotelian substratum" and the "lowest instincts" the genre caters to (*Great Jones Street* 49-50), Fenig switches to "fantastic terminal fiction" (222). Significantly, at this point he comes to fathom the importance of his "privacy" (222) as well as his having been "used" by the "market,"[3] reduced in his humanity and pushed toward "fascism." "I failed at pornography," he explains, "because it put me in a position where I the writer was being manipulated by what I wrote. This is the essence of living in P[orn]-ville," he goes on. "It makes people easy to manipulate.... I the writer was probably more aware of this than whoever the potential reader might be because I could feel the changes in me, the hardening of mechanisms, the subservience to lust-making and lust-awakening.... Every pornographic work brings us closer to fascism. It reduces the human element. It encourages antlike response" (223-24).

Social feedback preoccupies rock-star Bucky Wunderlick, too. Characteristically, he struggles to escape the "antlike" reaction of "the crowd's passion and wrath," the "immense ... pressure of their response ... blasting in with the force of a natural disaster" (14-15). Similarly to Gray, he no longer agrees to "sell" (perform, record, etc.), to give interviews or make the public appearances that would unavoidably enlarge his charisma. Remarkably, his manager does not ask him to play but solely to "appear" (198), always a symbolic ritual in DeLillo. His "silence strike" is another phenomenon of artistic rebellion that corporate giants such as Transparanoia or Happy Valley Farm Commune eventually manage to contain. Like the publishing house in *Mao II*, they want him just to show up, be merely seen in public and cynically respond to—or rather correspond with—the "need to be illiterate in the land of the self-erasing word" (139).

Literacy in media-saturated, market-oriented systems exerts a real fascination on DeLillo. The "digital" temple of contemporary society (Ruthrof 195-96; O'Donnell), the supermarket, brings to the fore in *White Noise* a new, "postcultural" docta ignorantia, which the author tackles with devastating irony. The hypnosis of the "consumerized space" (Wilson) and the ruthless media assault go hand in hand with the regression toward a new form of "brilliant" ignorance. "[T]here are full professors in this place who read nothing but cereal boxes" (*White Noise* 10), Murray Jay Siskind tells

Gladney, the chairman of the "Hitler studies" department at the midwestern College-on-the-Hill. To be sure, not all consumers ought to be devout readers. Nonetheless, *White Noise* insists precisely on reading as consumption, on readers increasingly "created" and reacting as consumers, perusing more and more solely what they literally consume for survival or leisure. The fabulous supermarket articulates the emblematic narrative of postmodernity, maps out the symbolic site wherein consumption-based existence and reading overlap. More specifically, it is the place where the former drastically alters the latter. The huge store designates the readable locus of our time, the seemingly "easy-to-read" ("reader-friendly") "catalogue"-space in which perusal is part of the mechanics of shopping and readers nonsensically "decipher" (shop for) elusive meanings. As Siskind contends, in the supermarket

Everything is concealed in symbolism, hidden by veils of mystery and layers of cultural material. But it is psychic data, absolutely.... All the letters and numbers are here, all the colors of the spectrum, all the voices and sounds, all the code words and ceremonial phrases. It is just a question of deciphering, rearranging, peeling off the layers of unspeakability. Not that we want to, not that any useful purpose would be served. (37-38)

Reading here oddly hinges on significantly "non-spiritual" activities, "Eating and Drinking," the "Basic Parameters" (171). Knowledge, expertise, and literacy have lost their original sense and object, and refocus on the superficial (or, as we shall see, "surfacial") world of consumption. Genres, practices, and domains traditionally treated as marginal in the economy of scholarly discourse and academic interest now supply the core of sybi. What is more, teaching in a media-informed world has become teaching of the media. The means have swallowed up the initial goals and now constitute their own telos, as "coupon analysis" (*Ratner's Star* 344) or "car crushing," "Elvis," and "Hitler studies" programs at the College-on-the Hill prove. People peruse food wraps and religiously watch food commercials between terrifying reports featuring natural catastrophes and massacres. In fact, a new, "postmodern" philology is about to arise from the relentless studying of "package narratives." *White Noise* is perhaps DeLillo's most devastating account of literacy's predicament in a marketplace-dominated "postliterate" age (Jameson 17). As critic John Frow writes, "the supermarket is the privileged place for a phenomenology of surfaces" (427), which shapes into a glowing, alienating "labyrinth" (Pireddu 140). Here, the consumer faces his or her own consumption, a paradoxical disappearance not beneath surfaces but on them, which eliminates the difference between the consumer and the consumed. Symbolically, the mall and the media cannot be sorted out. "Full of psychic data" (*White Noise* 37), the former demarcates the very site of the ultimate "event": consumers' metamorphosis into media signifiers, their insertion in the commercial narrative as new, self-aware "products," "exposed" and "featured" on the same glittering surfaces. As Gladney observes, there is an odd transfer of objectifying, immobile narcissism from the displayed goods—which looked "self-conscious," "carefully observed, like four-color fruit in a guide to photography" (170)—to consumers. "My family,"[4] he notices, "gloried in the event.... I kept seeing myself unexpectedly in some reflecting surface.... Brightness settled around me.... Our images appeared on mirrored columns, in glassware and chrome, on TV monitors in security rooms" (84).

This image-becoming of the subject molds the whole life of academic exiles in the college town Blacksmith. It "reveal[s] precisely the epistemological crisis that affects contemporary reality" (Pireddu 129) once the opposition between commodities and customers, media objects and media watchers no longer holds. Yet simply because these distinctions have been blurred, the crisis is not merely epistemological, but also ontological. It is the copy that legitimates, if not engenders, reality. Again, much like in Baudrillard's analysis of simulacra, the duplicate predates—in all senses—its model, enjoys a socially higher significance. Babette, Gladney's wife, for example, becomes suddenly far more interesting for her family when they see her on TV, when her body turns into an image, "second-order information" (King 72). Unlike Gray in *Mao II*, Babette must make a "detour" through the media in order to become "visible," for her relatives and friends react to information "rather than to entities" (LeClair 209). In general, people are spellbound by the rhetoric of their appearance—not a new theme in DeLillo, as we know—because they live in a culture of spectacular narratives. Gladney, e.g., "automatically" puts his dark glasses on when entering the campus (*White Noise* 211). Similarly to Siskind working on "Elvis" in his own cultural studies project, he treats Hitler like a star. Gladney's "postmodern attitude toward history as a kind of museum" or "supermarket of human possibilities, where people are free to shop for their values and identities" (Cantor 41), takes Hitler as a paragon of appearance. In his courses, Gladney deals with the Führer as a celebrity (Conroy 107-8), drawing on superficial, anecdotal details of his biography. Accordingly, teaching—also teaching grounded in specific (mis)readings—represents another instance of aborted cultural response. Intriguingly enough, Babette herself teaches modes of "appearing." Her odd course in "posture" illustrates a peculiar kind of "inscribing practice" (Hayles 156 ff). Most remarkably, it is the media that control this practice: people learn how to "appear," to embody different postures, take on various positions and, by implication, sociocultural "positionalities" from TV, the archimodel of appearance. One can therefore claim that they have turned into "terminal identities" of sorts, to evoke Bukatman's ambiguous title, that their bodies are gravely affected by, if not utterly turned into effects of, television.[5]

Generally speaking, teaching, reading, watching, and intellectual exchange are carried out within the circular universe of superficiality dominated by the autotelic logic of media narratives. Babette ritually reads out porno literature to her husband—an echo of *Running Dog*—and tabloid stories to her evening class of blind people. There is hardly any "analysis" or critical filtering involved in this act. According to Ben Agger, such a "passive," "moronized" reading signals the "degradation of signification" (6-8) in "fast capitalism." Symptomatically, "books become things provoking their thoughtless readings as things become books" (5). Thus one witnesses an all-pervasive "narrativization" of the surrounding world, which individuals make into a legible story, "People read," Agger argues, "different things—television, popular magazines, money" (75-76). Reading and readable objects have changed indeed. Babette cannot help but peruse "the wrong things" (76), and even if she may still read "actual" narratives, she does it the "wrong way." Overall, though, she prefers to pore over advertisements for "diet sunglasses," cover stories strangely entitled "Life After Death Guaranteed with Bonus Coupons" or accounts of the "country's leading psychics and their predictions for the coming year." These are the new heroic epics, as they fit the pattern of the "eventful" story: UFOs invading Disney World, "dead living legend John Wayne ... telepathically" helping President Reagan "frame U.S. foreign policy," and superkillers surrendering "on live TV" (*White Noise* 146). Such materials are stories run by the media, but also, more or less, stories on the media and entertainment industry, and thereby part of the same self-referential strategy of establishing communication instruments as information. Furthermore, as Mark Conroy insists, tabloid stories' omnipresence may indicate "the current fate of several traditional forms of cultural transmission" (97). "Master narratives," whether "discursive" or "scriptive," no longer provide the only "canonical" readings. The "iconographic" (107), in its multifarious forms, usually accompanies narrative information, catches the reader's attention, more often than not replacing reading with a sort of "blind" gaze lingering on surfaces, shapes, and colors.

There are at least two "catastrophic" results of these readings, DeLillo seems to suggest. First, they neglect "real," aesthetically valid narratives, replacing them with "trashy" or simply trivial materials. Second, reading as a traditionally conceived and completed process collapses, is reduced to mere repetition/recital of texts. Moreover, it carries negative overtones, being sensed as an act of manipulation, political control, and intrusion. In this view, it is noteworthy, e.g., that Gladney's "first and fourth" wife, while working "part-time [!] as a spy," also reviews "fiction for the CIA, mainly long serious novels with coded structures" (*White Noise* 213). For one thing, she performs a very "special" kind of reading. This does not differ considerably, though, from what Selvy, a secret agent in *Running Dog*, does. He is a "reader," too (*Running Dog*, 54)—he "reads" (that is, surveils) Senator Percival (28): when Selvy gets a new, "temporary assignment," he also receives copious "reading matter" (156). CIA "readers" in *Running Dog* and *Libra* can even use Kafkian-looking "reading machines," which scan people's most intimate stories, translate their private meanings into "readable" graphics.

DeLillo's pungent critique of "late capitalist" reading practices ultimately points to a, say, "postmodern" crisis of the classic notion of literacy. Nonetheless, while tackling this crisis, DeLillo resists gesturing nostalgically toward some Romantic myth or cult of authorship. Nor is he deploring the post-World War II crumbling away of modernism's "Great Divide," which, according to critics like Andreas Huyssen, separated high art and mass culture. He is rather taking aim at an expanding mode of consumption that loses sight of the "differential" nature of the consumed objects. His work is carrying out a critique of contemporary reading habits and literacy, a critique emphasizing the importance of local, non-homogenizing reading practices which are likely to value, enhance, indeed incorporate the defining differences between various types of texts read. In other words, DeLillo seems to be working out, from within postmodernism itself, a critical analysis of styles and scenarios of cultural absorption that appear to undercut postmodernism's largely recognized celebration of "regional" responses and differentiated practices of representation, production, and reception. Again, it is the social discount of such a contextual, nuanced treatment of narratives, to wit, postmodernism's failure to engender modes of consumption in tune with its own modes of production, that has brought about this crisis.

This cultural impasse may be more serious than we think. Most of DeLillo's readers are "intelligent and literate" but somewhat "deprived of the deeper codes and messages that mark [our] species as unique." Even when they "turn against the medium" (*White Noise* 50), fighting off the "mystical" experience of TV-watching, the "lethal" exposure and the "contamination" of the mind this experience induces persist. In this view, there is no substantial difference between TV "events" and the "toxic airborne event," between the media and Blacksmith's environmental catastrophe, finally, between any broadcasted narrative and a nuclear accident. All are devices of the same "terminal" rhetoric of delusive surfaces, of the same "fake" consummation that actually leads to reality's consumption by simulation, its voracious and usurping double.

The whole apparatus of "unnatural," mechanical reading, of false appropriation of narratives is even more meticulously decomposed in *Libra*. To be sure, while it is always highly relevant what and how DeLillo's people read, Lee H. Oswald's readings deserve particular scrutiny. They exemplify that type of narrative misreading which highlights and aggravates the character's fallacious perception and self-perception. One could argue that his readings carry the responsibility for his acts, that Oswald has misread himself into the "lone gunman" story. He has furnished the ideal materials for "his own fabrication in the name of a given desired effect" (Michael 151) pursued by the real plotters. Win Everett actually "understands that there is no difference between the scripted Oswald and the 'real thing'" (Mott 139), or, in Frank Lentricchia's words, between the "assassin as writer" ("*Libra* as Postmodern Critique" 447) and the assassin written by Everett. Win "reads" and uses in his turn Oswald's misreadings, which reveal themselves as self-misreadings since the texts Oswald "peruses" give him a false image of himself. "My boy Lee loves to read," Lee's mother acknowledges (*Libra* 107). "Reading Marx as a teenager," as Lentricchia maintains, "altered [Oswald's] room, charged it with meaning, propelled him into a history shaped by imagination" ("*Libra* as Postmodern Critique" 447). Marx and Engels, Trotsky, George Orwell's *Nineteen Eighty-Four*, H. G. Wells, or military manuals have devastating effects. It is not that "revolutionary," "anarchistic" or "utopian" literature "victimizes" him by its content, but that Oswald simply reads "wrong," literally, "following the text with his index finger, word by word by word" (*Libra* 49). His comprehension is rudimentary and procrustean. He unconsciously indulges in "affective" or "factual" fallacies, one could say, while "struggling" to grasp the opaque material—and failing:

> The books were struggles. He had to fight to make some elementary sense of what he read. But the books had come out of struggle. They had been struggles to write, struggles to live. It seemed fitting to Lee that the texts were often masses of dense theory, unyielding. The tougher the books, the more firmly he fixed a distance between himself and others.
>
> He found enough that he could understand. He could see the capitalists, he could see the masses. They were right here, all around him, every day. (34-35)

"Forbidden," "hard to read" books alert Lee to "the drabness of his surroundings, his own shabby clothes were explained and transformed by these books. He saw himself as part of something vast and sweeping" (41), performing "night missions that required intelligence and stealth" (37). This is another instance of narcissistic perception, when the reader unwittingly bestows upon himself a new, heroic identity. Oswald gradually becomes his own narrative project, "plots" himself, as it were, and therefore stages his own death. Like *Running Dog*'s "project" or *White Noise*'s and *Mao II*'s obsession with "deathward" plots (*White Noise* 26, 199; *Mao II* 200), Oswald's "overreadings" lay the premises for the actual plotters' "extending the fiction into the world" (*Libra* 50). Most notably, these readings supply Win Everett with essential epic material, with the "pocket litter" (50) necessary to credibly "construct" (Carmichel) Lee as a "lone assassin." The Communist Manifesto and similar pieces get woven into the plotters' strategy of narrative "make-believe" (term used as such by Win); Oswald is just another "character in the plot" (*Libra* 78), the narcissistic reader turned, by his false readings and his cunning "readers" alike, into a character of a (literally) homicidal story. Thus Oswald has unwittingly helped his "readers" to "write" him, to script and in-scribe him and his readings in a deadly intertextual scenario (a textual crypt), in a "realistic-looking thing" (119).

The simulated realism of writing-as-plotting rules out any real explanation, any accurate account of what happened in Dallas on November 22, 1963. Nicholas Branch, "a retired senior analyst of the Central Intelligence Agency, hired on contract to write the secret history of the assassination of President Kennedy" (15), has to deal exactly with this simulative writing if he wants to "rewrite" and eventually dislodge the "real story." Branch is another writer-in-the-text, a fictive narrator who duplicates "en abyme" the figure of the author. Likewise, the writing of his story takes an enormous amount of reading. Before narrating his own version of the Dallas "event," Branch has to go through the "historical record," to recall the "author's note" on *Libra*'s last page. He is literally flooded with information—both real and fabricated—on the assassination, provided by the Agency to help him put together a "history [that maybe] no one will read" (60). This (hi)story, Branch thinks, "is the megaton novel James Joyce would have written if he'd moved to Iowa City and lived to be a hundred," the Joycean Book of America ... the novel in which nothing is left out" (181-82). It follows that the indefinite "branching off" of Branch's story, its failure to "furnish factual answers" (see again the mentioned "author's note"), is also already "programmed" through his readings in another way: these supply him with "entropic" information whose excess obliterates the real data that may have yielded a coherent "story." The abundance of narratives, records, reports, and testimonies clearly blocks out the "facts." The "revelatory" tale overflows and grows more and more complicated, winding up in the swamp of language:

> Everything is here. Baptismal records, report cards, postcards, divorce petitions, canceled checks, daily timesheets, tax returns, property lists, postoperative x-rays, photos of knotted string, thousands of pages of testimony, of voices droning in hearing rooms in old courthouse buildings, an incredible haul of human utterance. It lies so flat on the page, hangs so still in the lazy air, lost to syntax and other arrangement, that it resembles a kind of mind-spatter, a poetry of lives muddied and dripping in language. (181)

As we can notice, the endless, sterile reading of unextinguished, "censored" or dubious sources reinforces the same "superficial" phenomenology at play in *White Noise* and other works by DeLillo. Despite or, better put, because of the amount of readings, Branch gets stuck on the surface of things, entangled in the huge narrative archive. Significantly, the novel does not present him in the act of story-writing or story-telling, but rather as a custodian of available files, photographs, and books, a "*Libra*rian" lost in *Libra*'s Borgesian *Libra*ry. An extreme case in DeLillo's inquiry into narrative consumption, Branch is just another consumer of supplied texts, a virtual author condemned to remain a reader. The epic version he is assigned is bound to merely further the extant "Dallas narrative," to cast him in a safely fictitious part of the ever-expanding text. We may expect Branch to "disappear," to be "digested" by his own project while trying to digest himself the information he is provided with and nourishing the illusion that he will ever tell his own story. Yet, due to his "programmed" failure as a reader, he stands no chance to become a true author. DeLillo's drama of narrative authorship and reception has come full circle.

Notes

1. As Fredric Jameson points out, in postmodern culture the commodification of objects and the commodification of human subjects are similar. The latter "are themselves commodified and transformed into their own images" (11).

2. In his essay on "the economics of publishing," Dan Lacy talks about the writer's own transformation into a "material" of the "communication industries" (408). See Newman for a more recent critique of "the preemption by the media of the writer as celebrity" (616). For a full account of the media's role in DeLillo, see Keesey.

3. See Osteen (170) for the ethics of "mastering commerce" in *Great Jones Street*.

4. Robert E. Lane sees shopping as "an intrinsically rewarding family experience" (539 ff). Unlike Lane, DeLillo hints at the lack of "reward" such a glorious "family event" entails. Also see Ferraro's essay, "Whole Families Shopping at Night," for DeLillo's view of "the contemporary American family" (15).

5. See Duvall for a full-fledged analysis of television in *White Noise*.

WORKS CITED

Agger, Ben. *Fast Capitalism: A Critical Theory of Significance*, Urbana and Chicago: University of Illinois Press, 1989.

Barthes, Roland. *Camera Lucida: Reflexions on Photography*. Trans. Richard Howard. New York: Hill and Wang, 1981.

Bukatman, Scott. *Terminal Identity: The Virtual Subject in Post-Modern Science Fiction*. Durham and London: Duke University Press, 1993.

Cantor, Paul A. "'Adolf, We Hardly Knew You.'" *New Essays on* White Noise. Ed. Frank Lentricchia. 39-62.

Conroy, Mark. "From Tombstone to Tabloid: Authority Figured in *White Noise*." *Critique* XXXV. 2 (Winter 1994): 97-110.

DeLillo, Don. "'An Outsider in This Society': Interview with Don DeLillo." Realized by Anthony DeCurtis. *South Atlantic Quarterly* 89.2 (Spring 1990): 281-304.

———. *End Zone*. Boston: Houghton Mifflin Company, 1972.

———. *Great Jones Street*. Boston: Houghton Mifflin Company, 1973.

———. *Libra*. New York: Penguin, 1989.

———. *Mao II*. New York: Viking, 1991.

———. *Running Dog*. New York: Alfred A. Knopf, 1978.

———. *White Noise*. New York: Penguin, 1986.

Doctorow, E.L. *The Book of Daniel*. New York: Random House, 1971.

Duvall, John N. "The (Super)Marketplace of Images: Television as Unmediated Mediation in DeLillo's *White Noise*." *Arizona Quarterly* 50.3 (Autumn 1994): 127-53.

Escarpit, Robert. *Sociology of Literature*. Trans. Ernest Pick. Second Edition. With a new introduction by Malcolm Bradbury and Dr. Bryan Wilson. London: Frank Cuss & Co., 1971.

Ferraro, Thomas J. "Whole Families Shopping at Night." *New Essays*, 15-38.

Frow, John. "The Last Things Before the Last: Notes on *White Noise*." *South Atlantic Quarterly* 89.2 (Spring 1990): 413-29.

Hayles, N. Catherine. "The Materiality of Informatics." *Configurations* 1.1 (Winter 1992): 147-70.

Horkheimer, Mark and Adorno, Theodor W. *Dialectic of Enlightenment*. Trans. John Cumming. New York: Continuum, 1982.

Jameson, Fredric. *Postmodernism, or, The Cultural Logic of Late Capitalism*. Durham and London: Duke University Press, 1991.

Keesey, Douglass. *Don DeLillo*, New York: Maxwell Macmillan, 1993.

King, Noel. "Reading *White Noise*: floating remarks." *Critical Quarterly* 33.3 (Autumn 1991): 66-83.

Lacy, Dan. "The Economics of Publishing, or Adam Smith and Literature." *The Sociology of Art and Literature. A Reader*. Milton C. Albrecht, James H. Barnett and Mason Griff, eds. New York. Washington: Praeger Publishers, 1970, 407-25.

Lane, Robert E. "The Road Not Taken: Friendship, Consumerism, and Happiness." *Critical Review* 8.4 (Fall 1984): 521-54.

LeClair, Tom. *In the Loop: Don DeLillo and the Systems Novel*. Urbana and Chicago: University of Illinois Press, 1987.

Lentricchia, Frank. "*Libra* as Postmodern Critique." *South Atlantic Quarterly* 89.2 (Spring 1990): 432-53.

———— ed. New Essays on *White Noise*. Cambridge: Cambridge University Press, 1991.

Michael, Magali Cornier. "The Political Paradox within Don DeLillo's *Libra*." *Critique* XXXV. 3 (Spring 1994): 146-56.

Mott, Christopher M. "*Libra* and the Subject of History." *Critique* XXXV. 3(Spring 1994): 131-45.

Newman, Charles. *The Post-Modern Aura: The Act of Fiction in an Age of Inflation*. With a Preface by Gerald Graff. Evanston, Ill.: Northwestern University Press, 1985.

O'Donnell, Patrick, "Engendering Paranoia in Contemporary Narrative." *Boundary* 2 19.1 (Spring 1992): 181-204.

Osteen, Mark. "'A Moral Form to Master Commerce': The Economics of DeLillo's *Great Jones Street*." *Critique* XXXV. 3 (Spring 1994): 157-72.

Pireddu, Nicoletta. "Il rumore dell'incertezza: sistemi chiusi e aperti in *White Noise* di Don DeLillo." *Quaderni di lingue e letterature* 17 (1992): 129-40.

Ruthrof, Horst. "Narrative and the Digital: On the Syntax of the Postmodern." *AUMLA. Journal of the Australian Universities Language and Literature Association* 74 (Nov. 1990): 185-200.

Sontag, Susan. *On Photography*. New York: Doubleday, 1990.

Wilson, Elizabeth. "The Rhetoric of Urban Space." *New Left Review* 209 (Jan.-Feb. 1995): 146-60.

LOU F. CATON

Romanticism and the Postmodern Novel: Three Scenes from Don DeLillo's White Noise

A critical exploration of romanticism in Don DeLillo's eighth novel *White Noise* may initially seem misguided or odd.[1] And yet, some of the values and topics commonly associated with popular notions of romanticism, like sympathy, unity, authenticity, and an interest in the "unknown," do emerge in this supposedly postmodern novel. They emerge not from overarching themes but rather from the common thoughts and desires associated with the novel's viewpoint character, Jack Gladney. By judging such characterization as romantic, that is, supportive of these broad transhistorical values, I find a deeply qualified postmodernism within *White Noise*.

Granted, in spite of these observations, a first response to DeLillo's fiction is probably not romantic; after all, his novels frequently show contemporary society struggling with a nostalgic palimpsest of old-fashion values that have been layered over by the textual, semiotic materialism of marketing, commodification, and computer codes. Cited as quintessentially postmodern, DeLillo reportedly writes a novel of simulacra with an endless regress of mediation. John Frow portrays DeLillo's curiosity here about simulation and iteration as "a world of primary representations which neither precede nor follow the real but are themselves real...."[2] Bruce Bawer has gone so far as to claim that DeLillo merely presents "one discouraging battery after another of pointless, pretentious rhetoric. [DeLillo] does not

From *English Language Notes* XXV, No. 1, September, 1997, pp. 38-48.

develop ideas so much as juggle jargon."[3] Paul Cantor directly calls sections of *White Noise* "self-reflexive" and "mediated;" a bit later, he claims *White Noise* transforms the "autonomous self" into the "inauthentic self."[4]

Clearly such declarations portray DeLillo as uninterested in old-fashion romantic notions like a mysterious unknown or authenticity and sympathy.[5] However, this sentiment centers itself on DeLillo's cultural critiques, his novel's "messages," while disregarding the possibility of any romantic human nature in his characters. For instance, John Kucich quickly looks past the psychology of DeLillo's male characters by stating only that they "persist" in the outdated belief that "oppositional stances can be differentiated and justified."[6] Kucich, in other words, sees DeLillo's characters naively embracing the tired belief that cultural difference can be adjudicated, that a truth-system of correspondences can still order the arbitrary nature of reality. Such views by these characters must be devalued, according to Kucich, because DeLillo's larger postmodern message denies the possibility of truth statements; the supposed central idea of *White Noise* is that a romantic, nostalgic character like Jack Gladney is only deceiving himself. The novel forecloses on a character's romantic desires as it erects a technological society where metaphysical truth is replaced by the materialistic codes of media and capitalism. The hard truth for DeLillo, Kucich and others seem to say, is that Gladney's romantic belief in a unified, shared definition of cultural truth no longer exists.[7]

What such an argument misses, though, is that DeLillo's romantic characterizations turn what might otherwise be thought of as an already clearly developed ideological position into a complex problem. Kucich is certainly right in stating that Gladney does believe in the unfashionable notion of an orderly universe; however, such a belief operates in healthy opposition to the postmodern anxiety within *White Noise*. Gladney's romantic assumptions regarding family unity and sympathy must be analyzed on their own merits; such views are more than mere foils for the novel's worries about mediation and representation.

In effect, I am contesting Frank Lentricchia's observation that DeLillo is a political writer who "stands in harsh judgment against American fiction of the last couple of decades, that soft humanist underbelly of American literature...."[8] This "humanist" tradition that DeLillo supposedly critiques is, among other things, a tradition that invokes transhistorical notions of consciousness (thus, romantic as well as humanist notions are being maligned here). According to Lentricchia, DeLillo's mind is made up; he advocates a contemporary political position which dismantles the mystified rhetoric of universals and timeless values about human nature:

But the deep action of this kind of fiction [the non-DeLillo, old-fashion, transhistorical kind] is culturally and historically rootless, an expression of the possibilities of "human nature," here, now, forever, as ever. This is realism maybe in the old philosophical sense of the word, when they affirmed that only the universals are real.[9]

Lentricchia presents DeLillo as already convinced, the problem of the romantic (i.e. transhistorical beliefs) and the postmodern having already been resolved; DeLillo becomes a cultural worker writing within a skeptical, antinomian tradition that prevents "readers from gliding off into the comfortable sentiment that the real problems of the human race have always been about what they are today."[10]

Lentricchia is wrong here; DeLillo's novels question rather than endorse this historicist stance. The transhistorical perspective entangles the historical; their supposed separate spheres, I intend to demonstrate, rely on rather than compete against each other.[11] Jack Gladney the naive sentimentalist, foil of the postmodernist (who still insists on universals, human nature, and the mythology of a human nature), recognizes but mourns the emergence of a constructed political postmodern culture (which rejects any universal subjectivity and sees all knowledge as interested and ideological). In appreciation of this conflict, DeLillo maintains a romantic uncertainty throughout *White Noise*.

Each of the following three scenes presents evidence for this uncertain romanticism composing the character of Jack Gladney. On the one hand, he is a traditionally unified character: a romantic who questions society but all along deeply values his personal relations and family. He is a communal person who desires to tell a simple story about a man trying to understand the eternal human questions of life. His is, as DeLillo describes him, "a reasonable and inquiring voice—the voice of a man who seeks genuinely to understand some timeless human riddle" (194).

Colliding with that, however, is his other growing awareness: that the world is turning him into a post-industrial, computer generated individual, someone who is slowly gaining a "non-authentic self" which is socially constructed, essentially valueless, and enveloped by an unstable matrix of material goods. This becomes clear to him when the SIMUVAC attendant reminds Jack that he is only "the sum total of [his] data. No man escapes that" (141).

Jack Gladney, then, is both "timelessly" searching for unification and arbitrarily fragmented. This double-self, a self both materially constructed by a fragmented, commercial community and one authentically trying to construct a unified community, reflects the movement of the introductory scene. The novel's first paragraph uses the possessions of a college student to enact this clash of values about identity formation.

DeLillo's vision of cars as a stream of machines slowly weaving through a pastoral landscape implies that these students are products of an assembly-line culture. The opening procession of station wagons doubles as a mechanical pilgrimage or industrial wagon train (3). Similar to a metallic snake sliding and easing itself into the center of the university, the focus here is on the mechanical residue from the industrial age. Indeed, even the students appear to be machine-like as they "spring" out of their vehicles. Moreover, these students and parents seem not to stand in opposition to their possessions but, instead, to be themselves erected by these very same objects. Accenting their hard opacity, DeLillo refuses to give these students emotional and personal details; instead they are defined by the things that surround them. A college student seems, in this scene at least, to be a constructed product, not a transcendent being: "The stereo sets, radios, personal computers; small refrigerators and table ranges; the cartons of phonograph records and cassettes; the hairdryers and styling irons..." (3).

And on and on. Eighteen lines of clothing, sporting equipment, electronics, grooming aids, and junk food, from nondescript "books" to specific "Kabooms" and "Mystic mints," the student becomes another commodity built from commodities. Even the parents seem propped up by this commercial world. They have "conscientious suntans" and "well-made faces" (3).

However, these families do not simply add up to the products of an empty consumerism. DeLillo complicates the social constructivism of this scene with romantic, community matters; he sees the current obsession with materialism as ironically satisfying a deeper, spiritual urge. DeLillo completes the scene by brashly joining this consumerism with a unity provided by spiritual and communal rhetoric: "The conscientious suntans. The well-made faces and wry looks. They feel a sense of renewal, of communal recognition ... they are a collection of the likeminded and the spiritually akin, a people, a nation" (3-4).

DeLillo here folds into the scene a dimension of spiritual identity. Our transcendent sense of who we are, the romantic desire to experience ourselves as part of a greater whole, strives for identity within the dynamics of capitalism. Even though the earlier emphasis on machinery would appear to devalue spiritual issues, DeLillo's combined use of religious and communal terms at the end of the scene reinstates these more metaphysical concerns. Instead of reading this mixture of social construction and spirituality as an ironic comment on the inferior position of religion in a postmodern world, one should interpret the scene as emphasizing the undying force of spiritual and communal urgings, whether fashionably inferior or not.

As things and students spill out, parents feel both renewed in a supersensible manner and materially affirmed; on the one hand, the virtuous and almost sacred gestalt of children and parents separating translates itself into the terms of material goods. Parents and students objectify this exalted moment. The parents are commodified by financial interests. DeLillo claims "something about them suggesting massive insurance coverage" (3). Their money and things blend with all the other station wagons until they "earn" a sense of spiritual collectivism. And yet, on the other hand, students and parents do not uniquely accept this elite position of "buying" a college education; they also experience it as a celebratory, communal moment. The gathering of the wagons becomes almost a religious ceremony: "more than formal liturgies or laws" (4). The upper-middle class has cashed in their material possessions for a taste of something which might have been denied them without the money to buy it: community and spirituality. The romantic desire for community may exist only ironically, only in this tainted capitalistic and privileged fashion; however, it still exists, resisting commodification and vying for its own legitimacy.

In the same manner of sensing spiritual desires among material possessions, DeLillo presents his viewpoint character, Jack Gladney, as being both essentially authentic and culturally constructed. Jack's narrative role as the story-teller infuses his cultural observations with a personal authority that makes it impossible to separate society's ills from Jack's personality. That is, DeLillo recognizes the influence of a psychological, unified ego, but simply sends it to the edges of the narrative; in its place a constructed, commodified lead character stalks center stage.

Jack Gladney speaks of himself only at the end of this first scene. His voice, seemingly of a single consciousness, feels subordinate, inferior to the grand reporting of the materiality of common things which preceded it. Indeed, even the description of the town takes precedence over any desire to humanize the ego of the only interior voice of the novel. In fact, the town itself is de-personalized, divested of any particular character; this dreary city called Blacksmith is home to a narrating voice as flat and common as the city itself.

Nothing seems very remarkable in Blacksmith. What details DeLillo gives are the details of sameness, of any small, college town: "There are houses in town....There are Greek revival and Gothic churches. There is an insane asylum with an elongated portico, ornamented dormers and a steeply pitched roof.... There is an expressway..." (4). Not only does the town seem boring and sleepy but the method of using "there is" and "there are" is equally gloomy and uninspired. And yet such arid prose belies a deeper issue.

DeLillo counters this deadness with a brief, almost hidden recognition of the possibility of a mysterious, spiritual unknown. As the expressway traffic speeds by, it develops into "a remote and steady murmur around our sleep, as of dead souls babbling at the edge of a dream" (4). Here the dead are mythically revived, muttering and rippling at the edge of consciousness. Their voices belong to past story-tellers who have refused to be silenced. They represent an imaginary over-soul that resists this culture's particular ideology. The reference to souls and dreams babbling suggests an unknowable world of rivers and voices that refuses to be reified by the marketplace ethics of station wagons and stereos. The socially constructed world of commodification meets the myth of an universal consciousness that will not die.

This is the introductory conflict between matter and spirit embodied in the character of Jack Gladney. The immediate introduction of this viewpoint character is not metaphysical, philosophical, or even psychological but occupational: he is the chairman of Hitler studies. DeLillo offers a practical, materialistic definition of this narrator: he is what he produces; we are what our jobs say we are. However, like before, this recognition of material reality does not stand alone. DeLillo undercuts it with a closing sentimental, one might say "romantic," paragraph regarding lost dogs and cats. The concluding image in Jack Gladney's introduction arises in the crude, primitive vision of innocent youth. As the mechanized police in their "boxlike vehicles" prowl the streets, children cry for the intimacy of domestic animals: "On telephone poles all over town there are homemade signs concerning lost dogs and cats sometimes in the handwriting of a child" (4).

DeLillo ends this first scene with one of the many romantic collisions that erupt throughout the novel. In this particular configuration the question is as follows: how can the desire to live in an innocent world persevere while at the same moment we experience ourselves as isolated, socially constructed, economic units? DeLillo retains this question, along with others, in order to inject a romantic mystery into *White Noise*.

A version of this same conflict reappears a few pages later when Jack and Murray visit the most photographed barn in America. Jack accompanies Murray as a student to a teacher. They approach the barn after seeing several signs declaring this barn to be "THE MOST PHOTOGRAPHED." Only the teacher talks; Jack listens silently to Murray's explanation as to why no one sees the "real" barn. For Murray, the commercial interests of marketing have replaced any natural, original, or unique qualities that the barn may have had: "Once you've seen the signs about the barn," Murray instructs, "it becomes impossible to see the barn" (12). Speaking like a McLuhan disciple, Murray claims that one can never see the barn; one can only experience it as a consumer. Its marketplace representation as a commodity overrides any hopes of seeing the original, unaffected, unadulterated "barn." Murray's declaration that perception is predicated on economic forces links the viewer to that collective consciousness of consumerism. As with the students and parents in the previous scene above, forms of mass-marketing construct how we experience the world. And yet this selling and buying motif continually collides with Jack's spiritual desires.

In the post-Christian era, we religiously embrace whatever image popular culture devises for us; in this case, DeLillo's characters see themselves as consumers. They are financially essential, not only targeted but coveted by business strategists. Our objectified, exchange-value lives are sacred in the world of commerce. And that world of profit-and-loss commodification becomes the world from which they define themselves, according to Murray. It is one's information-age identity. Murray glories in this obscene recognition of a capitalistic spirituality: "Being here is a kind of spiritual surrender. We see only what the others see. The thousands who were here in the past, those who will come in the future. We've agreed to be part of a collective perception. This literally colors our vision. A religious experience in a way, like all tourism."(12)

Business and tourist interests merge into a spiritual and collective recognition of consumerism: "We're not here to capture an image, we're here to maintain one. Every photograph reinforces the aura. Can you feel it. Jack? An accumulation of nameless energies" (12).

Murray's "nameless energies" are the combined forces of spiritual desire and advertizing expertise. The barn represents a new-age mix of spirituality, media, and cultural constructions. Murray accelerates his pitch until his voice becomes that of a postmodern preacher; he basks in his realization that the contemporary consciousness has been manipulated and formed by advertising executives. We are what advertisements have made us: "'We can't get outside the aura,' Murray exclaims gleefully. 'We're part of the aura. We're here, we're now.' He seemed immensely pleased by this" (13).

The economic representation has itself become the object. In fact, the conventional ontological object, the barn as a romantic object, dissolves. Jack is left only with perception. Frank Lentricchia contends that this scene presents a "strange new world where the object of perception is perception itself. What they view is the view of the thing."[12] The experience of a correspondence between an object and its mental image has been altered; a single representative activity has faded into a fascination for an endless egress of images that forever occlude the original object.

Murray's upbeat mood regarding these disclosures underscores by contrast Jack's silence. Rather than jubilation, Jack registers caution and a death-like voicelessness. After all, this play involving the real versus the simulation also implies a loss, a kind of moral fall. For Murray, the primacy of simulation brilliantly bankrupts any urge to locate an original, romantic object. For Jack, however, the moment is less celebratory. His reticence implies a resistance to this contemporary account of a world empty of stable realities and non-commodified experiences. Jack's behavior later in the novel will confirm that, for him, the commodification of culture's self-referring systems of codes and arbitrary signifiers has not replaced or destroyed the spiritual myths of community and authenticity. Indeed, it is Jack's recognition of the potential, divine loss involved with Murray's analysis that propels the narrative toward these romantic themes.

Finally, I want to use my last scene to highlight how the romantic and communal base of Jack's personality challenges any totalized vision of a postmodern relativistic universe. In this third scene, DeLillo moves to his largest question: How can one communicate in a radically indeterminate world? Jack's exchange with his son Heinrich demonstrates the emotional cost around such a crucial contemporary dilemma.

Jack begins this scene in the role of an empiricist. The world can be known and trusted, he seems to say; it is not fundamentally a theoretical construct but, instead, a knowable and physical environment displaying somewhat predictable natural laws. He enters into a confrontation with his son in an effort to answer a simple question: Is it or is it not raining? The replies lead to a comic, and sometimes absurd, interchange while Jack drives Heinrich to school:

> "It's raining now," I said.
>
> "The radio said tonight...."
>
> "Look at the windshield," I said. "Is that rain or isn't it?"
>
> "I'm only telling you what they said."
>
> "Just because it's on the radio doesn't mean we have to suspend belief in the evidence of our senses." (22-3)

Heinrich's responses are deeply skeptical and distrustful; his answer to the question depends not on what he can see or assume but on the meteorologist speaking through the radio, an expert who clearly claims that it will rain later, not now. Thus, Heinrich defers his answer to Jack's question as to whether or not it is raining at that exact moment: "I would't want to have to say" (23), he demurely replies.

Heinrich's non-answer frustrates Jack. His desire to gain assent from his son in regards to this banal but ingenuous question represents a common fatherly effort to meet with a son in conversation. For Jack, the question has little to do with rain but more to do with his romantic desire to join with his son in an appreciation of an intimate and shared physical event. Heinrich, instead, plays the mixed role of relativist, materialist, and cynical skeptic. He views the question not as a social, communal event but as a request for exact information, for verifiable data. Jack, however, pushes him to informally affirm the rain in order to achieve a simple, everyday, familial union; he wants confirmation of their common ground. Why not meet through the faith in our universal human situation, our shared physical senses, Jack seems to ask. Heinrich answers as a doubtful contemporary critic, not a son: "Our senses? Our senses are wrong a lot more often than they're right. This has been proved in the laboratory" (23).

The dialogue continues in this vein; Heinrich meets each of Jack's desires for affirmation and community with the well-known skepticism and undecidability of the postmodern theorist. In the age of deconstruction, all we can know is our inability to know. Even the common social bonding implied in a father and son conversation about the weather has been subverted into an academic debate about the principle of uncertainty:

> "You're so sure that's rain. How do you know it's not sulfuric acid from factories across the river? How do you know it's not fallout from a war in China? You want an answer here and now. Can you prove, here and now, that this stuff is rain? How do I know that what you call rain is really rain? What is rain anyway?" (24)

Heinrich denies Jack the romantic bond of community between a father and son. This great theme of romance, the dialectic of love and union between a father and a son, becomes a nostalgic, outdated, dream for a naive world that no longer exists. And yet Jack's hunger to experience this common ground never dies in *White Noise*; in fact, it only gains authority as the novel progresses to its tragi-comical ending.

NOTES

1. Don DeLillo, *White Noise* (New York: Viking Penguin, 1985). Further citations will appear parenthetically in the text.

2. John Frow, "The Last Things Before the Last: Notes on *White Noise*," *South Atlantic Quarterly* 89.2 (1990): 421.

3. Bruce Bawer, "Don DeLillo's America," *The New Criterion* 3.8 (1985): 40.

4. Paul Cantor, "Adolf, We Hardly Knew You," *New Essays on* White Noise, ed. Frank Lentricchia (Cambridge: Cambridge UP, 1991) 42-3.

5. This postmodern desire to undercut any stable definitions of the "real" and the authentic I claim are themselves already undercut by the romantic desires of Delillo's viewpoint character, Jack Gladney.

6. John Kucich, "Postmodern Politics: Don DeLillo and the Plight of the White Male Writer," *Michigan Quarterly Review* 27.2 (1988): 337.

7. Posing the romantic against the postmodern also suggests a commonsense antagonism. For example, Kathy Acker has noted, "I might not know what the postmodern means but I know it isn't romanticism" (personal conversation, May 4, 1993).

8. Frank Lentricchia, introduction, *New Essays on* White Noise, ed. Frank Lentricchia (Cambridge: Cambridge UP, 1991) 5.

9. Lentricchia, *New* 6.

10. Lentricchia, *New* 6.

11. Lentricchia does admit that since DeLillo "insists ... upon a comprehensive cultural canvas ... there remains ... a space for the poetry of mystery, awe, and commitment." The caveat, though, is that these possible universals die rapidly; they are, according to Lentricchia, quickly "laid to waste by contemporary forces" (*New* 7).

12. Frank Lentricchia, "Don DeLillo," *Raritan* 8.4 (1989): 8.

DANA PHILLIPS

Don DeLillo's Postmodern Pastoral

A decade after its publication, the contribution of Don DeLillo's *White Noise* to our understanding of postmodern cultural conditions has been thoroughly examined by literary critics (see, for example, the two volumes of essays on DeLillo's work edited by Frank Lentricchia). The novel has been mined for statements like "Talk is radio," "Everything's a car," "Everything was on TV last night," and "We are here to simulate"—statements that critics, attuned to our culture's dependence on artifice and its habit of commodifying "everything," immediately recognize as postmodern slogans. What has been less often noticed, and less thoroughly commented on, is DeLillo's portrait of the way in which postmodernity also entails the devastation of the natural world.

Frank Lentricchia, in his introduction to the *New Essays on* White Noise, has pointed out that "The central event of the novel is an ecological disaster. Thus: an ecological novel at the dawn of ecological consciousness" (7). But Lentricchia does not develop his insight about the "ecological" character of the novel. Neither does another reader, Michael Moses, who in his essay on *White Noise*, "Lust Removed from Nature," argues that "postmodernism, particularly when it understands itself as the antithesis rather than the culmination of the modern scientific project, confidently and unequivocally banishes from critical discussion the questions of human

From *Reading the Earth: New Directions in the Study of Literature and Environment*, edited by Michael P. Branch, Rochelle Johnson, Daniel Patterson, and Scott Slovic. University of Idaho Press, 1998, pp. 235-46.

nature and of nature in general" (82). Moses does not pursue this point, but I would argue that one of the great virtues of DeLillo's novel is the thoroughgoing and imaginative way in which *White Noise* puts the questions not just of human nature but of "nature in general" back on the agenda for "critical discussion."

The dearth of commentary on DeLillo's interest in the fate of nature is explained, not just by the fact that contemporary literary critics tend to be more interested in the fate of culture, but also by the fact that one has to adjust one's sense of nature radically in order to understand how, in *White Noise*, natural conditions are depicted as coextensive with, rather than opposed to, the malaise of postmodern culture. This adjustment is not just a task for the reader or critic: it is something the characters in the novel have to do every day of their lives.

As a corrective to the prevailing critical views of the novel, *White Noise* might be seen as an example of what I will call the postmodern pastoral, in order to foreground the novel's surprising interest in the natural world and in a mostly forgotten and, indeed, largely bygone rural American landscape. At first glance the setting of the novel and its prevailing tone seem wholly unpastoral. But then the pastoral is perhaps the most plastic of modes, as William Empson demonstrated in *Some Versions of Pastoral*. The formula for "the pastoral process" proposed by Empson—"putting the complex into the simple" (23)—is one which might appeal to the main character and narrator of *White Noise*, Jack Gladney. Gladney is someone who would like very much to put the complex into the simple, but who can discover nothing simple in the postmodern world he inhabits, a world in which the familiar oppositions on which the pastoral depends appear to have broken down. And thus the postmodern pastoral must be understood as a blocked pastoral—as the expression of a perpetually frustrated pastoral impulse or desire. In qualifying my assertion that *White Noise* is an example of postmodern pastoral in this way, I am trying to heed Paul Alpers's warning that "modern studies tend to use 'pastoral' with ungoverned inclusiveness" (ix). However, Alpers's insistence that "we will have a far truer idea of pastoral if we take its representative anecdote to be herdsmen and their lives, rather than landscape or idealized nature" (22) would prevent altogether the heuristic use of the term I wish to make here. With all due respect to herdsmen, the interest of the pastoral for me lies more in the philosophical debate it engenders about the proper relation of nature and culture and less in its report on the workaday details of animal husbandry or the love lives of shepherds.

Jack Gladney is not a shepherd, but a professor of Hitler Studies at the College-on-the-Hill, which is situated in the midst of an unremarkable sprawl of development that could be called "suburban," except that there is no urban center to which the little town of Blacksmith is subjoined. Like almost everything else in *White Noise*, the town, to judge from Jack Gladney's description of it, seems displaced, or more precisely, unplaced. Jack tells us that "Blacksmith is nowhere near a large city. We don't feel threatened and aggrieved in quite the same way other towns do. We're not smack in the path of history and its contaminations" (85). He proves to be only half-right: the town is, in fact, subject to "contaminations," historically and otherwise. Jack's geography is dated: Blacksmith is not so much "nowhere" as it is Everywhere, smack in the middle—if that is the right phrase—of a typically uncentered contemporary American landscape of freeways, airports, office parks, and abandoned industrial sites. According to Jack, "the main route out of town" passes through "a sordid gantlet of used cars, fast food, discount drugs and quad cinemas" (119). We've all run such a gantlet; we've all been to Blacksmith. It is the sort of town you can feel homesick for "even when you are there" (257).

Thus, despite a welter of detail, the crowded landscape in and around Blacksmith does not quite constitute a place, not in the sense of "place" as something that the characters in a more traditional novel might inhabit, identify with, and be identified by. Consider Jack's description of how Denise, one of the Gladney children, updates her "address" book: "She was transcribing names and phone numbers from an old book to a new one. There were no addresses. Her friends had phone numbers only, a race of people with a seven-bit analog consciousness" (41). Consciousness of place as something that might be geographically or topographically (that is, locally) determined has been eroded by a variety of more universal cultural forms in addition to the telephone. Chief among them is television—Jack calls the TV set the "focal point" of life in Blacksmith (85). These more universal cultural forms are not just forms of media and media technology, however; the category includes such things as, for example, tract housing developments.

Despite the prefabricated setting of *White Noise* and the "seven-bit analog consciousness" of its characters, an earlier, more natural and more pastoral landscape figures throughout the novel as an absent presence of which the characters are still dimly aware. Fragments of this landscape are often evoked as negative tokens of a loss the characters feel but cannot quite articulate, or more interestingly—and perhaps more postmodern as well—as negative tokens of a loss the characters articulate, but cannot quite feel. In an early scene, one of many in which Jack Gladney and his colleague Murray Jay Siskind ponder the "abandoned meanings" of the postmodern world (184), the two men visit "the most photographed barn in america," which lies "twenty-two miles into the country around Farmington" (12). In his role as narrator, Jack Gladney often notes details of topography with what seems to be a specious precision. But the speciousness of such details is exactly the issue. Even though it is surrounded by a countrified landscape of "meadows and apple orchards" where fences trail through "rolling fields" (12), Farmington is not at all what its name still declares it to be: a farming town. The aptness of that placename, and of the bits of rural landscape still surrounding the barn, has faded like an old photograph. As Murray Jay Siskind observes, "Once you've seen the signs about the barn, it becomes impossible to see the barn" (12). The reality of the pastoral landscape has been sapped, not just by its repeated representation on postcards and in snapshots, but also by its new status as a tourist attraction: by the redesignation of its cow paths as people-movers. The question of authenticity, of originality, of what the barn was like "before it was photographed" and overrun by tourists, however alluring it may seem, remains oddly irrelevant (13). This is the case, as Murray observes, because he and Jack cannot get "outside the aura" of the cultural fuss surrounding the object itself, "the incessant clicking of shutter release buttons, the rustling crank of levers that advanced the film" (13)—noises that drown out the incessant clicking of insect wings and the rustling of leaves that once would have been the aural backdrop to the view of the barn.

As the novel's foremost authority on the postmodern, Murray is "immensely pleased" by the most photographed barn in america (13). He is a visiting professor in the popular culture department, known officially as American environments" (9), an official title that signals the expansion of the department's academic territory beyond what was formerly considered "cultural." Jack dismisses Murray's academic specialty as "an Aristotelianism of bubble gum wrappers and detergent jingles" (9)—that is, as a mistaken attempt to uncover the natural history of the artificial. Jack finds the barn vaguely disturbing.

But *White Noise* is about Jack's belated education in the new protocols of the postmodern world in which he has to make his home. Jack learns a lot about those protocols from Murray and his colleagues, one of whom lectures a lunchtime crowd on the quotidian pleasures of the road (arguably a quintessentially postmodern American "place"). Professor Lasher sounds something like Charles Kuralt, only with more attitude:

"These are the things they don't teach," Lasher said. "Bowls with no seats. Pissing in sinks. The culture of public toilets. The whole ethos of the road. I've pissed in sinks all through the American West. I've slipped across the border to piss in sinks in Manitoba and Alberta. This is what it's all about. The great western skies. The Best Western motels. The diners and drive-ins. The poetry of the road, the plains, the desert. The filthy stinking toilets. I pissed in a sink in Utah when it was twenty-two below. That's the coldest I've ever pissed in a sink in." (68)

Lasher's little diatribe may seem to suggest that DeLillo is satirizing the much-heralded replacement of an older cultural canon by a newer one: Lasher would throw out the Great Books, if he could, in favor of "the poetry of the road." But in *White Noise* it is not so much the replacement as it is the displacement of older forms by newer ones, and the potential overlapping or even the merger of all those forms in an increasingly crowded cultural and natural landscape, that DeLillo records. "The great western skies," the "Best Western motels," "the road, the plains, the desert"—all are features of a single, seamless landscape.

Because of their ability to recognize so readily the odd continuities and everyday ironies of the postmodern world, the contentious members of the department of American environments seem better-adapted than their more cloistered colleagues. Their weirdness is enabling. By pursuing their interest in and enthusiasm for things like the culture of public toilets, they collapse the distinction between the vernacular and the academic and shorten the distance between the supermarket, where tabloids are sold, and the ivory tower, where the *Library* is housed. It is instructive that whenever one of their more extreme claims is challenged, members of the department tend to reply in one of two ways: either they say, "It's obvious" (a refrain that runs throughout the novel), when of course it (whatever it may be) isn't at all obvious. Or they simply shrug and say, "I'm from New York." In *White Noise*, all knowledge is local knowledge, but one must understand how shaped by the global the local has become. We're all from New York.

While it is true that we can "take in"—as the saying goes—a landscape, the literal ingestion of nature (that is, of discrete bits and selected pieces of it) is probably the most intimate and most immediate of our relations with it. In a telling passage from the opening pages of the novel, Jack and his wife Babette encounter Murray Jay Siskind in the generic food products aisle of the local supermarket:

His basket held generic food and drink, nonbrand items in plain white packages with simple labeling. There was a white can

labeled canned peaches. There was a white package of bacon
without a plastic window for viewing a representative slice. A jar
of roasted nuts had a white wrapper bearing the words irregular
peanuts. (18)

What is striking about the contents of Murray's cart is the way in
which, despite the determined efforts of all those labels to say in chorus the
generic word food, they seem to be saying something else entirely. These
"nonbrand items" actually seem to be all brand, nothing but brand; their
categorical labels seem like mere gestures toward the idea of food, evocations
of its half-forgotten genres. Remember uncanned peaches? Visible bacon?
regular peanuts? The packaging and the labels do not resolve the question of
contents. They raise it; that is, they heighten it, so that it seems more
important than ever before.

The jar of irregular peanuts in particular has a disturbing, perhaps even
slightly malign quality, as Murray explains: "'I've bought these peanuts
before. They're round, cubical, pock-marked, seamed. Broken peanuts. A lot
of dust at the bottom of the jar. But they taste good. Most of all I like the
packages themselves. [...] This is the last avant-garde. Bold new forms. The
power to shock'" (19). Siskind's identification of the jar of peanuts as part of
"the last avant-garde" suggests that cultural production has reached the ne
plus ultra of innovation, that henceforward it will consist not in making
things new, but in the repackaging of old things, of the detritus of nature and
the rubble of culture. "Most of all," Murray says, "I like the packages
themselves." So there will not be any more avant-gardes after this one—it is
not the latest, but "the last." Those irregular peanuts mark the end of history:
more than just irregular, they are apocalyptic peanuts. No wonder Murray
savors them. Each is a bite-size reminder of the "end of nature" and the "end
of history," two of the postmodernist's favorite themes.

The canned peaches, the invisible bacon, and the irregular peanuts also
demonstrate very clearly how postmodern culture does not oppose itself to
nature (as we tend to assume culture must always do). Instead, it tries to
subsume it, right along with its own cultural past. But one would like to
protest that despite all this repackaging and attempted subsumption, the fact
is that peanuts—even irregular ones—do not result from cultural
production, but from the reproduction of other peanuts. One wants to say
that natural selection (plus a little breeding), and not culture, has played the
central and determining role in the evolution of peanuts of whatever kind.
But the role of nature as reproductive source, even as an awareness of it is
echoed in certain moments of the novel, tends to get lost in the haze of

cultural signals or "white noise" that Jack Gladney struggles and largely fails to decipher, probably because all noise is white noise in a postmodern world. Murray Jay Siskind, as a connoisseur of the postmodern, is sublimely indifferent to factual distinctions between, say, the natural and the cultural of the sort that still worry less-attuned characters like Jack Gladney.

That they must eat strange or irregular foods is only part of the corporeal and psychological adjustment Jack and his family find themselves struggling to make. At least they remain relatively aware of what they eat, in that they choose to eat it. But "consumption" is not necessarily always a matter of choice in *White Noise*: there are things that enter the orifices, or that pass through the porous membranes of the body, and make no impression on the senses. These more sinister invaders of the body include the chemicals generated by industry, many of them merely as by-products, chemicals that may or may not be of grave concern to "consumers"—not entirely the right term, of course, since few people willingly "consume" toxins. After all, we do not have to eat the world in order to have intimate relations with it, since we take it in with every breath and every dilation of our pores. This suggests that the much-bewailed runaway consumerism of postmodern society is not the whole story: there are other kinds of exchange taking place that do not necessarily have to do with economics alone. The cash nexus is certainly economic, but the chemical nexus is both economic and ecological; the economy of by-products, of toxic waste, is also an ecology. Economic or ecological fundamentalism makes it hard to tell the whole story about postmodernism, as DeLillo is trying to do.

During the novel's central episode, the "airborne toxic event," Jack Gladney is exposed to a toxin called Nyodene Derivative ("derivative" because it is a useless by-product). Nyodene D and its possible effects are first described for Jack by a technician at the simuvac ("simuvac" is an acronym for "simulated evacuation") refugee center: "'It's the two and a half minutes standing right in it that makes me wince. Actual skin and orifice contact. This is Nyodene D. A whole new generation of toxic waste. What we call state of the art. One part per million can send a rat into a permanent state'" (138-39). The technician's last phrase is richly ambiguous: does "a permanent state" mean death or never-ending seizure or a sort of chemically induced immortality? This ambiguity terrifies Jack, and he begins to seek some surer knowledge of the danger he is in. At this point in the narrative, DeLillo's novel speaks most clearly about the effect the postmodern condition has on our knowledge of our bodies (and thus on our knowledge of nature). Having crunched all Jack's numbers in the simuvac computer, the technician informs him, "I'm getting bracketed numbers with pulsing stars," and he adds that Jack would "rather not know" what that means (140). Of, course, that is precisely what Jack would most like to know. The attempt at clarification offered by the technician at the end of their conversation does nothing to explain to Jack exactly when, why, and how he might die: "It just means that you are the sum total of your data. No man escapes that." (141).

The remainder of the novel is taken up with Jack Gladney's attempt to escape the reductive judgment of his fate given by the simuvac technician and his computer (whose bracketed numbers with pulsing stars "represent" Jack's death, but do so opaquely, in a completely nonrepresentative way, rather like the white package marked bacon that conceals the supermarket's generic pork product). As the repository of junk food and as a host for wayward toxins and lurking diseases, Jack's body has become a medium, in much the same way that television or radio are media. His postmodern body is hard to get at in the same way that the nameless voices on television—the ones that throughout the novel say macabre things like "Now we will put the little feelers on the butterfly" (96)—cannot always be identified, much less questioned or otherwise engaged in dialogue. In *White Noise*, the body itself is mediated, occult, hard to identify, and unavailable for direct interrogation by any solely human agent or agency. The postmodern body is, then, a curiously disembodied thing. It no longer makes itself known by means of apparent symptoms that can be diagnosed by a doctor, nor by means of feelings that can be decoded by the organism it hosts (it may be a little old-fashioned to think of this organism as a "person"). During his interview with Dr. Chakravarty, Jack utters a tortured circumlocution in response to the simple question, "How do you feel?" His carefully qualified reply, "To the best of my knowledge, I feel very well," demonstrates how distant from him Jack's body now seems (261). That this body just happens to be his own gives Jack no real epistemological advantage. In a postmodern world, technology and the body are merely different moments of the same feedback loop, just as the city and the country are merged in a common landscape of death. Because it is the place in which distinctions between bodies and machines, and between the city and country, have collapsed, "Autumn Harvest Farms" is an exemplar of postmodern pastoral space: at Autumn Harvest Farms, the machine not only belongs in the garden, it is the garden.

However confused he may be, and however paralyzed by his half-living, half-dead condition, Jack Gladney does seem to "feel," at times, a certain lingering nostalgia about and interest in "nature in general." This longing, if not for the prelapsarian world, then at least for some contact with a nature other than that of his own befuddled self, is apparent even in the lie Jack tells the Autumn Harvest Farms clinician in response to a question about his use of nicotine and caffeine: "Can't understand what people see in all this artificial stimulation. I get high just walking in the woods" (279). The only time in the novel when Jack actually goes for something like a walk "in the woods" is when he visits a rural cemetary. Like everything else in the novel, this cemetary has an overdetermined quality: it is called "the old burying ground," and it is both authentic—actually an old burying ground, that is—and a tourist trap. It is both what it is and an image or metaphor of what it is. And so the old burying ground seems uncanny, with the same kind of heightened unreality about it that gives Murray's jar of irregular peanuts and the most photographed barn in america their peculiar auras.

Nonetheless, it may be at the old burying ground that Jack comes closest to feeling some of the peace that the countryside can bring:

> I was beyond the traffic noise, the intermittent stir of factories across the river. So at least in this they'd been correct, placing the graveyard here, a silence that had stood its ground. The air had a bite. I breathed deeply, remained in one spot, waiting to feel the peace that is supposed to descend upon the dead, waiting to see the light that hangs above the fields of the landscapist's lament. (97)

But in this remnant of an older, more pastoral landscape set in the midst of a contemporary sprawl—across the Lethean river separating the graveyard from the factories in town, but still sandwiched between the town, the freeway, and the local airport—Jack does not quite have the epiphany he is so clearly seeking. His hope of living within the natural cycle of life and death suggested to him by his visit to the old burying ground has already been foreclosed by events. Direct encounter with nature, "walking in the woods," is no longer possible, not only because nature seems to have become largely an anecdotal matter of broadcast tidbits of information about animals (bighorn sheep, dolphins, etc.), but also because nature, like the body, has been ineluctably altered by technology. the old burying ground, landscaped as it is, and given its purpose, is a crude example of this alternation, however comforting Jack finds it.

The supermarket is the place that the characters in the novel depend on most for a sense of order, pattern, and meaning, and thus it fulfills something of the cultural function that used to be assigned to the pastoral. The difference is that the supermarket has an obscure relationship to the rest of the world, particularly to the natural world whose products it presumably displays. The supermarket is a pastoral space removed from nature.

Unfortunately, even this artificial haven is disturbingly altered by the novel's end: "The supermarket shelves have been rearranged. It happened one day without warning. There is agitation and panic in the aisles, dismay in the faces of the older shoppers" (326). The "agitation and panic in the aisles" of the supermarket links the postmodern condition back to an older set of fears and confusions that predate the repose that the pastoral is supposed to offer. DeLillo makes this very clear earlier in the novel when he has Jack Gladney use the word "panic" to describe his anxiety upon awakening in the middle of the night: "In the dark the mind runs on like a devouring machine, the only thing awake in the universe. I tried to make out the walls, the dresser in the corner. It was the old defenseless feeling. Small, weak, deathbound, alone. Panic, the god of woods and wilderness, half goat" (224). Thus Jack finds himself in the wilderness even while he is supposedly safe at home in Blacksmith. The order and rationality, the civilized space, that modernity (like the pastoral) supposedly created seems to be no longer a feature of the postmodern landscape.

The postmodern pastoral, unlike its predecessors, cannot restore the harmony and balance of culture with nature, because the cultural distinctions that the pastoral used to make—like that between the city and the country—have become too fluid to have any force and are dissolved in the toxic fog of airborne events. Neither culture nor nature are what they used to be. But perhaps DeLillo's point is that they never were, that the distinction between culture and nature cannot be taken as an absolute. As a novelist, he knows just how thoroughly "all of culture and all of nature get churned up again every day" (2), as Bruno Latour puts it in his appositely-titled book, *We Have Never Been Modern* (from which it follows that we cannot possibly be "postmodern" in the strict sense of the term). DeLillo is also aware of another point on which Latour insists: he realizes that the everyday churning up of nature and culture is not just a matter of media representations. Latour argues that "the intellectual culture in which we live does not know how to categorize" the "strange situations" produced by the interactions of nature and culture because they are simultaneously material, social, and linguistic, and our theories are poorly adapted to them (3). They are not cognizant of what Latour likes to call "nature-culture."

It seems to me that Latour—and DeLillo—are right, and that postmodernist theorists (unlike postmodern novelists, whose work is often finer grained than theory) have invested too much in the ultimately false distinction between nature and culture. They have tried to argue what amounts to a revision of Frederick Jackson Turner's frontier thesis, first promulgated in his 1893 essay, "The Significance of the Frontier in

American History." Turner argued that the closing of the frontier and the disappearance of wilderness was a turning point in American culture; the postmodernists—especially the more radical or pessimistic postmodernists like François Lyotard and Jean Baudrillard, or Fredric Jameson—argue that the disappearance of nature is a turning point in global culture. Postmodernism is a frontier thesis for the next millenium, more dependent on what has been called "the idea of wilderness" than its exponents have realized.

WORKS CITED

Alpers, Paul. *What Is Pastoral?* Chicago: U of Chicago P, 1996.

Delillo, Don. *White Noise*. New York: Viking Penguin, 1985.

Empson, William. *Some Versions of Pastoral*. Norfolk: New Directions Books. n.d.

Latour, Bruno. *We Have Never Been Modern*. Trans. Catherine Porter. Cambridge: Harvard UP, 1993.

Lentricchia, Frank, ed. *Introducing Don DeLillo*. Durham: Duke UP, 1991.

———. *New Essays on* White Noise. Cambridge: Cambridge UP, 1991.

Moses, Michael. "Lust Removed from Nature." In *Introducing Don DeLillo*. Ed. Frank Lentricchia. Durham: Duke UP, 1991: 63-86.

Turner, Frederick Jackson. "The Significance of the Frontier in American History." In *The Frontier in American History*. Tucson: U of Arizona P, 1986. 1-38.

TONY TANNER

Afterthoughts on Don DeLillo's
Underworld

"The true underground is where the power flows. That's the best-kept secret of our time....The presidents and prime ministers are the ones who make the underground deals and speak the true underground idiom. The corporations. The military. The banks. This is the underground network. This is where it happens. Power flows under the surface, far beneath the level you and I live on. This is where the laws are broken, way down under, far beneath the speed freaks and cutters of smack."

—Great Jones Street

"All plots tend to move deathward. This is the nature of plots. Political plots, terrorist plots, lovers' plots, narrative plots, plots that are part of children's games. We edge nearer death every time we plot. It is like a contract that all must sign, the plotters as well as those who are the targets of the plot."

Is this true? Why did I say it? What does it mean?

—White Noise

"You think the stories are ture?"
"No," Eric said.
"Then why do you spread them?"
"For the tone of course."
"For the edge."
"For the edge. The bite. The existential burn."

—Underworld

From *Raritan* 17, No. 4, Spring, 1998, pp. 48-71.

Some years ago—it must be about a dozen—I was sitting in an airport, flipping through Time magazine, and I came across a brief news item to the effect that the American writer, Don DeLillo, was working on a novel about the Kennedy assassination. My heart, as they say, sank. I had been reading DeLillo's novels with growing admiration and excitement—but how could even he, for all his wonderfully strange ways of getting at what he generically calls "the American mystery" (for which read "the mystery of America"), avoid being beset and distracted by all the cliches of paranoia and conspiracy theory which swarmed to the event as flies to honey. I need not, of course, have worried. *Libra* is a triumph; all the possible pitfalls, as I see it, brilliantly by-passed or side-stepped. Let me remind you of his concluding "Author's Note":

> In a case in which rumors, facts, suspicions, official subterfuge, conflicting sets of evidence and a dozen labyrinthine theories all mingle, sometimes indistinguishably, it may seem to some that a work of fiction is one more gloom in a chronicle of unknowing.
>
> But because this book makes no claim to literal truth, because it is only itself, apart and complete, readers may find refuge here—a way of thinking about assassination without being constrained by half-facts or overwhelmed by possibilities, by the tide of speculation that widens with the years.

You may remember the concluding meditation of Nicholas Branch, the retired CIA analyst, hired to write a secret history of the assassination (and thus, in part, a DeLillo stand-in):

> If we are on the outside, we assume a conspiracy is the perfect working of a scheme. Silent nameless men with unadorned hearts. A conspiracy is everything that ordinary life is not. It's the inside game, cold, sure, undistracted, forever closed off to us.... All conspiracies are the same taut story of men who find coherence in some criminal act.

But maybe not. Nicholas Branch thinks he knows better. He has learned enough about the days and months preceding November 22, and enough about the twenty-second itself, to reach a determination that the conspiracy against the President was a rambling affair that succeeded in the short term due mainly to chance. Deft men and fools, ambivalence and fixed will and what the weather was like.

Amidst swamps of temptations, and against pretty high odds, DeLillo keeps his poise, not to say his sanity, and does not succumb to the darkly glamorous seductiveness of the murderously appealing material he is handling. But by the time of his next novel, *Mao II*, something has gone wrong.

From a recent *New Yorker* profile by David Remnick, we learn that DeLillo has for a long time been interested in a passage in John Cheever's journals where he wrote, after a ballgame at Shea Stadium: "The task of the American writer is not to describe the misgivings of a woman taken in adultery as she looks out of the window at the rain but to describe 400 people under the lights reaching for a foul ball.... The faint thunder as 10,000 people, at the bottom of the eighth, head for the exits. The sense of moral judgments embodied in a migratory vastness." So-no more pottering about with old Flaubert, groping for his miserable mot juste; but off to the ballgame with Whitman, and "the city's ceaseless crowd" in which Whitman rejoiced (as he rejoiced in baseball: "it's our game: that's the chief fact in connection with it: America's game: has the snap, go, fling, of the American atmosphere"). DeLillo has long been fascinated by crowds (and Elias Canetti's Crowds and Power)—at least since *Great Jones Street* ("The people. The crowd. The audience. The fans. The followers.")—so perhaps it is not suprising that he starts *Mao II*, very arrestingly, with a powerful description of the vast undifferentiated horde of a Moonie mass wedding at Yankee Stadium. (Also not suprising that he starts *Underworld* with a swirling, hundred-eyed account of a famous baseball game.) The crowd motif is taken up with references to the Hillsborough football disaster and Khomeini's funeral, with Mao's Chinese millions milling in the background. "The future belongs to crowds"—so the introductory section blankly, bleakly concludes.

So much might be prophecy, or warning, or simply downhearted sociology; but, of itself, it does not generate narrative. Accordingly we have some (concluding, as it turns out) episodes from the life of an intensely reclusive writer named Bill Gray—who incorporates, I imagine, a glance at J. D. Salinger, a nod to Thomas Pynchon, and perhaps a wink from DeLillo himself ("When I read Bill I think of photographs of tract houses at the edge of the desert. There's an incidental menace." That "incidental menace" fits; and the desert features in nearly all of DeLillo's novels as a sort of "end zone" of meaning—silent, nonhuman, absolute, ultimate). Bill Gray tells us things that DeLillo's fiction has been telling us from the start: "There's the life and there's the consumer event. Everything around us tends to channel our lives toward some final reality in print or film." When David Bell sets out on his questing journey in *Americana* looking for origins, he isn't sure if he is discovering his real, unmediated family and country, or just so much print and film. America—or *Americana*? What kind of "real" life people can shape for themselves in a mediated, consumer culture swamped in images and information, is an abiding concern. But Bill Gray also has some things to say about the novel and the novelist which bear thinking about.

The novel used to feed our search for meaning. Quoting Bill. It was the great secular transcendence. The Latin mass of language, character, occasional new truth. But our desperation has led us toward something larger and darker. So we turn to the news, which provides an unremitting mood of catastrophe. This is where we find emotional experience not available elsewhere. We don't need the novel. Quoting Bill.

Quoting Bill, not Don. Certainly. But here is David Remnick quoting Don:

> I think there's something in people that, perhaps, has shifted. People seem to need news, any kind-bad news, sensationalistic news, overwhelming news. It seems to be that news is a narrative of our time. It has almost replaced the novel, replaced discourse between people. It replaced families. It replaced a slower, more carefully assembled way of communicating, a more personal way of communicating.

When Bill Gray is on a ship bound for Lebanon, he appreciates the families crowded on deck, together making "the melodious traffic of a culture." In *The Names*, James Axton relishes the gregarious, sociable street life in Athens.

> People everywhere are absorbed in conversation. Seated under trees, under striped canopies in squares, they bend together over food and drink.... Conversation is life, language is the deepest thing.... Every conversation is a shared narrative, a thing that surges forward, too dense to allow space for the unspoken, the sterile. The talk is unconditional, the participants drawn in completely. This is a way of speaking that takes such pure joy in its own openness and ardor that we begin to feel these people are discussing language itself.

So to the concluding paragraph of the novel (prior to the Epilogue), at the Parthenon:

> People come through the gateway, people in streams and

clusters, in mass assemblies. No one seems to be alone. This is a place to enter in crowds, seek company and talk. Everyone is talking. I move past the scaffolding and walk down the steps, hearing one language after another, rich, harsh, mysterious, strong. This is what we bring to the temple, not prayer or chant or slaughtered rams. Our offering is language.

Clearly this kind of crowd, and this way of conversing are, alike, admirable and much to be desired. But it is not entirely churlish to point out that the American onlookers cannot be assumed to have understood a word that was spoken. This is communicating community as exotic (and idealized) spectacle. Or perhaps we might say that it is like a Catholic mass, where it doesn't matter to the experience if the communicants do not understand the Latin words. The point here is that back in DeLillo's America where people do understand the words, there is precious little communicating-or communing. "Discourse between people" has gone; "families" have gone; as a result, following DeLillo's line of thinking, the novel has become, effectively, redundant. "So we turn to the news"—which is just what DeLillo has done in *Underworld*.

I'll come back to this, but I want to call on some more of Bill's pronouncements about the novelist. There's a curious knot that binds novelists and terrorists. Years ago I used to think it was possible for a novelist to alter the inner life of the culture. Now bomb-makers and gunmen have taken that territory. They make raids on human consciousness. What writers used to do before we were all incorporated.... What terrorists gain, novelists lose. The degree to which they influence mass consciousness is the extent of our decline as shapers of sensibility and thought. The danger they represent equals our own failure to be dangerous.... Beckett is the last writer to shape the way we think and see. After him, the major work involves midair explosions and crumbled buildings. This is the new tragic narrative.

Quoting Bill—I know. But I feel that DeLillo is standing dangerously close to him. *Libra* was only the culmination of a long-standing—and perfectly legitimate—fascination with terrorism and terrorists (just such an interest gave us *The Secret Agent* and *Under Western Eyes*); but Bill's proposition that the novelist once was a fully operative terrorist who now, in his neutered state, has ceded his ground to real terrorists, is, when thought about, ridiculous. Henry James may be said, I would suppose, to have "altered the inner life of the culture," yet it would be absurd to make of him even a metaphorical terrorist. In *Americana* the (failed) writer, Brand, wants to write a novel that will "detonate in the gut of America like a fiery bacterial bombshell." But he didn't; and anyway, it wouldn't. This is all metaphor. With much "Blasting" and fulminating gnashing of teeth, Wyndham Lewis tried to demolish the difference between literary and literal terrorism; and, rebarbatively enough, failed. Perhaps DeLillo might consider giving him a careful, pensive read. And to suggest that midair explosions and crumbling walls are the novels de nos jours is, really, mad if meant seriously (silly if not). Owen Brademas, seemingly privileged as wise in *The Names*, aphoristically muses: "In this century the writer has carried on a conversation with madness. We might almost say of the twentieth-century writer that he aspires to madness." To the real, loony, Moonie, Khomeini, Red Guard thing? Aspire to that? Come now.

Bill Gray betakes himself to the Middle East, now engaged in some of that clandestine activity so important in DeLillo's fiction. (In a Rolling Stone article of 1983 DeLillo suggested that the great leaps in science and technology had helped to create a kind of "clandestine mentality. We all go underground to some extent. In an era of the massive codification and storage of data, we are all keepers and yielders of secrets." It is the mentality of many of his characters.) But he succumbs to a "helpless sense that he was fading into thinness and distance." So he does—and so does the novel. It isn't going anywhere, so it just peters out—as they used to say when a vein of ore came to an end. The best of novelists can produce a disappointing book (Pynchon gave us *Vineland*), and it would be gross to go on belaboring *Mao II*. But I do think the book opens up certain problems which become rather important in *Underworld*, and in this connection I fear I must make a final negative comment.

An ancillary character named Karen (an ex-Moonie) figures in the book. Drifting around New York, she comes upon a "tent city" in a park. It is a shantytown abode of the down-and-outs, the thrown-aways, the insulted and the injured, the despised and rejected-the human junk of the modern city. We get it itemized. "There was a bandshell with bedding on the stage, a few bodies stirring, a lump of inert bedding suddenly wriggling upward and there's a man on his knees coughing blood.... Stringy blood looping from his mouth." And so on. Karen goes into a nearby tenement. "In the loft she went through many books of photographs, amazed at the suffering she found. Famine, fire, riot, war. These were the never ceasing subjects.... It was suffering through and through." A voice says "It's just like Beirut." At the end, a photographer is driving through the real Beirut. "The streets run with images.... The placards get bigger as the car moves into deeply cramped spaces, into many offending smells, open sewers, rubber burning, a dog all ribs and tongue and lying still and gleaming with green flies...." No one doubts the reality of unspeakable suffering and squalor; but just heaping it up in a novel in this way seems a bit easy, even opportunistic, and, by the same token, slightly distasteful. It begins to read like a form of atrocity tourism. I suppose that if you think that people "need bad news" and "don't need the novel," then you may as well give them lists of horrors to sup on. But, even then, it doesn't work like "news." A direct report from Beirut by Robert Fisk of the London Independent has far more impact than anything in DeLillo's novel. But "news" is what we get in *Underworld*.

News is, of course, "bad news, sensationalistic news, overwhelming news"; and, in the relative absence of significant characters or narrative plot (matters to which I will return), the book presents us with a string of more or less sensationalist news items or crises from 1951 to, presumably, the present day—as another way of getting at "the American mystery." The shock of Sputnik, the Cuban missile crisis, the Kennedy assassination, the Madison anti-Vietnam riot, civil rights marches and police brutality, the midair explosion of the Challenger space shuttle, the Texas Highway murders, the great New York blackout, J. Edgar Hoover, AIDS, and so on—and over everything the shadow of "the bomb" ("they had brought something into the world that out-imagined the mind." Again, it seems as if the novelist is ceding his imaginative rights to a superior power). There is also a certain amount of atrocity tourism—"They saw a prostitute whose silicone breast had leaked, ruptured and finally exploded one day, sending a polymer whiplash across the face of the man on top of her.... They saw a man who'd cut his eyeball out of its socket because it contained a satanic symbol." Near the end, a visit to a "Museum of Misshapens" in Russia, which houses damaged fetuses and victims of radiation from near the early test sites, allows DeLillo to present us with a gallery of grotesques ("there is the cyclops. The eye centered, the ears below the chin, the mouth completely missing. Brain is also missing"), and a clinic full of "disfigurations, leukemias, thyroid cancers, immune systems that do not function." I don't know if such a place exists, but in DeLillo's dark world it seems plausible. And that's the agenda. Bad news, and "suffering through and through."

As I am sure readers know, DeLillo presents his "news" items in a roughly reverse order. After the opening ballgame in 1951, there are six sections which run—Spring 1992; Mid 1981s to early 1990s; Spring 1978; Summer 1974; Selected Fragments Public and Private in 1950s and 1960s (twenty-one of these, discontinuous and unrelated); Fall 1951 to Summer 1952; and an Epilogue with a more or less present day—or timeless—feel to it. Two things to say about this. Of course novelists can and often should disrupt and rearrange unilinear chronology—think only of the scrambled narrative of Conrad's *Nostromo*. And of course, something is bound to happen if you juxtapose apparently unrelated fragments-you might sense an uncanny similarity, or register an ironic parallelism (Henry in his court; Falstaff in his tavern); or you might experience a shock of cognitive dissonance, or a disorienting sense of incongruity. But in a work of art, unless it is avowedly or manifestly aleatory, you usually feel that the scramblings and wrenched juxtapositionings have some point. Conrad was certainly getting at late Victorian attitudes to history and progress in a very corrosive way. But—it may of course be my obtuseness—I just did not see the point of DeLillo's randomizings. He has admitted to being strongly influenced by the cinematic techniques of Jean-Luc Godard, and in an interview with Tom LeClair (referred to in LeClair's very interesting book on DeLillo called *In the Loop*), DeLillo said that the cinematic qualities which influenced his writing were "the strong image, the short ambiguous scene ... the artificiality, the arbitrary choices of some directors, the cutting and editing." These qualities are all evident in *Underworld*, and the phrase I would hold on to in particular is "arbitrary choices." At the end of the opening account of the ballgame, a drunk is running the bases and leaps into a slide. "All the fragments collect around his airborne form. Shouts, bat-cracks, full bladders and stray yawns, the sand-grain manyness of things that can't be counted." In an over eight hundred-page book, you may be sure that DeLillo has quite a go at "the sand-grain manyness of things," and the sheer voracious energy of his appetitive attention is genuinely impressive. But the fragments do not collect around anything-unless you think that "Cold War America" will do the gathering-in work of the airborne drunk.

DeLillo must feel, I suppose, that he is assembling some of what he calls "those distracted events that seemed to mark the inner nature of the age." Where the novelist can go crucially one better than the news reporter is, presumably, in imaginatively illuminating the "underground network" of society, intimating the unofficial history of the period, tracing out some of those power flows, "under the surface, far beneath the level you and I live on." Surface events may seem random and discrete enough-a ballgame here, an atom-bomb test therebut, ah! what if they are in some way connected? DeLillo's fiction has long concerned itself with what Axton, in *The Names*, calls "Complex systems, endless connections," and that last word is used to exhaustion in *Underworld*. Indeed it would not be entirely facetious to say that if anything does connect the fragments of American "manyness" that pack the book, it is the word connection. Far-flung listeners to the ballgame commentary are "connected by the pulsing voice on the radio"; "The Jesuits taught me to examine things for second meanings and connections";

"technology ... connects you in your well-pressed suit to the things that slip through the world otherwise unperceived"; "I. wrote down all the occult connections that seemed to lead to thirteen"; "the feel of a baseball in your hand, going back a while, connecting many things"; "They sensed there was a connection between this game and some staggering event that might take place on the other side of the world" (There you are!); "she drew News and Rumors and Catastrophes into the spotless cotton pores of her habit and veil. All the connections intact" (this is a nun); "'Knowing what we know.' 'What do we know?' Simms said....'That everything's connected,' Jesse said." The baseball which, as I am sure you know, "passes through" the novel from owner to owner, is said to make "connections." "He was surrounded by enemies. Not enemies but connections, a network of things and people"; "He felt he'd glimpsed some horrific system of connections in which you can't tell the difference between one thing and another"; "Because everything connects in the end, or only seems to, or seems to only because it does." "Find the links. It's all linked" (that's J. Edgar Hoover). Then, finally, on the world wide web: "There is no space or time out there, or in here, or wherever she is. There are only connections. Everything is connected.... Everything is connected in the end." There is lots more about "undivinable patterns"; "something ... saying terrible things about forces beyond your control"; "underground plots," not to mention a Conspiracy Theory Cafe; and—of course—paranoia. "There's genuine paranoia. That's the only genuine anything I can see here." "He thought of the photograph of Nixon and wondered if the state had taken on the paranoia of the individual or was it the other way around?"; "Paranoid. Now he knew what it meant, this word that was bandied and bruited so easily, and he sensed the connections being made around him, all the objects and shaped silhouettes and levels of knowledge—not knowledge exactly but insidious intent. But not that either—some deeper meaning that existed solely to keep him from knowing what it was." There are so many forms and manifestations of paranoid consciousness (or paranoid voices) in this novel that I abandoned my list of examples since it promised to be not much shorter than the book itself. It may be claimed that paranoia is as American as violence and apple pie (as I believe they used to say), but in the case of *Underworld* it gives the book a rather wearingly uniform paranoid texture. Even figures who say they aren't paranoid, pretend to be. This is the significance of my third epigraph. Matt and Eric do secret underground work at a missile site, and Eric enjoys spreading "astounding rumours" about terrible things happening to workers at the Nevada Test Site who lived "downwind" of the aboveground shots and were exposed to fallout: "here and there a kid with a missing limb or whatnot.

And a healthy woman that goes to wash her hair and it all comes out in her hands.... Old Testament outbreaks of great red boils.... And coughing up handfuls of blood. You look in your cupped hands and you see a pint of radded blood."

> "You think the stories are true?"
> "No," Eric said.
> "Then why do you spread them?"
> "For the tone, of course."
> "For the edge."
> "For the edge. The bite. The existential burn."

This sounds like playing at dread, thereby devaluing it; and you may feel that it would be better kept for the real thing. Now it may be reprehensible on my part, but in Eric's answers I hear DeLillo. It certainly gives his work its "tone," ever alert to hints of "insidious intent"; but finally the paranoia comes to seem factitious and manufactured, we weary at the iterated insistence on never-explained "connections," and the "existential burn" fades.

At the risk of repeating what may have been already endlessly pointed out, in all this DeLillo is engaged in a prolonged and repetitious quoting, or reworking, of Pynchon (for whose work he has stated his admiration). Just to remind you—in *Gravity's Rainbow* Pynchon diagnosed two dominant states of mind—paranoia and anti-paranoia. Paranoia is, in terms of the book, "nothing less than the onset, the leading edge of the discovery that everything is connected, everything in the Creation, a secondary illumination—not yet blindingly one, but connected." Of course, everything depends on the nature of the connection, the intention revealed in the pattern; and just what it is that may connect everything in Pynchon's world is what worries his main characters, like Slothrop. Paranoia is also related to the Puritan obsession with seeing signs in everything, particularly signs of an angry God. Pynchon makes the connection clear by referring to "a Puritan reflex of seeking other orders behind the visible, also known as paranoia." The opposite state of mind is anti-paranoia, "where nothing is connected to anything, a condition not many of us can bear for long." As figures move between the System and the Zone, they oscillate between paranoia and anti-paranoia, shifting from a seething blank of unmeaning to the sinister apparent legibility of an unconsoling labyrinthine pattern or plot. In *V* these two dispositions of mind are embodied in Stencil and Benny Profane, respectively (and behind them are those crucially generative figures for the western novel—Don Quixote and Sancho Panza). And there is the poignant figure of Oedipa Maas at the end of *The Crying of Lot 49*: "Either Oedipa in the orbiting ecstasy of a true paranoia, or a real Tristero. For there either was some Tristero beyond the appearance of the legacy of America, or there was just America and if there was just America then it seemed the only way she could continue, and manage to be at all relevant, was as an alien, unfurrowed, assumed full circle into some paranoia." Pynchon is a truly brilliant and richly imaginative historian and diagnostic analyst of binary, either—or thinking, and its attendant dangers. DeLillo, by contrast, rather bluntly disseminates a vaguely fraught atmosphere of defensive voices, sidelong looks, and intimations of impending eeriness. And, crucially, *Underworld* has no Tristero.

There is one character in *Underworld* who stoutly insists that he is free of all paranoid delusions. "I lived responsibly in the real. I didn't accept this business of life as a fiction.... I hewed to the texture of collective knowledge, took faith from the solid and availing stuff of our experience.... I believed we could know what was happening to us.... I lived in the real. The only ghosts I let in were local ones." This is Nick Shay, intermittently a first-person narrator, and effectively the main figure in the book (the last section recreates his Bronx childhood-which must overlap with DeLillo's—and culminates with his shooting a man). But Nick is not your sane, well-rounded, genial empiricist. For a start, the local ghosts loom large, as his brother Matt explains, telling "how Nick believed their father was taken out to the marshes and shot, and how this became the one plot, the only conspiracy that big brother could believe in. Nick could not afford to succumb to a general distrust.... Let the culture indulge in cheap conspiracy theories. Nick had the enduring stuff of narrative, the thing that doesn't have to be filled in with speculation and hearsay." But this "narrative" is no more securely grounded than the conviction of the man who sees Gorbachev's birthmark as being a map of Latvia and thus a sign of the imminent collapse of the Soviet Union. Nick has simply put all his superstitions into one basket. Welcome to the club, Nick.

But as a character, Nick is just not there at all; and, more to the point, nor does he want to be. Like nearly all DeLillo's characters-call them voices-he seems to aspire to the condition of anonymity. "He was not completely connected to what he said and this put an odd and dicey calm in his remarks." This is said of a character in *Mao II*, but it applies to Nick, indeed across the board. Another figure in *Mao II* says: "If you've got the language of being smart, you'll never catch a cold or get a parking ticket or die," and defensive "smart language" is what Nick talks. It is a form of cultivated self-alienation, and is common in DeLillo's world. Lyle is one of the players in *Players*, and there is "a formality about his movements, a tiller-distinct precision" which preserves a "distance he's perfected." To keep himself at arm's length he engages in tough-guy routines at work. As does Nick. "I made breathy gutter threats from the side of my mouth.... Or I picked up the phone in the middle of a meeting and pretended to arrange the maiming of a colleague." Even, perhaps especially, when he has to convey something important—such as the fact that he has killed a man. "I had a rash inspiration then, unthinking, and did my mobster voice. 'In udder words I took him off da calendar.'" Invent-and-spread-the-bad-news Eric "affected a side of the mouth murmur," but that's the way to talk round here. A woman artist has "a tough mouth, a smart mouth"—pity anyone who hasn't.

"He gave me a flat-eyed look with a nice tightness to it"—compare the supremely "indifferent" work of Andy Warhol which "looks off to heaven in a marvelous flat-eyed gaze." Nice. Marvelous. Rub out the affect. Be "laconic"; go for "a honed nonchalance." Nick reads approvingly in a woman's eyes an "unwillingness to allow the possibility of surprise." Henry James spoke of "our blessed capacity for bewilderment," recognizing it as the essential precondition for true learning. Well forget that, all ye who enter DeLillo's world. The thing here is never to be caught off-guard or risk being wrong-footed. Seal yourself off. "We talked on the phone. In monosyllables. We sounded like spies passing coded messages." It's as if it is too risky, no—impossible—to speak in a natural, unself-consciously communicating voice, such as Axton imagines he is hearing at the Parthenon. Intimacy seems not a possibility, perhaps not a desirability. Nick's father "always kept a distance.... Like he's somewhere else even when he's standing next to you." Nick is felt by his younger brother to have "the stature of danger and rage," but this hardly constitutes an identity. He admits "I've always been a country of one," maintaining "a measured separation." He uses an Italian word to explain his temperament to his wife: "lontananza. Distance or remoteness, sure. But as I use the word, as I interpret it, hard-edged and finegrained, it's the perfected distance of the gangster, the syndicate mobster—the made man. Once you're a made man, you don't need the constant living influence of sources outside yourself. You're all there. You're made. You're a sturdy Roman wall." It's not clear that anything in the book would disapprove of, or regret, this aspiration to cultivate just such a hard, self-dehumanizing remoteness. Indeed, at the very end, Nick says: "I long for the days of disorder ... when I was alive on the earth ... heedless ... dumb-muscled and angry and real ... when I walked real streets and did things slap-bang and felt angry and ready all the time, a danger to others and a distant mystery to myself." Nothing wrong with this, if that's how you feel-but you cannot expect such a limited and self-restrictive presence—or voice—to maintain a thread of human interest as the book trawls through the news archives. (DeLillo has owned to having some of this "lontananza" himself, intimating that it might have something to do with his having been brought up an Italian Catholic. "I suppose what I felt for much of this period was a sense of unbelonging, of not being part of any official system. Not as a form of protest but as a kind of separateness. It was an alienation, but not a political alienation, predominantly. It was more spiritual." By coincidence, I read this in the *Guardian* in a piece by Hugo Young, also brought up a Catholic. "I also absorbed and relished the sidelong stance, the somewhat distanced obliqueness as regards the established state, which the Catholic inheritance conferred." You feel DeLillo would agree.)

In bringing us voices rather than more traditionally delineated characters, DeLillo is working in an honorable line—*Ulysses* is, after all, a novel of voices. And DeLillo catches and transcribes American voices as no other writer can. You feel that, as with Bill Gray, it makes "his heart shake to hear these things in the street or bus or dime store, the uninventable poetry, inside the pain, of what people say." His ear is, indeed, marvellously attuned to the poetry inside the pain—or, as I sometimes feel, the panic inside the plastic—"of what people say." For some of the exchanges between voices in his book—flat, deadpan, comic, menacing, weird, cryptic, gnomic, enigmatic, absurd, disturbing, moving—you can think of Beckett (or Ionesco, or Pinter) in America. But there is a risk. Speaking specifically of the characters in his *End Zone*, but by implication more generally, DeLillo said they "have a made-up nature. They are pieces of jargon. They engage in wars of jargon with each other. There is a mechanical element, a kind of fragmented self-consciousness." Tom LeClair, who conducted the interview, comments: "without stable identities as sources of actual communication, the characters often seem, like one character's favorite cliche, 'commissioned, as it were, by language itself.'" *End Zone* was a seventies novel—the time we were hearing a lot about our being "serfs du langage" and "being spoken" rather than "speaking." But DeLillo sometimes takes this very far, and a robotic feeling starts to creep in. And in *Underworld*, the many voices start to seem just part of one, tonally invariant, American Voice. There are hundreds of names in the book, but I would be prepared to bet that—apart from the real figures such as Sinatra, Hoover, Lenny Bruce, Mick Jagger—none will be remembered six months after reading the novel. As I find, for instance, are Pynchon's Stencil and Benny Profane; Oedipa Maas(!); Tyrone Slothrop and Roger Mexico; and—I predict—Mason and Dixon. It is not a question of anything so old-fashioned as "well-rounded characters"; rather I'm thinking of memorably differentiated consciousnesses.

The real protagonist of this novel is "waste." I don't know when garbage moved to center stage in art (as opposed to occasional litter). In a recent exhibition I came across "Household Trashcan" by Arman dated 1960, and it was, indeed, trash in a Plexiglas box. A book called *Rubbish Theory* by Michael Thompson came out in 1979, and I made use of it in a small book on Pynchon I wrote shortly thereafter. For Pynchon is the real lyricist of rubbish. No one can write as poignantly or elegiacally about, for example, a second-hand car lot, or an old mattress. And what other writer, in the course of a long and moving passage about Advent in wartime, would consider embarking on a curiously moving meditation triggered off by the thought of "thousands of old used toothpaste tubes" (in *Gravity's Rainbow*)? Many actual rubbish heaps or tips appear in his work-not as symbolic wastelands (though those are there too), but exactly as "rubbish." One of Tristero's enigmatic acronyms is W.A.S.T.E., and by extension Pynchon's work is populated by many of the categories (or noncategories) of people whom society regards as "rubbish," socially useless junk: bums, hoboes, drifters, transients, itinerants, vagrants; the disaffected, the disinherited, the discarded; derelicts, losers, victims—collectively "the preterite," all those whom, for the Puritans, God in His infinite wisdom has passed over, overlooked. Pynchon forces us to reassess, if not revalue, all those things—and people—we throw away. And DeLillo follows in the master's footsteps.

There is a memorable trash bag in *White Noise*:

> An oozing cube of semi-mangled cans, clothes hangers, animal bones and other refuse. The bottles were broken, the cartons flat. Product colors were undiminished in brightness and intensity. Fats, juices and heavy sludges seeped through layers of pressed vegetable matter. I felt like an archaeologist about to sift through a finding of tool fragments and assorted cave trash.... I unfolded the bag cuffs, released the latch and lifted out the bag. The full stench hit me with shocking force. Was this ours? Did it belong to us? Had we created it? I took the bag out to the garage and emptied it. The compressed bulk sat there like an ironic modern sculpture, massive, squat, mocking.... I picked through it item by item.... why did I feel like a household spy? Is garbage so private? Does it glow at the core with personal heat, with signs of one's deepest nature, clues to secret yearnings, humiliating flaws? What habits, fetishes, addictions, inclinations? What solitary

acts, behavioral ruts? I found crayon drawings of a figure with full breasts and male genitals....I found a banana skin with a tampon inside. Was this the dark underside of consumer consciousness?

Terrific! DeLillo absolutely cresting. But in *Underworld* it all gets rather labored and repetitious.

Nick Shay is professionally involved with waste, which, perhaps not very subtly, allows for heaps of the stuff in the novel. "My firm was involved in waste. We were waste handlers, waste traders, cosmologists of waste.... Waste is a religious thing." He lives it; he thinks it. He and his wife "saw products as garbage even when they sat gleaming on store shelves, yet unbought." His workmate Brain goes to a landfill site on Staten Island: "He looked at all that soaring garbage and knew for the first time what his job was all about.... To understand all this. To penetrate this secret.... He saw himself for the first time as a member of an esoteric order." Another workmate, Big Sims, complains that, now, "Everything I see is garbage."

"You see it everywhere because it is everywhere."

"But I didn't see it before."

"You're enlightened now. Be grateful."

Nick's hard-hat humor never lets him down. Perhaps inevitably, there is a former "garbage guerrilla," now "garbage hustler," with his theories:

> Detwiler said that cities rose on garbage, inch by inch, gaining elevation through the decades as buried debris increased. Garbage always got layered over or pushed to the edges, in a room or in a landscape. But it had its own momentum. It pushed back. It pushed into every space available, dictating construction patterns and altering systems of ritual. And it produced rats and paranoia.

Everywhere, there are abandoned structures and artifacts—"the kind of human junk that deepens the landscape, makes it sadder and lonelier"; along with any number of Pynchon's "preterite"—"wastelings of the lost world, the lost country that exists right here in America." Perhaps unsurprisingly, there is the contention that "waste is the secret history, the underhistory" of our society. And Nick maintains that "what we excrete comes back to consume us." An unattributed, oracular voice (DeLillo's?) announces at one point: "All waste defers to shit. All waste aspires to the condition of shit." Nick's final appearance in the novel is—of course—at a "waste facility," where he and his granddaughter have brought "the unsorted slop, the gut squalor of our lives" for recycling. The light streaming into the shed gives the machines "a numinous glow," and the moment prompts a final meditation. "Maybe we feel a reverence for waste, for the redemptive qualities of the things we use and discard. Look how they come back to us, alight with a kind of brave aging." Clearly there is waste and waste, since we hardly think of "shit" as coming back to us "with a kind of brave aging."

What there is is waste turned into art—"We took junk and saved it for art," says one artist in the book. And of course, there are the Watts Towers—"a rambling art that has no category"—visited once by Nick, and once by the artist, Klara. "She didn't know a thing so rucked in the vernacular could have such an epic quality."

She didn't know what this was exactly. It was an amusement park, a temple complex and she didn't know what else. A Delhi bazaar and Italian street feast maybe. A place riddled with epiphanies, that's what it was.

And that is what waste primarily is for DeLillo—epiphanic. That, presumably, is why "waste is a religious thing."

For a Catholic the Epiphany is the manifestation of Christ to the Magi—by extension any manifestation of a god or demiged. Joyce defined an epiphany as "a sudden spiritual manifestation," but without a specifically religious implication. It occurs when a configuration of ordinary things suddenly takes on an extra glow of meaning; when, in Emerson's terms, a "day of facts" suddenly becomes a "day of diamonds," leaving you with, perhaps, a nonarticulable sense of "something understood" (George Herbert). A writer can create secular epiphanic moments—Jack Gladney's exploration of his garbage is an epiphany of a rather dark kind. But simply asserting that something is "riddled with epiphanies" does not, of itself, bring the precious glow. Epiphanies have to be caused rather than insisted on, and *Underworld* suffers somewhat from this failing.

Whether DeLillo still is, or no longer is, a Catholic is none of my business; but he is clearly disinclined to abandon what seems like a proto-religious response to the world. Mystery is a much-cherished word in his fiction. "Mysteries of time and space" is how he begins his essay on the Kennedy assassination, later saying "Establish your right to the mystery; document it; protect it." In his statement of admiration for some of the great modernist works—*Ulysses, The Death of Virgil, The Sound and the Fury, Under the Volcano*—he says: "These books open out onto some larger mystery. I don' t know what to call it. Maybe Broch would call it 'the world beyond speech.' "His fiction is eager to sense out moments in which existence begins to turn mysterious. Pynchon also does this of course-economically, but to quite dazzling effect in *The Crying of Lot 49*, for example. No one can better catch that slowly rising sense of the "je ne sais quoi de la sinistre" which can creep into a seemingly ordinary scene. DeLillo seems keener on an almost overtly religious dimension. For instance, in *White Noise*, Gladney hears his young daughter murmuring in her sleep—"words that seemed to have a ritual meaning, part of a verbal spell or ecstatic chant."

Toyota Celica.

A long moment passed before I realized this was the name of an automobile. The truth only amazed me more. The utterance was beautiful and mysterious, gold-shot with looming wonder. It was like the name of an ancient power in the sky, tablet-carved in cuneiform. It made me feel that something hovered. But how could this be? A simple brand name, an ordinary car. How could these near-nonsense words, murmured in a child's sleep, make me sense a meaning, a presence? She was only repeating some TV voice.... Whatever its source, the utterance struck me with the impact of a moment of spendid transcendence.

That's another word favored by DeLillo: "he liked the voices, loud, crude, funny, often powerfully opinionated, all speechmakers these men, actors, declaimers, masters of insult, reaching for some moment of transcendence." In some ways, DeLillo is, indeed, some kind of latter-day American urban Transcendentalist. The closing pages of *White Noise* touch on matters of religion, or religious-type feelings, in three ways. First: Gladney says to a nun in hospital: "Here you still wear the old uniform. The habit, the veil, the clunky shoes. You must believe in tradition. The old heaven and hell, the Latin mass. The Pope is infallible, God created the world in six days. The great old beliefs." The nun gives him a dusty answer, and explains:

> "It is our task in the world to believe things no one else takes seriously. To abandon such beliefs completely, the human race would die. That is why we are here. A tiny minority. To embody old things, old beliefs. The devil, the angels, heaven, hell. If we did not pretend to believe these things, the world would collapse."
> "Pretend?"
> "Of course pretend. Do you think we are stupid? Get out from here."

She adds that "Hell is when no one believes. There must always be believers." It is an interesting position; and one rather wonders where DeLillo himself stands on this. Shortly after, in the last chapter, there is what may or may not be a miracle when Gladney's young son rides his tricycle mindlessly across a busy highway, and survives unhurt. After this the Gladneys start going to the overpass, joining other people watching the sunsets in seemingly patient expectation.

This waiting is introverted, uneven, almost backward and shy, tending toward silence. What else do we feel? Certainly there is awe, it is all awe, it transcends previous categories of awe, but we don't know whether we are watching in wonder or dread, we don't know what we are watching or what it means, we don't know whether it is permanent, a level of experience to which we will gradually adjust, into which our uncertainty will eventually be absorbed, or just some atmospheric weirdness.

Immediately after this, the novel concludes in a supermarket, where there is "agitation and panic in the aisles" because all the items have been rearranged. "There is a sense of wandering now, an aimless and haunted mood, sweet-tempered people taken to the edge." There is of course an element of comic exaggeration in all this; but I wonder how comic the very last lines of the book are, as the shoppers approach the cash point.

A slowly moving line, satisfying, giving us time to glance at the tabloids in the racks. Everything we need that is not food or love is here in the tabloid racks. The tales of the supernatural and the extraterrestial. The miracle vitamins, the cures for obesity. The cults of the famous and the dead.

Ironic? Or perhaps not. One character, Murray Siskind, goes to the supermarket as to a church. "This place recharges us spiritually, it prepares us, it's gateway or pathway. Look how bright. It's full of psychic data." It is here that he seeks to fulfill his ambition—"I want to immerse myself in American magic and dread." Siskind is the most eloquent spokesman for "the American mystery." As a lecturer in popular culture he is an amusing character. He is also a sinister one, as when he persuades Gladney to attempt a murder. Yet, according to LeClair in *In the Loop*: "It's in Siskind's realm, the supermarket, that the tabloids, which DeLillo states are 'closest to the spirit of the book,' are found. These tabloids, DeLillo says, 'ask profoundly important questions about death, the afterlife, God, worlds and space, yet they exist in an almost Pop Art atmosphere,' an atmosphere that Siskind helps decode." DeLillo writes of "the revenge of popular culture on those who take it too seriously," and I wonder what he really thinks of the low lunacies of the tabloids. Has the "religious sense" come to this?

In *Underworld*, the lights from night-flying B-52s give Klara "a sense of awe, a child's sleepy feeling of mystery." The fireball from a missile—"like some nameless faceless whatever"—so impresses a boy that "It made him want to be a Catholic." Matt believes in "the supernatural underside of the arms race. Miracles and visions." Old postbeats are "still alert to signs of marvels astir in the universe." In his Jesuit school, Nick studies "thaumatology, or the study of wonders." No doubt drawing on his Jesuit education, Nick discusses *The Cloud of Unknowing* with an unsuspecting pick-up. "I read this book and began to think of God as a secret, a long unlighted tunnel, on and on. This was my wretched attempt to understand our blankness in the face of God's enormity.... I tried to approach God through his secret, his unknowability.... We approach God through his unmadeness ... we cherish his negation." (In theology, I believe this approach to God is called apophasis—it feels a little out of place here.) The need or hunger for some kind of "religious" experience seems ubiquitous. "Sometimes faith needs a sign. There are times when you want to stop working at faith and just be washed in a blowing wind that tells you everything."

But in DeLillo's world there is more than one kind of faith or belief. At the end, when Sister Edgar learns that a young vagrant girl, Esmeralda, has been brutally raped, murdered, and thrown from a roof, she "believes she is falling into crisis, beginning to think it is possible that all creation is a spurt of blank matter that chances to make an emerald planet here, a dead star there, with random waste in between. The serenity of immense design is missing from her life, authorship and moral form.... It is not a question of disbelief. There is another kind of belief, a second force, insecure, untrusting, a faith that is springfed by the things we fear in the night, and she thinks she is succumbing." In DeLillo's world, where there is always "some unshaped anxiety" hovering, where things are as often "ominous" as they are "shining," it is this other kind of belief which seems to have the stronger purchase on people. Yet the novel ends—again—with a sort of miracle which both is—and-isn't-but-might-be an epiphany. The beatified face of the dead Esmeralda appears on a billboard whenever a passing commuter train's lights fall on it. Watching crowds gasp and moan—"the holler of unstopped belief." The skeptical Sister Grace explains it as "a trick of light," but Sister Edgar feels "an angelus of joy." And so the key question is posed—the last of many in a long book:

> And what do you remember, finally, when everyone has gone home and the streets are empty of devotion and hope, swept by river wind? Is the memory thin and bitter and does it shame you with its fundamental untruth-all nuance and silhouette? Or does the power of transcendence linger, the sense of an event that violates natural forces, something holy that throbs on the hot

horizon, the vision you crave because you need a sign to stand against your doubt?

Sister Edgar dies "peacefully," and we assume happy in her recovered faith. And the book ends there (apart from a short, visionary coda). For me, the novel deliquesces into something close to sentimental piety; and here, perhaps, is the source of my reservations about DeLillo's writing in this book. It can either be very hard—all those "marvellous" flat-eyed looks and that smart, brittle talk; or it goes rather soft, inserting easy intimations of transcendence. In a little essay called "The Power of History," which appeared in the *New York Times Magazine*, DeLillo wrote: "The novel is the dream release, the suspension of reality that history needs to escape its own brutal confinements.... At its root level, fiction is a kind of religious fanaticism, with elements of obsession, superstition and awe. Such qualities will sooner or later state their adversarial relationship with history." But, having pretty much given up on people and plots (conventional ones, anyway), DeLillo in *Underworld* is totally reliant on history from the opening events of 1951, onwards (he has "turned to the news"). By all means be adversarial to the so-called official versions of the times—as Melville said in *Billy Budd*, such histories have a way of "considerably" "shading off" any discreditable events into "the historical background." But it seems odd to write of "the brutal confinements of history" per se, particularly when your subject is, manifestly, Cold War America. And I cannot see it as the novelist's task to substitute "religious fanaticism" for the cold prose of the real. There is—God knows—enough of it around already.

JEOFFREY S. BULL

"What About a Problem That Doesn't Have a Solution?": Stone's A Flag for Sunrise, DeLillo's Mao II, and the Politics of Political Fiction

The political novel, says Irving Howe, is a work of fiction alive with the "internal tensions" born of abstract ideologies colliding with "representations of human behavior and feeling" (20)—and since World War II, by his estimation, such fiction has only been produced outside the West (254). In his 1986 epilogue to *Politics and the Novel*, Howe describes authors such as V. S. Naipaul, Nadine Gordimer, and Milan Kundera—among others—as creators of "a literature of blockage, a literature of impasse" (252) that offers "no way out of the political dilemmas with which they end their books." He praises their ability to document "utterly intractable" circumstances while pointedly refusing to accept the totalist stances propounded by the subject of so many of their novels (253-54).

I argue that Howe's definition underestimates recent attempts by American novelists to create political fictions—that is, that writers such as Robert Stone and Don DeLillo, to name two, also make the themes and discourse of blockage and impasse important parts of their novels. For example, both Stone's *A Flag for Sunrise* (1981) and DeLillo's *Mao II* (1991) explore the seemingly unresolvable conflict between liberal pluralism and revolutionary certitude. Mapping the limitations of both certainty and cynicism in a world where the boundaries between religious faith, political orthodoxy, and "apolitical" evasion meet and cross, Stone and DeLillo are

From *Critique* 40, No. 3, Spring, 1999, pp. 215-29.

ideal constituents of Howe's literature of impasse, writers who reveal the full effects of political action in an age when clear-cut solutions no longer seem to exist. By documenting the West's increasing uncertainty concerning its own democratic tenets, Stone and DeLillo question how one can find a reason to believe in (let alone act for) as fragile an enterprise as democracy, even as they critique the propensity to spurn dialogue in favor of totalism. Their works expose the limitations of all orthodoxies, while illustrating the sources of their allure. At the same time, both writers resist the temptation to simplify or solve the dynamic (active, potent, energetic) conflict between certitude and pluralism, thereby generating in their novels a perception of politics that reflects the novel's inherent receptivity to differing interpretations and opposing voices.

Uncomfortable separating "observation and participation" (Whalen-Bridge 198), a number of American novelists are now creating political fictions attuned to "the postmodern condition," the notion that metanarratives (i.e., all-inclusive explanations of human purpose and practice) fail to account for the variety and contingency of human experiences (Lyotard xxiv). Any "faith"—any political ideology, any theocratic design, any dogmatic espousal of "freedom" and the "mission" of the United States—is itself such a metanarrative, and as such is now thought to be worth examining. Stone and DeLillo, drawing on the very complicities and failings of the American sense of mission, reveal the complexities of their homeland's relationship with itself and with the world. Their novels also reveal the complexities of the novelist's own relationship with his or her culture, the "politics of the novel," and its relationship with democracy.

The last fifteen years have seen numerous compelling declarations of the democratic spirit of the novel. For example, the Czech novelist Milan Kundera praises the ability of novelists to defend individuality and indeterminacy against those who insist that all bow to an unassailable Law. Believing that religions and ideologies "can cope with the novel only by translating its language of relativity and ambiguity into their own apodictic and dogmatic discourse [...] (Kundera 7), he declares that "the spirit of the novel" is, as a rule, "incompatible with the totalitarian universe," because totalitarian conceptions of truth reject any vision of "relativity, doubt, questioning" (14), whereas the novel "does not by nature serve ideological certitudes, it contradicts them" (Kundera, quoted in Rorty, Essays 73).

Richard Rorty echoes that view when he affirms that, in place of "contemplation, dialectic, and destiny," novelists offer "adventure, narrative, and chance"—inherently anti-essentialist concepts that subvert the search for some "greater truth" beyond or behind events, something "more important" than suffering or joy (*Essays* 74). Rorty's novelist, unwilling to see suffering as simply "mere appearance" and recognizing that there is no way to completely describe (i.e., subsume) any person, chooses to create "a display of [the] diversity of viewpoints, a plurality of descriptions of the same events" that does not "privilege one of these descriptions" or "take it as an excuse for ignoring all the others" (Rorty, *Essays* 74). That novelist insists upon desacralizing all ideologies and orthodoxies, submitting them to careful analysis and orientation against the specific contexts of a work. The novelist's neologism "postmodernist bourgeois liberalism" (*Objectivity* 197), whatever its flaws, can serve as a name for this pronarrative "politics." A self-subverting ideology that owes "more to our novelists than to our philosophers or to our poets" (Rorty, *Essays* 81), postmodernist bourgeois liberalism celebrates efforts to undermine dogmatism while making a virtue of the deterioration of certitude.[1] Against totalist appraisals of culture and history, the postmodern bourgeois liberal seeks to create a haven for difference while upholding a central tenet of traditional bourgeois liberalism: the notion that there can be an anti-ethnocentric ethnos, a "we ("we liberals") that is dedicated to enlarging itself, to creating an even larger and more variegated ethnos" (Rorty, *Contingency* 198). Salman Rushdie's post-fatwa lecture "Is Nothing Sacred?" makes similar positive claims for inclusiveness, instability, and "unholiness." Literature, says Rushdie, "tells us that there are no answers; or, rather, it tells us that answers are easier to come by, and less reliable, than questions. If religion is an answer, if political ideology is an answer, then literature is an inquiry" (422). Insisting that distrust of metanarratives must not itself become a metanarrative, that novelists ("we") "must not become what we oppose," Rushdie feels that literature must remain "the arena of discourse, the place where the struggle of languages can be acted out" (427).[2]

The politics of the novel, therefore, are founded on the properties of the genre itself. E. L. Doctorow suggests that "the most important political function of the writer is to be a witness" (Whalen-Bridge 198)—and the novel's inherent tendency to measure and question all metanarratives, upholding the ethos of the ethnos discussed above, assists in that act of witness. The novel's excellence as a vehicle for "opposition," its capacity for refusing to accept without question any single reading of existence (Howe 23), is a result of its propensity for allowing characters and their ideological stances to interact, to challenge each other, and to be challenged by events.

Although emerging from an entirely different cultural and critical orientation, Mikhail Bakhtin's "prosaics,"[3] his celebration of unfinalizability, variety, and freedom, makes similar claims for fiction. Bakhtin sacralizes the novel to some degree (Seguin 42-43), but the political significance of his ideas is clear: suggesting that metanarratives are of limited value.[4] Bakhtin challenges "theoretisms" (ideological abstractions) of any kind (Morson and Emerson 49-50). He envisages the novel as the place in which contesting discourses state their cases and challenge each other.

According to Bakhtin, Dostoevski's emphasis on creating a "genuine polyphony of fully valid voices," and his effort to see that both the form and content of his works support "the struggle against a reification of man, of human relations, of all human values [...]" (6.62), both help to reveal how human unfinalizability and indeterminacy are central themes of all novelistic discourse. Part of that effort includes creating a new and important role for ideas—including political ideologies—in his works. Whereas ideas in "monologic" (author-centered) texts are placed in character's mouths to be used as "simple artistic characterizing feature[s]," important only so far as they represent or are repudiated by the author's own ideology, ideas in Dostoevski's dialogic (ideologically decentered)[5] texts become "the subject of artistic representation," actors in their own right (85).[6] Both characters and ideas confront and test each other as autonomous actors: Dostoevski's polyphonic conception of fiction, the "ideology" of his works, demands that characters' ideas be both known and felt, born of dialogic contact with other consciousness in a world where "nothing conclusive has yet taken place [...where] the ultimate word of the world and about the world has not yet been spoken, the world is open and free, everything is still in the future and will always be in the future" (85-87, 166).

Bakhtin's Dostoevski, as David Lodge points out, "put the adventure plot 'at the service of the idea' [...] to make it the vehicle for exploring profound spiritual and metaphysical problems" (62).[7] Therefore, his narratives test both ideas and those who hold them, and feature characters in whom ideas and the idea of self are interdependent, unfinalized, in dialogue. Aspects of Menippean Satire—plot extravagance, the use of low settings such as bars, prisons, and brothels as the site of dialogues concerning ultimate questions, the clash of diametrically opposed viewpoints, and the use of ridiculous, "carnivalized" characters (Bakhtin 109-19)—are turned to charting the sense of spiritual crisis their author detected in modern secular society (typified by political extremism and the decline of commonly accepted bases for social stability) and to doing justice to the complexity of "the man in man."

Therefore, even though Dostoevski's own antidemocratic opinions are well documented,[8] the artist Bakhtin depicts possesses an aesthetic model that clearly draws on "the wisdom of the novel," that "imaginary paradise of individuals [...] where no one possesses the truth [...] but where everyone has the right to be understood" (Kundera 159).

In their works, Stone and DeLillo draw on and examine the political implications of such wisdom. *A Flag for Sunrise* and *Mao II*, latter-day examples of the Dostoevskian "philosophical adventure story" (Lodge 62), display all the passions and contradictions that politics and religion engender and set conflicts between characters and ideas in a heterogeneous adventure-story setting. Both novels depict how the differences between religious and political faith blur; guerillas, gun-runners, spies—and novelists—pose "ultimate questions" (What is the use of man? Do we seek freedom to act or freedom from action?) while participating in plots consistent with the contingencies of thrillers. In both books, political ideologies and the characters who hold them come to be tested through contact with each other and are woven into a "great dialogue" that illuminates the complexities of modern culture and character. In so doing, Stone and DeLillo reiterate the particular politics of the novel, the "wisdom" that measures all things before judging them.

Robert Stone, for one, draws on "what there is of the mythic in [the thriller's] kind of popular melodramatic form," both because it works as an "irreverent echo" [that is, conscious parody] of the heroic epic, and because it helps hold readers' attention (Schroeder 159-60). Indeed, *A Flag for Sunrise* "has the pace and suspense of a first-class thriller, [catching] the shifting currents of contemporary Latin American politics," while its author manages to "convert clichés into people, and people into questions" (Wood I). Contingent circumstances and the necessities of ideas control its plot. Characters move from place to place according to the dictates of hidden, often inexplicable motivations, thereby revealing the author's determination to allow his protagonists to struggle freely with antithetical ideas.[9]

Don DeLillo is also known for using popular genres as forums for debating "ultimate questions." Tropes of the conspiracy thriller, for example, vie with explorations of philosophical and political problems in many of his novels (Aaron 308). Frank Lentriccia praises DeLillo's novels for their "irredeemably heterogeneous texture," calling them anatomies, "montages of tones, styles, and voices that have the effect of yoking together terror and wild humor as the essential tone of contemporary America" (239-40). Even though *Libra* (1988) was DeLillo's only best-seller, the preponderance of "popular" genres in his works might lead one to ask, Is DeLillo "a highbrow or a populist writer?" (Johnston 261). In each of DeLillo's novels, "the subject matter or content normally associated with conventional or popular forms of the novel is crossed or overlaps with at least one other kind of content"—namely, complex philosophical and moral questions (Johnston 262). It is in genre variety of this sort, mixing the contingencies of the thriller with important philosophical and political matters, that DeLillo, like Stone, establishes a dialogue with American mass culture and with the political implications of that culture.

Stone's protagonist, Frank Holliwell, is neither able clearly to articulate why he came to be in Central America, nor why he allows himself to be drawn into the political upheaval there. That which has driven him south resists easy interpretation, as it depends more on longing than logic. Like many Americans before him, he finds himself drawn into events in this "sweet waist of America"—drawn to something sensually thrilling and seductively macabre that inhabits both the landscape and the politics of the fictional nation Tecan. For example, driving toward Tecan with Tom and Marie Zecca, employees of the U.S. Embassy, and Bob Cole, a "leftish" freelance journalist. Holliwell notes to himself that the giant volcanoes for which the country is famous seem to communicate "a troubling sense of the earth as nothing more than itself, of blind force and mortality. As mindlessly refuting of hope as a skull and bones" (Flag 157-58). Stone sets that observation against Cole's belief (as intuited by Holliwell) that there is something moral and just in history, something worthy of respect. Holliwell finds such optimism both touching and dangerous. For him, the truth of the land exists beyond hope, beyond politics; here "primary process" rules. That same feeling radiates from the menacing blankness he later encounters while scuba-diving below "Twixt," and from Pablo Tabor, the American drifter with whom Holliwell makes his escape from Tecan at the end of the book: all give off intimations of a darker power no justice can answer.

Already seductive, the macabre allure is only augmented by the chance to encounter the Catholic missionaries his "friends" in the C.I.A. have asked him to check up on—people in whom faith and hope might still abide. "It would be strange to see such Catholics," he thinks. "It would be strange to see people who believed in things, and acted in the world according to their beliefs" (101). With his own sense of hope "badly seared" by what he encountered in Vietnam (165), he has grown comfortable with the voyeurism allowed by his profession (anthropologist) and the cynicism born of his past and present experiences with American history in action. As a result, he feels within himself a simultaneous longing for and loathing of hope, a sort of false martyrdom of caustic despair that drives him forward.

That inchoate compulsion is the plot-device that allows Stone to place Holliwell in extreme situations, such as his conversation with the antiterrorist operative Heath or his ride in the open boat with Pablo Tabor.

Such situations test Holliwell's personal "ideology" of political indifference (an attempt to forget that silence is consent), his own mix of personality and philosophy. He believes himself to be a liberal, a free agent; he thinks he owes nothing to anyone. Nevertheless, the dictates of history and fear eventually beset his faith. In the polarized political world of Tecan, his "curiosity" seems to both the Left (the missionary Sister Justin) and the Right (Mr. Heath) little more than "'a moral adventure [he] can dine out on in the States'" (395). "'I don't know quite why I came [...],'" he angrily tells Heath. "'People do such things, you know. You may live in a world of absolute calculation but I don't'" (394). "[H]e had vainly imagined that truth was on his side—but of course there was no truth. There were only circumstances" (394). Amidst that ineluctable polarization of Left and Right, the needs of Holliwell's "dry spirit" and his abiding discomfort with such needs (apparent in his despairing skepticism and political uncertainty) combine to put him in peril. Curiosity and desire lead him deeper and deeper into the politics of the region—and closer and closer to the confrontation with himself and his own values that ends with his murder of Tabor, an act of calculated violence he had hoped to avoid, yet knew he could not escape. He had hoped to evade politics, evade involvement, leave the world to the sharks. In the end, of necessity, he is obliged to become one of them. He betrays Justin to the Guardia, and kills Tabor, Hallucinating after the murder, he "hears" sharks "talk" to him, joke with him, as they swim past the boat back toward Tabor's body. They tell him that now he has his proof, that there is no justice—"just us." Cole was entirely wrong. In the final scene the sun rises on a world, as Holliwell sees it, permanently lost, one in which history cannot be challenged or changed. He styles himself the man who "understands history" because his encounter with Tabor's brutality and his own has confirmed what the volcanoes and Twixt called forth: that sense that "blind force and mortality" are the only earthly powers.

In *Mao II* the central characters are also at the mercy of contingencies. They act out a plot less dependent on cause and effect than on the need to intertwine certain issues and circumstances to test idea against idea, person against person. The culmination of the novel comes when Brita Nilsson, a photographer who gave up her original project of photographing authors— because "it stopped making sense"—chooses instead to cover "the interesting things, barely watched wars, children running in the dust [...]" (229), meets Abu Rashid—the Maoist leader whose kidnapping of a Swiss relief worker and poet in Beirut provides much of the surface impetus of the plot. Rashid, recreating himself (like his idol, Mao Zedong) as a symbol of the "immortal truth" of his "total politics," epitomizes "the Terrorist," that figure the novelist Bill Gray (the central figure in the novel) believes has taken control of mankind's narrative (41). By making Rashid a Maoist in Beirut, DeLillo is able to play with the implications of both those proper nouns, thereby commingling political and theocratic absolutisms and complicating all definitions of belief. Although not typical of those who battled over Beirut and Lebanon during the 1970s and 1980s—the Christian and Muslim militias, the Islamic Jihad, the South Lebanon Army—but entirely believable within the parameters of that disaster or of the text itself.[10] Rashid works as both a contrivance ("the Terrorist" incarnate) designed to allow DeLillo to pose "ultimate questions" and as an example of those "men dazed by power" (DeLillo, "Art" 296) who turn to violence in the hope of fulfilling their political programs. Therefore, his encounter with Brita, erstwhile iconographer of old-style "authors" (those using words, not bombs, to create the world's narrative) allows DeLillo the chance to pose terrorism against "novelism" without unduly favoring either stance.

Brita is a paradoxical choice as a challenger to Rashid. Photographs, as Martin Jay suggests, have an uncanny ability to "stop time" violently, thereby "introducing a memento mori into visual experience." As Roland Barthes put it, photographs are "clear evidence of what was there" that ineluctably speak of "flat death" (quoted in Jay 135, 451-55). Brita calls her author photographs "[b]eautiful and a little sacred" (*Mao II* 36): they are both moving and unworldly. Depending on the context, they can become "the death of the author" made literal, if you will, monologizing depictions that type writers as saints, grant them existence simply as objects. Therefore, while her "'species count'" may be "'a form of knowledge and mystery'" (26, 25), it also participates in the emptying out of the image prevalent in postmodern culture, the depletion of meaning as (to paraphrase Bill Gray, the novelist-protagonist of the novel) Nature gives way to aura (44). On first arriving in New York, years before, she concentrated on photographing street people: "'But after years of this I began to think it was somehow, strangely—not valid. No matter what I shot, how much horror, reality, misery, ruined bodies, bloody faces, it was all so fucking pretty in the end. Do you know?'" (24-25). She moved on to making authors beautiful—creating the images of "celebrity" that, as Bill Gray suggests, do not "'begin to mean anything until the subject is dead'" (42). That Brita turns her attention to terrorists at the end of the novel seems to suggest that the ethos of novelists has been overwhelmed by the culture of terror and image, that "novelism" is static now, dead: and her lens needs to turn to a new theme.

Yet the author, and the character, simultaneously challenge that pat conclusion. The ambiguous effect of photographs does not allow for it.

Brita's camera can both undermine the absolutism of Rashid and help promote his message. Although it can subvert his totalist design by catching scenes that contradict his rule, it also fixes things, limits how they can be known. Unlike the novel (Rushdie's "arena of discourse"), photographs offer only scant shelter to debate. DeLillo implies as much by enabling us to imagine, side by side, the identical photographs of Rashid that his hooded disciples wear pinned to their uniforms in place of their own faces (233) and the set of newsphotos of the man that Brita compiles. Nevertheless, her roll of film also includes an "unauthorized" exposure of one of Rashid's boys unmasked, himself. By ending the novel with such an ambiguous challenge to Rashid's "total thought." DeLillo brings to the fore the unresolvable debate over images and ideas that make up the real "plot" of the novel.

Brita, for her part, wary of the price of "moral adventures," attempts to take her pictures without commenting on their content (i.e., on Rashid). She believes she can stay clear of "politics": "'I know that everybody who comes to Lebanon wants to get in on the fun,'" she tells him, "'but they all end up confused and disgraced and maimed, so I would just like to take a few pictures and leave, thank you very much'" (232). However, despite the fact that her actions and speech seem to indicate that terrorists have taken control of the West's narrative (as Bill predicted), she still challenges Rashid's demand that all surrender to "something powerful and great" (234). Impulsively unmasking one of Rashid's followers allows her to thwart, for an instant, anyway, the "longing for Mao" (236) Rashid promotes, the disintegration of self into "all man one man" (235). In that frame she saves an image of violence, contempt—and individuality—that subverts totalism. At the same time, DeLillo, lending complexity to his depiction of her act of witness, insists that the reader note how Brita's act is not founded in any inflexible idealism but bears all the imperfections of a "democratic shout" (159): "She does this because it seems important" (236).

Her almost accidental act of subversion, for which she has no clear explanation, remains unresolvably paradoxical. Although our culture suffers under a camera-borne barrage of increasingly substanceless images, those images can also challenge and subvert "monologic" political cures such as Rashid's. Brita's rash act of witness, set in the ruins of the dead city, is a central episode in the unresolved combat of ideologies in DeLillo's text and reflects the necessities of his self-consciously self-undermining narrative[11]— a narrative in which the ideas Brita and Rashid embody are as important as their personalities. Here, characters are ideologists; ideas themselves become subject to scrupulous testing. No metanarrative is allowed to pass by unexamined.

Stone also manages to investigate, and thereby unsettle, both ideological certitude and the politics of the novel. Holliwell's use of language and his meeting with Sister Justin are two examples of how Stone examines the limitations of both unquestioning belief and corrosive doubt. For example, Holliwell's political voyeurism, his attempt to watch American foreign policy in action in Tecan while trying to avoid becoming committed to either side, arises from his unwillingness to believe that change is now (or ever) possible, that history and hope might be related. By his estimation, the United States has put an end to that. Asked by an old friend (now a C.I.A. stooge) to present a lecture at the Autonomous University of Compostela, Tecan's neighbor (asked, he later finds out, so he will be "in the neighbourhood" of the missionaries). Holliwell decides to let his audience in on a crucial secret: not only has the United States buried the world under pop culture—to borrow his phrase, "'Mickey Mouse will see [us] dead'" (Flag 108)—but it has also committed cultural suicide by destroying its own secret, nonexportable culture: the United States no longer believes that it is "more" (109).[12] The peculiarly American brand of idealism, that problematic bonding of self to nation, born of the merger of secular and spiritual hope, is, as he understands it, a dying thing, "Its going sour and we're going to die of it" (109-10). Recent history has toppled American certainty and brought down with it Holliwell's faith in that nonexportable virtue.

As evidence of that decline, Holliwell's own speech, in several spots in the text, re-creates tropes adopted during the Vietnam War, phrases haunted by self-betrayal and futility (Wood 1). That "doubly-voiced discourse" (to borrow Bakhtin's term) lets Stone create a dialogized conception of history within Holliwell's own consciousness. Vietnam merges with Tecan: Driving into the capital Holliwell imagines that "the markets would be behind the bus station, where they always were, in Tecan as in Danang or Hue (163). "He had no business down there," he tells himself (245)—not down under the reef, where he had sensed some greater darkness in the depths, not down in Tecan, "far from God, a few hours from Miami" (71), and not "under that perfumed sky" (245) (a turn of phrase as appropriate to Saigon and the Perfume River as to Puerto Alvarado). Memories of the idioms and events of Vietnam return repeatedly to his thoughts, drawn out by the echoes and similarities with that former circumstance he recognizes in his new surroundings. The Zeccas, he is only half-surprised to learn, also served in Vietnam. His conversation with them is centered around a comparison of then and now, Vietnam and Tecan, which increasingly paints Tecan as "Vietnam" about to be reborn. Tom Zecca, an astute student of history, hopes that when the place goes up he will be long gone: "[m]y tour is almost up. Then they can send in the types who like the Guardia's style. The headhunters, the Cubans, the counter-insurgency LURPS's" (169). Spooks and assassins; the names move back and forth through time, make incursions into a new continent, bleed 1961 into 1981. Such overt and implicit comparisons engage the present (early 1980s) in a dialogue with the American past and work as reminders of both the danger of American confidence and the price of its loss. The death of the sense of mission is handled in its full complexity by that use of language: language containing both a memory of the price Americans exacted from others in order to pursue imperial dreams and a sense that the last and the finest of all human dreams—democracy for all—has been murdered by such pursuits.

The void left by the end of hope is filled. Holliwell believes, by a loss of affect. "Whirl" supplants the dying sense of purpose. Powerful ideals have given way to empty yet deadly simulations. "In suburban shopping centers [he thinks] the first chordates walk the pavement, marvels of mimesis. Their exoskeletons exactly duplicate the dominant species. Behind their soft octopus eyes—rudimentary swim bladders and stiletto teeth" (246).

Having lost the secret culture of democratic hope. Holliwell's United States has become no more than its commodities, "for sale to anyone who can raise the cash and the requisite number of semi-literate consumers" (108). Unable to believe in belief and possessed by nostalgia for a world in which people acted on their beliefs. Holliwell slides into a lasting cynicism. Reflecting on Sister Justin and her fragile sense that she can act in history— that is, act for others, fulfill her religious and political "mission"—Holliwell feels "admiration, contempt, and jealousy" (243). Drawn to her hope yet repelled by it, he lacks the courage to be sincere, "Positive thinkers" frighten him. Such people's beliefs, he feels, are turned by the brute force of existence into a species of moral blindness leading to murder. "The world paid in blood for their articulate delusions, but it was all right because for a while they felt better. And presently they could put their consciousnesses on automatic. They were beyond good and evil in five easy steps [...]" (245). He recognizes that his absolute doubt is a sign of despair, that last and greatest challenge to believer and political actor alike. "There was no reason to get angry," he thinks. "At his age one took things as they were. Despair was also a foolish indulgence, less lethal than vain faith but demeaning" (246). However, by the end of the book, despair becomes master of his speech and thought. He reifies that "ideology of despair," this sense that all is whirl and only whirl and insists that it governs every circumstance. When he tries to get Sister Justin to come away from the mission with him by arguing that the revolution is futile, she recognizes that for him "despair and giving up are like liquor [...]" (388). He believes he must warn her that "God doesn't work through history"—and even after she tells him that that's "too metaphysical" for her, he persists: "'The things people do don't add up to an edifying story. There aren't any morals to this confusion we're living in. I mean, you can make yourself believe any sort of fable about it. They're all bullshit'" (387).

What he fails to understand is that Justin is no longer interested in doubting or affirming any abstract ideology. Paradoxically, she moves away from metaphysics toward belief; she accepts the notion that "justice" might only be a word, yet she continues to see the revolution as a chance to end some suffering in one place, now. The paradoxes of religious and political belief settle in her as a desire for practical action, and she discovers a moment when a choice must be made and kept. Her conception of political practicalities alters the dynamic between Holliwell and herself so that the reader witnesses Holliwell becoming the "believer"—believing in the meaninglessness of belief—whereas Justin finds her use in a suffering world, "'I don't have your faith in despair,'" she tells him, "'I can't take comfort in it like you can'" (388). Her faith in action and her attention to the necessities of her particular situation allow her to go on: his controlling sense that action is futile, therefore worthless, binds him to the escapism of despair. Holliwell's internal conflict, the collision between his desire to "drink and drink and drink" of her goodness and his belief that all political action is foredoomed, allows Stone to play out "ultimate questions" arising from the American sense of self-doubt and thereby to establish and explore the longing and self-loathing within its politics.

In creating Bill Gray's series of discussions with the terrorists' spokesperson, George Haddad, DeLillo also brings together implacable and antithetical visions of the world and uses their contact to illustrate the limitations of faith and despair. Paralleling the meeting of Brita and Rashid (their successors, in a sense). Gray and Haddad's dialogue tests both the "longing for Mao" and "the democratic shout" of the "novelistic" world-view. Authors and terrorists, Bill believes, "'are playing a zero-sum game'" (156): "'What terrorists gain, novelists lose. The degree to which they influence mass consciousness is the extent of our decline as shapers of sensibility and thought. The danger they represent equals our own failure to be dangerous'" (157). Whereas Haddad believes that the terrorist, by default, has become the new hero of history. Bill refuses to concede the game. To his mind, absolutism is the terrorists' great failure, proof that both their means and ends are corrupt. They abolish choice, accident, and all faiths save one, universal and absolute. At that point, however, the text makes plain the ambiguities inherent in Bill's novelistic politics, his celebration of openness.

Are there no ideals worth dying for? Worth killing for? "' I think you have to take sides,'" Haddad declares. "'Don't comfort yourself with safe arguments. Take up the case of the downtrodden, the spat-upon. Do these people feel a yearning for order? Who will give it to them?'" (158). The novel's attention to that debate in itself supports Bill's "novelism," but his politics of inclusion and individuality, events in the book, such as Karen Janney's uncanny spiritual encounters with mass man (as a participant in a Unification Church mass wedding in Yankee Stadium, as a lay worker amongst the victims of modern culture living in Tompkins Square, even while watching Khomeini's funeral on TV) suggest that the longing of many humans for the "symbolic immortality" offered by totalist rulers and their "immortal"—that is, impregnably monologic—words certainly cannot be ignored.[13] The text contains a recognition of that dilemma and allows a place of absolute privilege to neither Bill's strident dismissal of absolutes nor Haddad's paean to "'total politics, total authority, total being'" (158).

DeLillo's own depiction of Karen's mission amongst the sufferers in Tompkins Square forces readers to pay attention to "the down-trodden, the spat-upon" that Haddad believes only total order can save. Nevertheless, the author also ensures that we note how Bill Gray, spokesperson for the novel, cannot present his case without resorting to the kind of tropes of certitude his work is supposed to resist. His dependence on those tropes increases alongside his sense of doubt concerning both himself and his art. Yet, unlike Rashid's Maoism, Bill's novelism puts its faith in failure and ambiguity. That antithesis is the basis for the success and the failings of his argument. "'Even if I could see the need for absolute authority,'" he tells Haddad, "'my work would draw me away. The experience of my own consciousness tells me how autocracy fails, how total control wrecks the spirit, how my characters deny my efforts to own them completely, how I need internal dissent, self-argument, how the world squashes me the minute I think it's mine'" (159). Novels are a "'spray of ideas. One thing unlike the next. Ambiguities, contradictions, whispers, hints.'" That is what Rashid's absolutism would destroy. However, the receptivity offers no sense of security, or certainty; only words. Bill's own dissolution into despair under the "shitpile" of his own "hopeless prose" offers little of promise to those Karen finds living in New York's streets, learning the "language of soot." Bill's discourse appears to be little match for the tropes of whirling terror—for bombs, kidnappings, "enormous and commanding [...] figure of absolute being" (158). Paradoxically, DeLillo's "great dialogue" reflects that ineffectualness even as its very existence declaims the validity of Bill's ideal. In the interplay of political circumstances and ideologies within the text, the possibilities inherent in the ideology of the novel are renewed even as that text describes hope's end. As a result, the book may be read as both a homage to the New Postmodernist vision of the novel as a democratic space and as a critique of the optimism of that vision.

Bill Gray, like Frank Holliwell, eventually finds himself adumbrating an ideology of despair and political inefficacy. In the "great dialogue" of the novel he repeatedly prophesies barrenness and negation. Telling Brita of the decay of the word, Bill relates consumerism with terrorism and ties them together as proof of the extinction of meaning. Describing how the Terrorist has seized our time's narrative from the Novelist, Bill does not forget to include the commercialization of art as a factor in art's defeat: "'[...] I used to think it was possible for a novelist to alter the inner life of the culture. Now bomb-makers and gunmen have taken that territory. They make raids on human consciousness. What writers used to do before we were all incorporated'" (41). In his view, the acceleration of consumerism exemplified by literary celebrity has had as much a part in the terrorists' victory as any other factor. All is commodity[14]: "There's the life and there's the consumer event," quoting Bill. "'Nothing happens until it's consumed. Or put it this way. Nature has given way to aura'" (42). He predicts that Brita's photographs of him, another commodity, will gain power after his death—and he is correct. In his absence, his assistant and hagiographer, Scott Martineau, creates the myth of "Bill Gray the Writer" by leaving Bill's uncompletable "botch" of a book unpublished, silent, "gathering aura and force," and using the pictures Brita has taken to deepen "Old Bill's legend, undyingly" (224).

Although events in the text almost completely validate Bill's affirmation of despair and the dissipation he suffers as he moves toward a confrontation with Rashid and his own death, ironic points of light appear to contradict the mood of destruction. That silence of the author-protagonist, his loss of faith in his power to draw out the "moral force" of a well-made sentence (48) (a decline evinced by his fading attempts to write some sense of the life of the hostage, to see dialogically, see another as himself) compels one toward accepting the text's suggestion that "our only language is Beirut" (239). However, as the book also reveals, that language still retains phrases capable of communicating the ineffable: the moment Brita pulls away the hood; the wedding party moving across the rubble, "transcendent, free of limits [...]" (240). Positioned at the end of the work, in ironic contrast with the mass wedding at the beginning, that last event subverts Bill's assumption that the full and final defeat of man has been prefigured by the emptying out of "facts" and the empty violence that calls forth. Like Holliwell, Bill comes to depend too much on despair; he grows perversely fond of ineffectiveness and affectlessness. DeLillo (as Stone did with Holliwell) engages Bill's overarching despair in dialogue with circumstances of immediate personal and political importance, moments of reprieve that offer some hope, some sense that human agency is not futile at all times. That commingling of ideology and the tangible concerns of human behavior and suffering allows DeLillo and Stone to illustrate the complexities of political faith and political action in an age that knows too well the dangers of blind certainty.

According to Stone, "There's a shared Marxist and American attitude that where there's a problem there must be a solution. What about a problem that doesn't have a solution?" (Plimpton 371). Stone and DeLillo's "answer" to that question is to enhance the tensions between idea, character, setting, and content that are the sources of the novel's effectiveness as an art form. Actual political crises (ghosts of Vietnam stirred up in Central America, censorship, and the rise of theocratic states[15]) become important figures in both texts, taking their places in the "arena of discourse." In playing out these historical events (drawing on fiction's ability to clarify and order experience, lend it scope) both writers are able to draw the conflict of ideologies down to the personal level, thereby establishing "the connection between political forces and individual lives" important to all successful political fiction (Stone, "Reason" 75-76). Their novels support Bill Gray's contention that the novel has its own bit of moral force (*Mao* 48), which abides in the novel's ability to represent the complex and changing relationships between the private desires and the political ideals of the characters.

NOTES

1. Mark Edmundson calls Rushdie, Rorty, and (to a lesser extent) Kundera positive-minded "new postmodernists" who both "disenchant the world" (standard operating procedure for the original "negative postmodernists") and affirm the merits of diversity and uncertainty (62-66).

2. As Howe put it in *Politics and the Novel*, ideologies become "active characters in the political novel" (21); they are brought to life and brought into live, set against each other.

3. A neologism coined by Gary Saul Morson (Morson and Emerson 15ff).

4. Bakhtin resists "semiotic totalitarianism, the assumption that everything has a meaning relating to the seamless whole [...] one could

discover if only one had the code. This kind of thinking is totalitarian in its assumption that one can, in principle, explain the totality of things" (Morson and Emerson 28). "Semiotic totalitarians typically assume that it is disorder that requires an explanation. Prosaics begins by placing the burden of proof the other way. [...] In the self, in culture, and in language, it is not [...] disorder or fragmentation that requires explanation: it is integrity" (31).

5. Bakhtin himself calls his ideas inadequate summaries, monologic representations of Dostoevski's dialogic creations (see Morson and Emerson 61). As Linda Hutcheon points out, he favored an ideology of anti-ideologism, whereas postmodern novelists recognize that paradox and use parodic re-enactments of traditional "centering" (which they promptly throw into doubt) to contest both centering and decentering. By the rules of Bakhtin's own analysis, "decentered" texts also have a "center," self-conscious though it may be (180).

6. Bakhtin's thoughts here match Howe's own interpretation of Dostoevski in *Politics and the Novel*. "Dostoevsky shows how ideology can [...] blind men to simple facts, make them monsters by tempting them into that fatal habit which anthropologists call 'reifying' ideas. No other novelist has dramatized so powerfully the values and dangers, the uses and corruptions of systematized thought" (71). He is the "great artist of the idea" because he does not "finish" ideas and characters who hold them: he keeps his distance, "neither confirming the idea nor merging it with his own expressed ideology" (Bakhtin 85).

7. See Bakhtin 106-66, where he discusses how the spirit of Dostoevski's works reflects the subversive power of carnival and compare with Kundera 20, on the wisdom of "the depreciated legacy of Cervantes."

8. One can only imagine what he'd say of "postmodernist bourgeois liberals"!

9. Compare Bakhtin 104: "The adventure plot relies not on what the hero is [or] the place he occupies in life, but more often on what he is not, on what [...] is unexpected and not predetermined."

10. DeLillo prefigures Rashid by having the words "Sendero Luminoso" (Shining Path, the Peruvian Maoist revolutionaries) and "Beirut" meet and mix beforehand. Written in spraypaint on "half-demolished walls," the former word is an uncanny caption for an apocalyptic New York (in which gas mains rupture and fireballs form "outside famous restaurants"), which has the locals muttering "Beirut, Beirut, it's just like Beirut" (173-75).

11. Compare Hutcheon 178-87.

12. That nonexportable element is "Idealism. A tradition of rectitude that genuinely does exist in American society and that sometimes has been

translated into government, [...] so much that is best in America is a state of mind you can't export" (Stone quoted in Plimpton 370).

13. Compare Lifton 7-8. Lifton describes how "the Thought of Mao Tse-tung," particularly during the Cultural Revolution, came to take on quasi-religious significance for the Chinese people: "Over the course of Mao's later career the word becomes not only flesh but his flesh. The man-word corpus is increasingly represented as absolutely identical with China's destiny" (91). Unlike Bakhtin's version of the author, just one voice amongst many in his text (Bakhtin 63), the writer Mao, inspiration for Haddad and Rashid, supplants all other voices, is every voice.

14. See Hutcheon 223. Postmodern texts, by "problematizing" our conceptions of reality itself, undermine any lament concerning emptiness by generating an elusive sense of possibility, an unresolvable tension between opposing conceptions. DeLillo's play with the powers of the camera, its ability to liberate and finalize at once, is an example of such a postmodern strategy.

15. Compare Stone quoted in Plimpton 371 and DeLillo quoted in Passaro 77.

WORKS CITED

Aaron, Daniel. "How to Read Don DeLillo." *South Atlantic Quarterly* 89.2 (1990): 305-19.

Bakhtin, Mikhail. *Problems of Dostoevsky's Poetics*. Ed. and trans. Caryl Emerson, Minneapolis: U of Minnesota P, 1984.

DeLillo, Don. "The Art of Fiction CXXXV [interview]." *Paris Review* 35 (Fall 1993): 273-306.

———. *Mao II*. New York: Viking Penguin, 1991.

Edmundson, Mark. "Prophet of a New Postmodernism." *Harper's* 279 (December 1989): 62-71.

Howe, Irving. *Politics and the Novel*, 1957, New York: Columbia UP, 1992.

Hutcheon, Linda. *A Poetics of Postmodernism: History, Theory, Fiction*. New York and London: Routledge, 1988.

Jay, Martin. *Downcast Eyes: The Denigration of Vision in Twentieth-Century French Thought*. Berkeley: U of California P, 1993.

Johnston, John. "Generic Difficulties in the Novels of Don DeLillo." *Critique* 30.4 (1989): 261-75.

Kundera, Milan. *The Art of the Novel*, 1986. Trans. Linda Asher. New York: Grove, 1988.

Lentriecia, Frank. "The American Writer as Bad Citizen—Introducing Don DeLillo," *South Atlantic Quarterly* 89.2 (1990): 239-44.

Lifton, Robert Jay. *Revolutionary Immortality: Mao Tse-Tung and the Chinese Cultural Revolution*. 1968. New York: Norton, 1976.

Lodge, David. *After Bakhtin: Essays on Fiction and Criticism*. London and New York: Routledge, 1990.

Lyotard, Jean-François. *The Postmodern Condition: A Report on Knowledge*. Trans. Geoff Bennington and Brian Massumi. Minneapolis: U of Minnesota P, 1984.

Morson, Gary Saul, and Caryl Emerson. *Mikhail Bakhtin: Creation of a Prosaics*. Stanford: Stanford UP, 1990.

Passaro, Vince. "Dangerous Don DeLillo." *New York Times Magazine* 19 May 1991: 34-37, 76-77.

Plimpton, George. ed. *Writers at Work: The Paris Review Interviews*. Eighth Series, Intro, Joyce Carol Oates. New York: Penguin, 1988.

Rorty, Richard. *Contingency, Irony, and Solidarity*. Cambridge: Cambridge UP, 1989.

———. *Essays on Heidegger and Others: Philosophical Papers Volume II*. Cambridge: Cambridge UP, 1991.

———. *Objectivity, Relativism, and Truth: Philosophical Papers Volume I*. Cambridge: Cambridge UP, 1991.

Rushdie, Salman. *Imaginary Homelands: Essays and Criticism 1981-1991*. London: Granta, 1991.

Schroeder, Eric James. "Two Interviews: Talks with Tim O'Brien and Robert Stone." *Modern Fiction Studies* 30.1 (1984): 135-64.

Seguin, Richard. "Borders, Contexts, Politics: Mikhail Bakhtin." *Signature* 2 (Winter 1989): 42-59.

Stone, Robert. *A Flag for Sunrise*. 1981. New York: Vintage Books, 1992.

———. "The Reason for Stories: Toward a Moral Fiction." *Harper's* 276 (June 1988): 71-76.

Whalen-Bridge. John. "Some New American Adams: Politics and the Novel Into the Nineties." *Studies In the Novel* 24.2 (1992): 187-200.

Wood, Michael. "A Novel of Lost Americans." Rev. of *A Flag for Sunrise*, by Robert Stone. *New York Times Book Review* 18 Oct. 1981: 1, 34-36.

Chronology

1936	Born on November 20, in the Bronx, New York, to Italian immigrant parents.
1953	Lives within seven blocks of Lee Harvey Oswald in the Bronx. His interest in Oswald would eventually lead to the writing of his highly acclaimed historical fiction *Libra*.
1958	Receives B.A. in communication arts from Fordham University.
1959	Begins work as a copywriter for the Ogilvie & Mather ad agency.
1960	"The River Jordon," his first published story, appears in *Epoch*.
1963	President John F. Kennedy assassinated by Lee Harvey Oswald in Dallas, Texas, on November 22.
1964	Quits his job at the ad agency and works as a freelance writer.
1966	Begins *Americana*.
1971	Publishes his first novel, *Americana*. Begins *End Zone*. Publishes a story in *Esquire*.
1972	Publishes *End Zone*. His essay, "Total Loss Weekend," appears in *Sports Illustrated*.
1973	Publishes *Great Jones Street*.
1975	Marries Barbara Bennet.

1976	Publishes *Ratner's Star*.
1977	Publishes *Players*.
1978	Publishes *Running Dog*.
1979	Publishes *The Engineer of Moonlight*, a drama. Receives a Guggenheim fellowship. Travels to Greece, where he researches and writes *The Names*.
1980	Publishes *Amazons* under the pseudonym Cleo Birdwell.
1982	Publishes *The Names*. Begins *White Noise*.
1983	Publishes the essay "American Blood: A Journey through the Labyrinth of Dallas and JFK," in *Rolling Stone*.
1984	Receives the Award in Literature from the American Academy and Institute of Arts and Letters. Begins work on *Libra*.
1985	Publishes *White Noise*.
1986	Receives the American Book Award for *White Noise*. *The Day Room* premieres as part of the "New Stages" series at the American Repertory Theater in Cambridge, MA.
1987	Publishes *The Day Room*.
1988	Publishes *Libra*. Wins the Irish Times-Aer Lingus International Fiction Prize, and is nominated for the American Book Award.
1989	Begins *Mao II*.
1990	His play "The Rapture of the Athlete Assumed into Heaven," is performed by the American Repertory Theater.
1991	*Mao II* is published.
1992	Receives the PEN/Faulkner Award for *Mao II*. His novella, *Pafko at the Wall*, is published.
1997	Publishes *Underworld*. Nominated for the National Book Critics Circle Award.
1999	Publishes the play *Valparaiso*.
2001	Publishes *The Body Artist*.

Contributors

HAROLD BLOOM is Sterling Professor of the Humanities at Yale University and Henry W. and Albert A. Berg Professor of English at the New York University Graduate School. He is the author of over 20 books, including *Shelley's Mythmaking* (1959), *The Visionary Company* (1961), *Blake's Apocalypse* (1963), *Yeats* (1970), *A Map of Misreading* (1975), *Kabbalah and Criticism* (1975), *Agon: Toward a Theory of Revisionism* (1982), *The American Religion* (1992), *The Western Canon* (1994), and *Omens of Millennium: The Gnosis of Angels, Dreams, and Resurrection* (1996). *The Anxiety of Influence* (1973) sets forth Professor Bloom's provocative theory of the literary relationships between the great writers and their predecessors. His most recent books include *Shakespeare: The Invention of the Human*, a 1998 National Book Award finalist, and *How to Read and Why*, which was published in 2000. In 1999, Professor Bloom received the prestigious American Academy of Arts and Letters Gold Medal for Criticism.

MICHAEL ORIARD has been a Distinguished Professor of American Literature and Culture at Oregon State University. His publications include *Reading Football: How the Popular Press Created an American Spectacle* and *Sporting With the Gods: The Rhetoric of Play and Game in American Culture.*

ROBERT NADEAU is a science scholar and writer. His publications include *The Non-Local Universe: The New Physics and Matters of the Mind.*

BRUCE BAWER is the author of several books including the critically acclaimed *A Place at the Table* and *The Aspects of Eternity: Essays by Bruce Bawer.* His book reviews and articles have appeared in *The New York Times Book Review*, *The Washington Post Book World* and *The Advocate*.

GREG TATE is a noted American cultural critic and essayist. His work has appeared in several journals including *The Village Voice* and the *VLS*.

GREGORY SALYER has been a professor of Religion at Huntingdon College in Alabama. His work has appeared in such journals as *Literature and Theology: An International Journal of Theory, Criticism and Culture*.

PAUL MALTBY is a literary scholar and essayist. His work has appeared in such journals as *Contemporary Literature*.

DAVID COWART is a scholar of twentieth-century American and British literature. He was appointed Fulbright Senior Specialist in 2001. His published works include *Literary Symbiosis: The Reconfigured Text in Twentieth-Century Writing* and *History and the Contemporary Novel*.

CHRISTIAN MORARU has been a professor of English and Comparative Literature. His published work includes *Rewriting: Postmodern Narrative and Cultural Critique in the Age of Cloning*.

LOU F. CATON has taught literature and writing at Auburn University. He has written on several contemporary writers including Don DeLillo, Jamaica Kincaid and Leslie Marmon Silko.

DANA PHILLIPS has taught in the Department of English at the University of Pennsylvania, and published in such journals as *Raritan* and *The Arizona Quarterly*.

TONY TANNER was one of the most recognized critical voices on American Literature. His critical volumes include *Henry James: the Writer and His Work* and *The American Mystery: American Literature from Emerson to DeLillo*.

JEOFFREY S. BULL is an essayist and scholar of American Literature. His work has appeared in such journals as *Critique*.

Bibliography

Bawer, Bruce. "Don DeLillo's America." *Diminishing Fictions: Essays on the Modern Novel and Its Critics.* Saint Paul: Graywolf Press, 1988. 252–66.

Begley, Adam. "Don DeLillo: *Americana, Mao II,* and *Underworld.*" *Southwest Review* 82, No. 4 (1997): 478–505.

Berman, Neil. "*End Zone:* Play at the Brink." *Playful Fictions and Fictional Players: Game, Sport and Survival in Contemporary American Fiction.* Port Washington, NY: National University Publications, 1981. 47–71.

Bryant, Paula. "Discussing the Untellable: Don DeLillo's *The Names.*" *Critique* 29.1 Fall, 1987): 16–29.

Bryson, Norman. "City of Dis: The Fiction of Don DeLillo." *Granata 2* (1980): 145–57.

Civello, Paul. *American Literary Naturalism and Its Twentieth–Century Transformations: Frank Norris, Ernest Hemingway, Don DeLillo.* Athens: University of Georgia Press, 1994.

Dee, Jonathan: "The Reanimators: On the Art of Literary Graverobbing." *Harper's Magazine* 298, No. 1789 (June 1999): 76–84.

DeLillo, Don with Adam Begley. "Don DeLillo: An Interview." *Paris Review* 35, No. 128 (Fall 1993): 274–306.

Edmundson, Mark. "Not Flat, Not Round, Not There: Don DeLillo's Novel Characters." *Yale Review* 83, No. 2 (April 1995): 107–124.

Engles, Tim. "ÔWho Are You, Literally': Fantasies of the White Self in *White Noise.*" *Modern Fiction Studies* 45, No. 3 (Fall 1993): 755–87.

171

Hagen, W.M. Review of *Underworld*, by Don DeLillo." *World Literature Today* 73, No. 1 (Winter 1999): 145–46.

Hantke, Steffen. *Conspiracy and Paranoia in Contemporary Fiction: The Works of Don DeLillo and Joseph McElroy.* New York: P. Lang Publishers, 1994.

Hayles, N. Katherine. "Postmodern Parataxis: Embodied Texts, Weightless Information." *American Literary History* 2.3 (Fall 1990): 394–421.

Johnson, Diane. "Terrorists as Moralists: Don DeLillo." *Terrorists and Novelists.* New York: Knopf, 1982. 105–110.

Knight, Peter. "Everything Is Connected: *Underworld*, Secret History of Paranoia." *Modern Fiction Studies* 45, No. 3 (Fall 1999): 811–36.

Kucich, John. "Postmodern Politics: Don DeLillo and the Plight of the White Male Writer." *Michigan Quarterly Review* 27.2 (Spring 1988): 328–41.

LeClair, Tom. *In the Loop: Don DeLillo and the Systems Novel.* Urbana: University of Illinois Press, 1988.

Lentricchia, Frank, ed. *Introducing Don DeLillo.* Durham: Duke University Press, 1991.

———, ed. *New Essays on White Noise.* New York: Cambridge University Press, 1991.

Moore, Lorrie. "Look for a Writer and Find a Terrorist." *New York Times Book Review* (June 9, 1991): 17–18.

Nadeau, Robert. "Don DeLillo." *Readings from the New Book on Nature: Physics and Metaphysics in the Modern Novel.* Amherst: University of Massachusetts Press, 1981.

O'Donnell, Patrick. "Obvious Paranoia: The Politics of Don DeLillo's *Running Dog*." *Centennial Review* 34.1 (Winter 1990): 56–70.

Osteen, Mark. "Becoming Incorporated: Spectacular Authorship and DeLillo's *Mao II*." *Modern Fiction Studies* 45, No. 3 (Fall 1999): 643–74.

———. *American Magic and Dread: Don DeLillo's Dialogue with Culture.* Philadelphia: University of Pennsylvania Press, 2000.

Phillips, Dana. "Don DeLillo's Postmodern Pastoral." *Reading the Earth: New Directions in the Study of Literature and Environment*, ed. Michael P. Branch, Rochelle Johnson, Daniel Patterson, and Scott Slovic. Boise: University of Idaho Press, 1998, pp. 235–46.

Ruppersburg, Hugh M., and Time Engles, eds. *Critical Essays on Don DeLillo.* New York: G.K. Hall, 2000.

Oriard, Michael. "Don DeLillo's Search for Walden Pond." *Critique* 20.1 (1978): 5–24.

Remnick, David. "Exile on Main Street." *New Yorker* 73, No. 27 (15 September 1997): 42–48.

Reeve, N.H. "Oswald Our Contemporary: Don DeLillo's *Libra*." *An Introduction to Contemporary Fiction*, ed. Rod Mengham. Polity Press, (1999): 135–49.

Salyer, Gregory. "Myth, Magic and Dread: Reading Culture Religiously." *Literature and Theology: An International Journal of Theory, Criticism and Culture*. Vol. 9, No. 3 (September 1995): 261–77.

Tate, Greg. "White Magic: Don DeLillo's Intelligence Networks." *VLS*, No. 68, (October 1988): 39–41.

Tyler, Anne. "Dallas, Echoing Down the Decades." *New York Times Book Review*. (July 24, 1988): 1, 22–3.

Wacker, Norman. "Mass Culture/Mass Novel: The Representation Politics of Don DeLillo's *Libra*." *Works and Days* 8.1 (Spring 1990): 67–87.

Will, George. "Shallow Look at the Mind of an Assassin." *Washington Post*. (22 September 1988): A25.

William, Skip. "Traversing the Fantasies of the JFK Assassination: Conspiracy and Contingency in Don DeLillo's *Libra*." *Contemporary Literature* XXXIX, No. 3 (Fall 1998): 405–33.

Young, James Dean. "A Don DeLillo Checklist." *Critique* 20.1 (1978): 25–26.

Zinman, Toby Silverman. "Gone Fission: The Holocaustic Wit of Don DeLillo." *Modern Drama* 34.1 (March 1991): 74–87.

Acknowledgments

"Don DeLillo's Search for Walden Pond" by Michael Oriard from *Critique: Studies in Modern Fiction*, Vol. XX, No. 1, (1978). Published by Heldref Publications, 1319 Eighteenth St., NW, Washington, DC 20036–1802. Copyright © 1978.

"Preface and Don DeLillo" by Robert Nadeau from *Readings from the New Book on Nature: Physics and Metaphysics in the Modern Novel*, © 1981 by University of Massachusetts Press.

"Don DeLillo's America" by Bruce Bawer from *The New Criterion*, Vol. III, No. 8, (April, 1985): 34-42, © 1985 by *The New Criterion*.

"White Magic: Don DeLillo's Intelligence Networks" by Greg Tate from *VLS*, No. 68, (October, 1988): 39-41, © 1988 by *VLS*.

"Myth, Magic and Dread: Reading Culture Religiously" by Gregory Salyer from *Literature and Theology: An International Journal of Theory, Criticism and Culture*, Vol. 9, No. 3, (September, 1995): 261-77, © 1995 by *Literature and Theology: An International Journal of Theory, Criticism and Culture*.

"The Romantic Metaphysics of Don DeLillo" by Paul Maltby from *Contemporary Literature*, Vol. XXXVII, No. 2, (Summer, 1996): 258-77, © 1996 by *Contemporary Literature*.

"For Whom the Bell Tolls: Don DeLillo's *Americana*" by David Cowart from *Contemporary Literature*, Vol. XXXVII, No. 4, (Winter, 1996): 602-19, © 1996 by *Contemporary Literature*.

"Consuming Narratives: Don DeLillo and the 'Lethal' Reading" by Christian Moraru from *The Journal of Narrative Technique*, Vol. 27, No. 2, (Spring, 1997): 190-206, © 1997 by *The Journal of Narrative Technique*.

"Romanticism and the Postmodern Novel: Three Scenes from Don DeLillo's *White Noise*" by Lou F. Caton from *English Language Notes*, Vol. XXV, No. 1, (September, 1997): 38-48, © 1997 by *English Language Notes*.

"Don DeLillo's Postmodern Pastoral" by Dana Phillips from *Reading the Earth: New Directions in the Study of Literature and Environment*, eds. Michael P. Branch, Rochelle Johnson, Daniel Patterson, and Scott Slovic, University of Idaho Press, 1998: 235-46, © 1998 by University of Idaho Press.

"Afterthoughts on Don DeLillo's *Underworld*" by Tony Tanner from *Raritan*, Vol. 17, No. 4, (Spring, 1998): 48-71, © 1998 by *Raritan*.

"'What About a Problem That Doesn't Have a Solution?': Stone's *A Flag for Sunrise*, DeLillo's *Mao II*, and the Politics of Political Fiction" by Jeoffrey S. Bull from *Critique*, Vol. 40, No. 3, (Spring, 1999): 215-29. Published by Heldref Publications, 1319 Eighteenth St., NW, Washington, DC 20036–1802. Copyright © 1978.

Index

Almanac of the Dead, (Silko)
    on blind and greedy officials and
      citizens, 48
    on end of white history, 34
    on technological mimesis, 45
    unraveling of Euro-American culture,
      46–47
Americana, 81, 132–133
    on America's bondage to the
      historical process, 74
    the communications network under
      investigation, 14
    complexity of determining authentic
      subject, 73
    on culture and image, 76
    on female land as maternal, 72
    on images and reality in the
      American mind, 72
    on innocence, 84
    on the media, 15
    on the narrator, 71
    a rethinking of the identity theme, 71
    search for source of life's meaning, 5
    on setting of, 6
    sexual play as game, 8
    on violation of the land, 72, 85
    the vision of reality revealed, 6
American Dream, An, (Mailer), 81
"Archaischer Torso Apollos," (Rilke), 77
Axton, James, 21
    on language, 28

Bakhtin, Mikhail, 151–152
Barth, John, 9
    on nuclear holocaust, 16
Barthes, Roland, 40, 62, 93
Baudrillard, Jean, 127
Bawer, Bruce
    on DeLillo's America, 21–28
    on DeLillo's characters, 27
    on DeLillo's heroes, 23
    on lack of interest in developing
      characters, 28
    on life in America today, 22–23
    on DeLillo's philosophy of language,
      27–28
    on DeLillo's point about Hitler, 27
    on a single theme, 21
    on theorizing about life, 24
Bell, David, 8, 16, 84
    as American protagonist, 14
    the American reality, 78
    on death, 79–80
    on failure, 77–78
    on looking for origins, 131–132
    as narrator, 71
    on the Oedipus complex, 79–81
    on seeker of truth, 78
    on his travels, 73–74, 77–78
    on visionaries, 7
Billy Budd, (Melville), 148
Bloom, Harold
    introduction, 1–3

Book of Daniel, The, (Doctorow), 93
Branch, Nicholas, 101–102
  on the conspiracy, 130
Bridge, The, (Crane), 84
Bull, Jeoffrey
  on DeLillo's debate over images and
    ideas, 157
  on DeLillo's *Mao* II and the Politics
    of Political Fiction, 149–163
  on popular genres as forums for
    debating, 153
  on DeLillo's subject matter, 153–154

Caton, Lou, F.
  on DeLillo and humanist tradition,
    108
  on DeLillo and romanticism, 107
  on DeLillo and spiritual identity, 110
  on Three Scenes from DeLillo's
    White Noise, 107–116
Ceremony, (Silko), 49
  on defining the Native American
    renaissance, 34
  on otherness, 41
  stories of conquest, 43
  words as filaments in stories, 43
Chandler
  and similarities with DeLillo, 30
Circle of Nations, A, (Silko), 47
Coover, Robert, 9
Cowart, David
  on DeLillo's *Americana*, 71–87
  on DeLillo's culture and image, 76
  on the identity theme, 71
  the psychoanalytic theory, 72
  on structure of *Americana*, 73
  on DeLillo's style and message, 75
  on the underclass omitted from the
    media, 78
Crying of Lot 49, The, (Pynchon), 21, 51,
    76, 139

DeLillo, Don
  and American asceticism, 7
  on America's bondage to historical
    process, 74
  off-beat humor, 6
  on changing to a more authentic life,
    77
  his characters, 5–6, 25
  on chronology, 135–136
  on the cliché, 10
  on complexities of political faith and
    political action, 163
  on our compulsion to define our
    being, 18
  on cultural consumption, 94
  on democracy, 150
  on displacement of old culture with
    new, 121
  on end of nature and history, 122
  on faith, 147
  and fascination with crowds, 131
  on final solutions and life, 8
  on first four novels, 5
  on games in his fiction, 8
  on Hitler, 26–27
  on humanistic tradition, 109
  on images and the reality in the
    American mind, 72
  insight of names, 54
  interest in CIA, 29
  language as themes, 9
  and limitations of faith and despair,
    160
  on nature and culture, 123
  on paranoia, 137–138
  on personal and national corruption,
    80
  philosophy of language, 27–28
  on possessing his characters, 30
  on postmodern terrorists, 126
  on psychoanalytic theory, 72
  on questioning problems of human
    race, 109
  on return to primitivism, 22–23

on romanticism and postmodernism, 107

and search for mystery of existence, 112

similarities with Pynchon, 14

on structure of *Americana*, 73

on sublimity, 62

on voices, 145

on waste, 144

Dostoevski, 152

Dubliners, (Joyce), 51

Einstein, 13

Emile, (Rousseau), 59

End Zone, 12, 22, 26, 74, 94

on comparing football and modern warfare, 16–17

on language, 9, 11, 27

and metaphor for positive violence, 10–11

on search for source of life's meaning, 5

on settings, 6–7

as seventies novel, 141

on success of, 9

and theme of, 21

on vision of reality revealed, 6

vulgarity in, 9

Essay on the origins of languages and confessions, (Rousseau), 56

Fiction and Repetition, (Miller), 37

Freud, 72, 83

on Oedipus complex, 78–79

Future Perfect, In The, (Abish), 59, 65

Gass, William, 9

Genesis of Secrecy, The, (Kermode), 36

"Gerontion," (Eliot), 83–84

Gladney, Jack, 25, 58, 99, 146

the barn, 120

on cemetery visit, 125

as connoisseur of destruction, 23

on death, 79, 96

on deceiving himself, 108

desired bond between father and son, 115

on epiphanies, 144

and fascination with Hitler, 26

on a meaningful experience, 37–38

a moment of transcendence, 49

on nature and himself, 124

on political postmodern culture, 109

on postmodern pastoral, 126

as protagonist, 36

on romanticism, 108

the toxic event, 60–61, 123

as viewpoint character, 107

a visionary moment, 53–58

his wife, 97

Graduate, The (film), 79

Gravity's Rainbow, (Pynchon), 138, 142

Gray, Bill, 97

his comeback, 91

discussions with terrorists, 160

on plotting his death, 92–93

as reclusive writer, 131

on symbol of photograph, 91–92

as vanishing novelist, 90

Great Gatsby, The, (Fitzgerald), 84

Great Jones Street, 23, 26, 94, 95, 129

on crowds, 131

on search for source of life's meaning, 5

on sensory overload, 22

on setting, 6

on theme, 21

and vision of reality, 6

Guardian, (Young), 141

Handmaid's Tale, The, (Atwood), 79

Harkness, Gary, 21

on football and nuclear war, 16–17

Have never been Modern, We, (Latour),
126
Holliwell, Frank
as believer, 160
on despair and political inefficacy,
162
on language, 158
as protagonist, 154–155
Household Trashcan, (Arman), 142
House Made of Dawn, (Momaday), 34
Howe, Irving, 149–150

Ikiru, (film), 80, 82

Jameson, Fredric, 127
Johnson, Lyndon, 76
Journal of the American Academy of
Religion, 33

Knife, Black, 84
on beliefs, 82–83

Laird, Melvin, 76
Le Clair, Tom, 65, 141, 146
Lentricchia, Frank, 117
the barn scene, 113–114
on DeLillo as political writer, 108
and transhistorical beliefs, 109
Libra, 29, 32, 90, 94, 130, 153
on death, 93
on fiction, 31
on misreading character, 100
on mystery of Lee Harvey Oswald,
30
on political violence, 31
on postmodernist text, 62
on spies for characters, 31
on terrorism, 133
Loop, In The, (Le Clair), 136
Lyotard, Fran, 127

Mad Memo-Writer, (Warburton), 79
Maltby, Paul
on DeLillo's characters beliefs, 63
on DeLillo's insight of names, 54
on mocking traditional faith, 53
postmodern responses to visionary
moment, 51–52
on Romantic Metaphysics of Don
DeLillo, 51–69
and the tabloids, 59–60
Mao II, 90–93, 134, 139, 155
on conflict between liberal pluralism
and revolutionary certitude, 149
on mass wedding, 131
on politics and religion, 153
McNamara, Robert, 76
Moraru, Christian
on Don DeLillo and 'The Lethal'
Reading, 89–105
on the masses, 92
on narrative consumption, 102
on post literate age, 96
on DeLillo's resistance to popularity,
89–90

Nadeau, Robert
on DeLillo and the media, 15
on DeLillo and numbers, 16
on Preface and Don DeLillo, 13–20
and revolution in physics and
metaphysics, 13
Names, The, 21, 25, 136
on failure of language, 54–55
on innocence, 84
and mystical power of names, 54
on violence, 23
Name of The Rose, The, (Eco), 82
New Yorker, (magazine), 131
Nixon, Richard, 76
Nostromo, (Conrad), 136

Oriard, Michael

on DeLillo's characters, 5–6
on DeLillo's examples of jargon, 10
and existence, 12
on DeLillo's importance in
    contemporary fiction, 12
on DeLillo's Search for Walden
    Pond, 5–12
Oswald, Lee, Harvey, 29–30, 62
on how he is portrayed, 31
on problem with language, 32

Phillips, Dana
on DeLillo's culture and nature, 126
on DeLillo's portrait of the way, 117
on DeLillo's postmodernism, 123
on DeLillo's Postmodern Pastoral,
    117–127
*Philosophical Enquiry into the Origin of
    Our Ideas of the Sublime and the
    Beautiful*, (Burke), 60
Players, 25, 140
on breaking pattern, 5
on characters, 5, 12
on couples life, 12
on game quality of life, 12
on main theme, 21
"Power of History, The," (essay), 148
Prelude, (Wordsworth), 51, 57, 64
on nature, 61
on visionary experience, 59
Pricksongs and Descants, (Coover), 59
Pynchon, Thomas, 19, 21, 51, 78, 144
on nuclear holocaust, 16
on the postmodern moment, 75
on real lyricist of rubbish, 142
and similarities with DeLillo, 14

Ratner's Star, 22–23, 93–94, 96
on compulsion to define our being,
    18
on culmination of four-part
    exploration, 12

on origin of human civilization, 18
in remaking language, 8
and search for source of life's
    meaning, 5
on setting, 6
on vision of reality revealed, 6
Rubbish Theory, (Thompson), 142
Running Dog, 98, 101

Salyer, Gregory
on challenges of cultural criticism, 35
on DeLillo's death, 39
on language, 36
on looking inward as critics, 33
on DeLillo's Myth, Magic, and
    Dread, 33–50
on storytelling, 37
Second Sex, The, (deBeauvoir), 45
Shay, Nick
on involvement with waste, 143, 144
as main character, 139
on study of wonders, 147
"Significance of the Frontier in
    American History, The," (essay),
    126–127
Silko, Leslie, Marmon, 41, 48
on destroyers and creators, 45
on history with a future, 47
Siskind, Murray, 23–25, 40, 57, 96–97,
    119, 121
on the barn, 112–114
on being a cultural critic, 35–36
on dread, 38–39
on symbolism, 58
Snow White, (Barthelme), 59, 62
SomeVersions of Pastoral, (Empsom), 118
Sot-weed Factor, The, (Barth), 84
Spivak, Gayatri, 34
Sullivan, 81–84
Suspiria de Profundis, (De Quincey), 59

Tanner, Tony

on bad news and suffering, 135
on chronology, 135–136
on cinematic qualities which
    influence DeLillo, 136
on crowds, 131
on DeLillo's *Libra*, 131
on DeLillo's *Underworld*, 129–148
on voices, 141, 145
Tate, Greg
    on DeLillo's fictional world view, 29
    on DeLillo's Intelligence Networks,
        29–32
    on Kennedy assassination, 30
    on Oswald, 31
Theologians, The, (Borges), 82
Thousand Acres, A, (Smiley), 81
Tintern Abbey, (Wordworth), 62
Tracks, (Erdrich), 34

Underworld, 1, 129, 143, 146
    on bad news and suffering, 135
    on cimematic qualities, 136
    on crowds, 131
    on epiphanies, 144
    on paranoia, 137–138
    on turning to the news, 133–134
Un Souffle au Coeur, (Malle), 81

Vineland, (Pynchon), 134

White Noise, 34, 41, 49, 79, 92, 94
    on barn scene, 35
    on challenges of cultural criticism, 35
    on characters, 24
    on cultural impasse, 99
    on dark humor, 28
    on death, 60
    on ecological disaster, 117
    and fascination with Hitler, 26
    on innocence, 84
    on language as identity, 28
    and postmodernism, 107
    as postmodern pastoral, 118
    on reading as consumption, 95–96
    on religion, 145
    a romantic uncertainty, 109
    on supermarket tabloids, 59–60
    on technological mimesis, 40–41
    on theme, 23
    and visionary moments, 53
Winter in the Blood, (Welch), 34
Wynant, Lyle, 12
    on murder and terrorists, 21
Wynant, Pammy, 12